Dear Ian

Many, many thanks for
all your amazing support
throughout this whole
process — from workshop
to edited collection, to
wonderful endorsement.
I am very grateful.
Un abrazo,
Cathy

STUDIES OF THE AMERICAS

edited by

Maxine Molyneux

Institute for the Study of the Americas
University of London
School of Advanced Study

Titles in this series are multidisciplinary studies of aspects of the societies of the hemisphere, particularly in the areas of politics, economics, history, anthropology, sociology, and the environment. The series covers a comparative perspective across the Americas, including Canada and the Caribbean as well as the United States and Latin America.

Titles in this series published by Palgrave Macmillan:

Cuba's Military 1990–2005: Revolutionary Soldiers during Counter-Revolutionary Times
By Hal Klepak

The Judicialization of Politics in Latin America
Edited by Rachel Sieder, Line Schjolden, and Alan Angell

Latin America: A New Interpretation
By Laurence Whitehead

Appropriation as Practice: Art and Identity in Argentina
By Arnd Schneider

America and Enlightenment Constitutionalism
Edited by Gary L. McDowell and Johnathan O'Neill

Vargas and Brazil: New Perspectives
Edited by Jens R. Hentschke

When Was Latin America Modern?
Edited by Nicola Miller and Stephen Hart

Debating Cuban Exceptionalism
Edited by Bert Hoffman and Laurence Whitehead

Caribbean Land and Development Revisited
Edited by Jean Besson and Janet Momsen

Cultures of the Lusophone Black Atlantic
Edited by Nancy Priscilla Naro, Roger Sansi-Roca, and David H. Treece

Democratization, Development, and Legality: Chile, 1831–1973
By Julio Faundez

The Hispanic World and American Intellectual Life, 1820–1880
By Iván Jaksić

The Role of Mexico's Plural *in Latin American Literary and Political Culture: From Tlatelolco to the "Philanthropic Ogre"*
By John King

Faith and Impiety in Revolutionary Mexico
Edited by Matthew Butler

Cross-Border Migration among Latin Americans

European Perspectives and Beyond

Edited by

Cathy McIlwaine

First published in 2011 by
PALGRAVE MACMILLAN®
in the United States—a division of St. Martin's Press LLC,
175 Fifth Avenue, New York, NY 10010.

Where this book is distributed in the UK, Europe and the rest of the world,
this is by Palgrave Macmillan, a division of Macmillan Publishers Limited,
registered in England, company number 785998, of Houndmills,
Basingstoke, Hampshire RG21 6XS.

Palgrave Macmillan is the global academic imprint of the above companies
and has companies and representatives throughout the world.

Palgrave® and Macmillan® are registered trademarks in the United States,
the United Kingdom, Europe and other countries.

ISBN: 978–0–230–10838–7

Library of Congress Cataloging-in-Publication Data

Cross-border migration among Latin Americans : European
perspectives and beyond / edited by Cathy McIlwaine.
p. cm.—(Studies of the Americas)
ISBN 978–0–230–10838–7 (alk. paper)
1. Latin America—Emigration and immigration.
2. Europe—Emigration and immigration. 3. Latin Americans—Europe.
I. McIlwaine, Cathy, 1965–

JV7398.C76 2011
304.8′408—dc23   2011021695

A catalogue record of the book is available from the British Library.

Design by Newgen Imaging Systems (P) Ltd., Chennai, India.

First edition: December 2011

10 9 8 7 6 5 4 3 2 1

Printed in the United States of America.

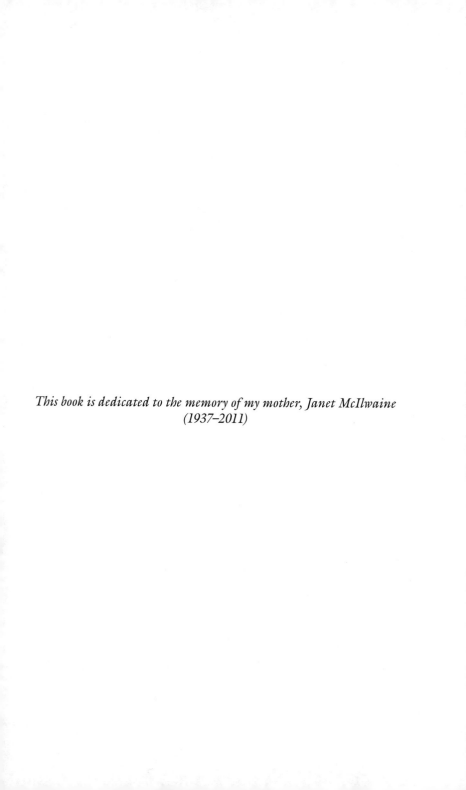

This book is dedicated to the memory of my mother, Janet McIlwaine
(1937–2011)

Contents

Section 2   Understanding Latin American Migration to the United Kingdom

Figures and Tables

Figures

Tables

Contributors

Adrian J. Bailey is currently Dean of the Social Sciences at Hong Kong Baptist University and Professor of Migration Studies at the University of Leeds, UK. His broad interest is in the nature of transnational society, and how this circulates inequality and vulnerability. A series of articles published in the *Annals of the Association of American Geographers* and *Global Networks* draw on field research in Central America and southern Africa to examine the possibilities for, and constraints upon, human creativity and collective action in the face of growing social inequality.

Anastasia Bermudez works at the *Instituto de Estudios Sociales Avanzados* (IESA-CSIC, Spain), monitoring and analyzing migration issues at the regional level. She is also a Visiting Research Fellow at Queen Mary, University of London. Since finishing her PhD in 2008, which looked at gender and transnational politics among Colombian migrants in Spain and the UK, Anastasia has focused her research on the transnational political practices of Latin American migrants, in the process contributing to the publication of a book and several journal articles and chapters.

Frances Carlisle is Director of the Latin American Women's Rights Service. She has a background in gender and community development, gained through working on women's and human rights in Mexico, Bolivia, and London, and has an MSc in Gender and Development. She has previously published on gender, employment, and Latin American migration to the UK in Oxfam's *Gender and Development* journal.

Juan Camilo Cock obtained a PhD in Human Geography from Queen Mary University of London. His dissertation, "Colombian Migrants, Latin American Publics," focused on the relationship between urban spaces, ethnicity, and transnationalism as lived by Colombian migrants in London. At present he is a project manager at the Migrants' Rights Network and has published on Latin American migration in the UK, the politics of migration in London, and community cohesion.

Magdalena Díaz-Gorfinkiel is a sociologist who currently works as an Assistant Professor at *Universidad Carlos III* in Madrid, Spain. Her research interests are related to the fields of gender relations, women's migration, and domestic work, and more specifically to the internationalization of care and the formation of global care chains. She has worked with different social organizations with the aim of raising awareness about these issues.

Angeles Escrivá (PhD) teaches sociology of work at the University of Huelva in Southern Spain. For nearly 20 years, she has followed the occupational and family trajectories of Peruvians in Spain who are employed as domestic workers. Drawing on this research, she has published several book chapters and journal articles in English and Spanish. More recently, she has been working in the intersection of aging and migration.

Gioconda Herrera is Professor of Sociology and Gender Studies at the Facultad Latinoamericana de Ciencias Sociales (FLACSO) in Quito, Ecuador. Her research is rooted in feminist approaches to migration and citizenship in the Andean Region. Her recent research has focused on transnational families and the social organization of care among Ecuadorian migrants. She has edited four books and several articles and chapters on these issues.

Rosa Mas Giralt is a doctoral candidate in the School of Geography at the University of Leeds. Her research interests revolve around transnational migration, social identities and belonging, and migrant and second-generation children. She has recently coauthored an article with Prof. A. J. Bailey (2010), "Transnational Familyhood and Liquid Life Paths of South Americans in the UK," *Global Networks* (forthcoming).

Cathy McIlwaine is a Reader in Human Geography at Queen Mary, University of London. Her research is rooted in geographies of development in relation to poverty, gender, and urban violence as well as the nature of North-South linkages through migration. Her recent research has focused on the Latin American community in London. She has published eight books, the most recent with colleagues entitled *Global Cities at Work* (Pluto), and a range of journal articles and chapters on these issues.

Caroline Moser is Professor of Urban Development and Director of the Global Urban Research Centre at the University of Manchester. She is an urban social anthropologist with research on urban poverty and vulnerability, the informal sector, gender planning, and urban violence. She recently completed a longitudinal study on asset accumulation and poverty reduction in Guayaquil, Ecuador, and is currently focusing on urban asset adaptation to climate change. She has published extensively on these issues.

Davide Però is Lecturer in Sociology at the University of Nottingham, where he also convenes the Identity, Citizenship and Migration Centre. Previously he was Researcher at the Centre on Migration, Policy and Society (University of Oxford). Davide Però has conducted ethnographic research on politics and migrants in Britain, Italy, and Spain. He is the author of *Inclusionary Rhetoric/Exclusionary Practices. Left-Wing Politics and Migrants in Italy* (Berghahn), numerous articles, and chapters, and is the coeditor of three volumes.

Olivia Sheringham is a doctoral student in the School of Geography at Queen Mary, University of London. Her academic background is in Modern Languages and Latin American Area Studies, and more recently this has developed into an interest in Latin American migrants and their experiences of living across borders. She has published two articles from her research into Brazilian migrants living in a small town in Ireland, as well as a review essay on the topic of Religion and Transnationalism, which relates to her more recent research into the role of religion in the lives of migrants in London.

Katie Wright is a Senior Lecturer in international development at the University of East London. Her research interests include gender and development, international migration, human well-being, and Latin America. She has conducted ESRC-funded research on the construction of human well-being among Peruvian migrants based in London and Madrid and their relatives in Peru. She is currently writing a book to publish the findings from this research with Palgrave Macmillan on the theme of international migration, development, and human well-being.

Acknowledgments

This collection is based on a conference funded by JISLAC (Joint Initiative for the Study of Latin America and the Caribbean) hosted by the Institute for the Study of the Americas at the University of London in December 2008 and conceived by James Dunkerley. This was a conference that aimed to present the "state of the art" on Latin American international migrants. When I was asked to take the lead in organizing it, although it was obviously important to invite speakers to talk about the US experience as well as the situation in Latin America itself among those left behind, I also took the opportunity to get together people working on Latin Americans in the UK. At this time, this was one of the first occasions that this issue had been addressed in this type of forum. While most people who presented at the conference are included in the collection, I would also like to thank other speakers including Alejandro Portes, Tania Bronstein, and Juan Pimienta together with the chairs, Kavita Datta, Jasmine Gideon, and Katie Willis. I am also grateful to both James Dunkerley and Maxine Molyneux for their support at the conference and to Maxine as the editor of this series for ensuring that this book was published. I would also like to thank Olga Jimenez without whom the conference would never have been organized. At Palgrave, I am especially indebted to Robyn Curtis, whose efficiency made this book a reality.

On a brief personal note, my interest in Latin American migration is the culmination of research that began in Latin America with Sylvia Chant in 1989 together with Sarah Bradshaw. I am incredibly grateful to both of them who continue to be colleagues and friends since our early days in Costa Rica. My research in Latin America continued with Caroline Moser whom I have to thank for introducing me to Colombia and Guatemala in the late 1990s, where we also established a friendship that endures today. It was the result of my experiences in Colombia in particular that led me to the gradual realization in the early 2000s that there was a Colombian migrant population living almost on my doorstep in London. This was partly through the research of two of my PhD students, Anastasia Bermúdez and Juan Camilo Cock, who were both working on fascinating topics in relation to Colombian migration. Simultaneously and since, separately and together, we have worked on issues of Colombian and wider Latin American migration in the UK. I am also very grateful to the support of my colleagues in the School of Geography at Queen Mary, University of London, and especially to Kavita Datta, Jane Wills, Jon May, Yara Evans, and Joanna Herbert with whom I worked on another project on low-paid migrant workers that included many Latin Americans and that provided many more invaluable insights into the community as well as to Alison Blunt and Al James with whom I have shared ideas in relation to many strands of my research.

Through all this research with the Latin American community in London, I am also indebted to several Latin American migrant community organizations with whom I have been working in some form since 2004. These include in particular IRMO, Carila, and the Latin American Women's Rights Service all of whom have been exceptionally generous with their time and sharing information. More recently, I have begun to work with the Children of the Andes as a trustee, which has allowed me to maintain my interest in the "Colombian end" of Latin American migration processes in London.

Finally, I would like to give special thanks to my long-suffering and supportive husband, Lee Drabwell, and my two amazing sons, Max and Alex.

CATHY MCILWAINE
May 2011

Chapter 1

Introduction: Theoretical and Empirical Perspectives on Latin American Migration across Borders

Cathy McIlwaine

Over the twentieth century, Latin America shifted from being a region that receives international migrants to one that sends them. Most of the outflows until the turn of the millennium were to North America and especially to the United States. Since then and partly prompted by the restrictions on movement implemented after September 11, 2001, Latin Americans have migrated to an increasingly diverse range of places across the globe (Solimano 2003). However, while some have moved within the continent from Colombia to Venezuela or from Bolivia to Argentina, or beyond to Japan and Australia, large numbers have migrated to Europe (Brea 2003). Although research on the migration of Latin Americans to the United States has burgeoned, especially since the early 1990s as flows intensified, the most recent migrations, especially to Europe, have only recently been examined. In turn, much of the latter work has focused on the case of Spain, where most Latin Americans have moved. Other types of Latin American migration within Europe have received much less attention, especially migration to the UK.

This edited collection therefore aims to address these lacunae in terms of a broad focus on Latin Americans in the European context, but with a specific focus on the UK, where research to date has been very limited. The book brings together a group of leading, established, and emerging scholars from various disciplines including geography, sociology, anthropology, and development studies, who have been forging new paths on research on Latin Americans and especially in the UK context.

Because of the empirical focus on Latin American cross-border movements, the conceptual scope of the collection is to explore the broad conceptual relevance of notions of transnationalism, diaspora, and integration among Latin Americans in the European context. However, the book does not only focus on Europe and on the UK; one chapter, by Giaconda Herrera, considers the situation in the source country, in this case, Ecuador, in order to provide some insights into the reasons why people leave, but crucially, to examine the effects of international migration on those left behind, and especially on families. This is complemented by another chapter that considers international domestic labor in Latin American and Spain (Escrivá and Díaz-Gorfinkiel). The chapter by Moser then considers the migration from Guayaquil, Ecuador, to Barcelona in Spain through the lens of a transnational assets framework. These chapters, together with Bailey and Mas Giralt's on transnational theory with a particular focus on transnational families, make up the first main section of the collection that emphasizes ways to conceptualize Latin American migration. The remaining chapters comprising the second section concentrate specifically on the British case addressing a range of different conceptual dimensions of transnationalism and integration.

Countering North-American–Centric Research on Latin American Migration

The huge body of research on Latin American migration to the United States has fostered some rich conceptualizations of how to make sense of these flows. Work on the so-called Latino population has developed from a range of different perspectives including their cultural, ethnic, and social identities (Gracia 2008), their working lives (Murphy, Blanchard, and Hill 2001), and their political situations (Oboler 1995). Furthermore, an entire field of study on "Latinos" has emerged exemplified by a range of edited collections (Darder and Torres 1998; Poblete 2003), and the establishment of a dedicated journal established in 2003 (*Latino Studies*). Related to this, many early conceptualizations of transnationalism and transnational migration were rooted in investigations of the lives of Latin American migrants in North America (Guarnizo, Portes, and Haller 2003, Portes, Escobar, and Radford 2002). Massey et al.'s (1987) early and influential study was one of the first to highlight the importance of connections between countries, in this case between Mexico and the United States. Since then, a large body of extremely influential work on a range of transnational linkages between the United States and Latin America has developed, much of it focusing on the experience of Latin American migrants (Guarnizo 1997; Grasmuck and Pessar 1991; Levitt 2001; Menjívar 2000; Portes, Guamizo, and Landolt 1999; Portes, Escobar, and Radford 2007; Portes, Haller, and Guamizo 2002, Smith 2003, among others).

While this research has been crucial in widening understandings of the dynamics of international migration, by the mid-2000s, scholars began to question "the scope and importance of the phenomena [transnationalism], arguing that too many claims were based on case studies, particularly those of Latin American and Caribbean migrants, who have a particular social and historical relationship to the United States" (Levitt and Jaworsky 2007, 131; also Waldinger and Fitzgerald 2004). Research on migration in Europe also burgeoned and certainly influenced wider theorizations of transnationalism and integration (Al-Ali, Black, and Koser 2001; Caglar 2006; Joppke and Morawska 2003; Soysal 1994, among others), and there were also explicit efforts to bring together European and U.S. scholars of migration to explore comparative theorizations of international migration (for example, Portes and DeWind 2007). However, little of this research mentions Latin American population movements in European contexts (although see Solé and Parella 2005; Pastor and Meneses 2005).

The reasons for this were primarily that migration flows from Latin America to Europe were limited until the first decade of the twenty-first century (Pellegrino 2004, see below). Therefore, until recently, research on Latin Americans in this context has been mainly confined to Spain, which has the largest populations (see Berg 2009; Bermudez 2010; Escrivá 2000; Margheritis 2007; Oso 2003; also Escrivá, Bermudez, and Moraes 2009), including some work on other countries such as Israel (Raijman, Schammah-Gesser, and Kemp 2003), Portugal (Feldman-Bianco 2001), Italy (Boccagni 2011), and Sweden (King and Ganuza 2005), covering a range of different issues. In the case of the UK, research on Latin Americans is growing, although it tends to be confined to one nationality group and especially Colombians (Guarnizo 2008) or Brazilians (Cwerner 2001; Evans et al. 2007), or is based on small-scale qualitative research (Mas Giralt and Bailey 2010; Wright 2010), with few attempts to consider more than one nationality group at a time (however, see Carlisle 2006; McIlwaine 2010; Román-Velasquez 1999, 2009). Indeed, this collection aims to bring together many of the scholars working on Latin Americans in the UK for the first time.

Patterns of Latin American Migration in Europe

Data on the patterns and volumes of Latin American migration to Europe are very limited with the exception of Spain, where more research has been conducted. However, as Pellegrino (2004, 7) notes: "With the growth of LAC [Latin American and Caribbean] migrant communities in Europe, the need to better understand the dynamics of such flows, the forces driving them and future trends has also grown." The problems with the data comparisons revolve around the fact that many European nations use citizenship to delineate their migrant populations in their censuses, while Latin American countries and the United States use country of birth (ibid.). In the specific case of the UK, the 2001 census and subsequent population surveys use country of birth, but more recent data such as the International Passenger Survey (IPS) use nationality, making it extremely difficult to compare across data sets (Linneker and McIlwaine 2011).

Acknowledging these challenges, recent research work allows for a basic picture to be built. As table 1.1 shows, the countries identified with significant proportions of Latin Americans by nationality are Spain, Italy, Portugal, Germany, the UK, France, and Sweden (in order of size). One of the core patterns to emerge from these figures is the dramatic increases in most countries between 1986 and 2005 and especially in Spain, where, for example, the proportion of Ecuadorians increased from 2,900 to 84,700 between 1996 and 2001 and where the total Latin American population in 2005 stood at 966,577. Also notable is the concentration of Brazilians in Portugal. However, Peixoto's (2009, 7) research also highlights the proportion of Latin Americans compared with other migrant groups. From this perspective (and excluding the Caribbean), Spain has by far the largest proportion (32 percent), followed by Portugal (15.1 percent), Italy (8 percent), Sweden (3.7 percent), the Netherlands (3.0 percent), Norway (2.4 percent), Switzerland (2.1 percent), the UK (1.7 percent), Germany (1.3 percent), Finland (1.1 percent), and France (0.9 percent).

Therefore, while Latin American migration established a foothold in Europe in the 1970s and 1980s, the most marked growth has been since 2000 and has been diversified but with marked concentrations in Spain, Italy, and Portugal (ibid.; Martínez Pizarro and Villa 2005; Padilla and Peixoto, 2007).

More recent research in the UK has shown that the census in 2001 enumerated the South American population as 73,785 (see Mas Giralt this volume). Even more recent work on the size of the Latin American population in the UK on the basis of country of birth, estimated

Table 1.1 Latin American population stock by nationality in selected European countries (in thousands)

	1986	1991	1996	2001	2005
Italy					
Peruvians	–	6.4	21.7	29.6	
All Latin Americans					178,796
Portugal					
Brazilians	10.5	12.7	20.0	23.5	
Venezuelans	4.9	5.1	4.2	3.5	
All Latin Americans					55,752
Spain					
Ecuadorians			2.9	84.7	
Peruvians*	2.2	6.5	18.0	33.8	
Dominican Republic	1.7	6.6	17.8	29.3	
Colombians	3.4	5.3	7.9	48.7	
Cubans	5.5	2.7	7.8	21.5	
Argentineans	12.2	20.0	18.2	20.4	
All Latin Americans					966,577
Sweden					
Chileans	10.2	19.1	12.4	9.9	17,593
United Kingdom					
All Latin Americans					47,351
France					
All Latin Americans					29,307
Germany					
All Latin Americans					76,729

Notes: * First column refers to 1989; 1986–2001 adapted from Pellegrino (2004, 16), 2005 adapted from Peixoto (2009, 7)

Source: Adapted from Pellegrino (2004) and Peixoto (2009)

that there were 186,469, of whom 61 percent lived in London, where Brazilians and Colombians were the most numerous groups, followed by Ecuadorians, Bolivians, and Peruvians. This represents 3.2 percent of the foreign-born population of London (McIlwaine, Cock, and Linneker 2011).

In terms of Europe as a whole, Spain is currently the "leading country for immigration" Vicente (2010, 1). Much of this is made up of Latin Americans, who comprised more than 2.3 million in 2009. In relative terms, this reflected an increase from 24 percent of the foreign-born population in 1999 to 37 percent in 2009. Among Latin Americans, Ecuadorians are the third-largest migrant group in the country (behind Romanians and Moroccans). Colombians and Argentineans are in the fifth and sixth places, respectively, followed by Bolivians and Peruvians in the ninth and tenth places (ibid.).

In terms of who is migrating from Latin America to Europe as a whole, this population is largely youthful with high employment rates. Education levels tend to be high with most having completed secondary school or having attended university. Many of the flows are highly feminized, particularly those from the Dominican Republic and Colombia and to a lesser extent from Ecuador and the Southern Cone (Martínez Pizarro and Villa 2005; Pellegrino 2004).

Processes of Latin American Migration in Europe

This leads us to the processes underlying these patterns of increased Latin American movement to Europe. Obviously, this reflects the intersection of a wide range of factors from the macrostructural position of Latin America in the world economy to the microlevel decisions of individual migrants that in combination have led to what Mas Giralt and Bailey (this volume) call the "deepening transnationalisation of Europe."

Early flows for political reasons beginning in the 1960s with Cuban migration to Spain (Berg 2009) increased and diversified in the 1970s, as political exiles fled various authoritarian regimes, such as those who left Chile for Sweden and Norway as well as the UK and Spain (Peixoto 2009). The increase in flows in the 1990s and 2000s, however, was largely down to economic factors. In particular, the neoliberal project from the 1980s until the 2000s led to marked levels of inequality as most countries in the region adopted free-market reforms, usually through Structural Adjustment Programs (SAPs). This inequality was interrelated with high levels of poverty, unemployment, and reduction in real wages; in turn, social protection measures were reduced (Gwynne and Kay 2000). As national economies became more integrated into the global economy in terms of trade liberalization, so international and national migration increased (Herrera this volume). In certain countries, protracted civil war and armed conflict between the 1980s and 2000s also encouraged outward migration (Pellegrino 2001; Moser and McIlwaine 2004 on Colombia and Guatemala).

As noted above, while until recently most Latin Americans looked toward the United States as a destination, accounting for three-quarters of the outward flows (Martínez Pizarro and Villa 2005), immigration to Europe diversified especially after September 11, 2001, as increasing restrictions on movement were imposed (see also Mas Giralt and Bailey this volume). The appeal of Europe, and especially southern Europe, was bolstered by historical ties forged through colonialism together with linguistic legacies. In addition, many immigrant communities in Latin America in the early twentieth century originated in southern Europe; it made sense for Latin Americans of Italian or Spanish origin to "return" to the country of their ancestors, especially if there was an opportunity of asserting citizenship rights (Pellegrino 2004). Therefore, the pull of ancestral as well as contemporary family roots has been important for many, as has the role of religion, where the Catholic church in particular, has been shown to bring immigrants to Italy and Spain (Peixoto 2009; see also Escrivá and Díaz-Gorfinkiel this volume; Sheringham this volume).

Also extremely important, especially in the case of Spain, was the preferential immigration legislation arrangements that favored Latin Americans (Peixoto 2009). For example, Spain and Ecuador signed a bilateral agreement in 2001 that regularized 25,000 unauthorized Ecuadorians (as did Colombia and the Dominican Republic). After 2003, although Ecuadorians required a visa, a regularization law was passed in 2004 granting legal status to more than 400,000 Ecuadorians. This followed five regularization programs from 1985 to 2001. Portugal and Italy also instituted regularization programs in 2001 and 2002, respectively (Peixoto 2009). This is not to say that there are no longer irregular Latin American migrants in these countries; on the contrary, there is a "sizeable presence of irregular immigrants" in southern European countries (ibid., 19).

Underlying these legislative changes in the Spanish case in particular was the demand for labor. Although in early waves of migration Latin Americans were able to work in professional occupations, especially Argentineans, Chileans, and Uruguayans who arrived in Spain in the 1970s or Brazilians who settled in Portugal in the 1980s, the more recent flows have been linked with labor demand in the care, cleaning. and construction sectors (Peixoto 2009). In the case of care and cleaning, this has been linked with the feminized nature of migration flows (see above). In particular, these have been predicated on the demand for female migrant labor (and to a lesser extent male labor) to provide for the social reproductive roles of the increasing proportion of middle-class professional women who have moved into paid employment. Coupled with weak welfare states in southern Europe, this has created what some have referred to a "global care chain" or an "international division of reproductive labor" spanning the borders between Latin America and Europe (see Escrivá and Díaz-Gorfinkiel this volume; Herrera this volume). While many male and female Latin Americans end up working in low-paid domestic service, in cleaning and caring jobs,

and in construction in Europe, this does not reflect their qualifications or skills, with most being well-educated (McIlwaine this
volume Section 2).

Beyond the southern European cases that have dominated the discussion so far, Latin American migration to other countries such as
the UK and Germany has been influenced by a range of primarily
economic factors. On the one hand, it is important to recognize that
there are secondary movements within Europe (see McIlwaine this
volume b). For example, it is not uncommon for Latin Americans
to move first to Spain, Italy, or Portugal in order to ensure EU citizenship (through ancestry or regularization of some form) and then
move on to other northern European countries where wages are often
assumed to be higher (Peixoto 2009; also Mas Giralt and Bailey this
volume; McIlwaine this volume b). In the case of the UK in particular, a combination of immigration legislation (that allowed exile
in the 1970s, asylum in the 1980s and 1990s, and the provision of
temporary visas in the first decade of the twenty-first century), labor
demand (mainly in elementary jobs), and existing social networks
that stretched back to the late 1970s when a group of Colombians
arrived in London on work permits to work in cleaning and catering,
attracted Latin Americans to the country. Central to this was the
expectation that wages would be higher in the UK than in southern
Europe. Despite little hard data, it also appears that flows to northern
Europe have intensified since the global economic crisis in 2008; evidence from the UK suggests that this has promoted migration from
Spain, where the crisis has been especially severe (McIlwaine, Cock,
and Linneker 2011).

Underlying many of these processes throughout Europe is the
need to remit money home. Indeed, remittances are essential to
many of the economies of Latin America. For example, in 2009,
remittances to Latin America totalled US$58.8 billion, which rep-
resented a decline from US$69.2 billion in 2008 because of the
global financial crisis. This is equivalent to foreign direct investment and much larger than overseas development assistance. On
average in Latin America, remittances represent 4.9 percent of GDP.
In 2006, remittances represented 3.3 percent of GDP in Colombia,
0.3 percent in Brazil, 7.8 percent in Ecuador, 8.7 percent in Bolivia,
and 3.1 percent in Peru.[1] Increasing proportions of remittances have
been sent from European countries in recent years as migration
flows have intensified, with Spain being the second most important
country of remittance sending for Latin America after the United
States (Meins 2009).

Transnationalism and Integration among Latin Americans in the European Context

As noted above, theorizations of transnationalism, integration, and diaspora have in various ways been influenced by the flows of Latin American migrants around the world. Indeed, it was research on Latin American migrants to the United States in particular that challenged early assimilation approaches to migration. While these early perspectives assumed that migrants would be absorbed into wider society that would not change, in the late 1980s and 1990s, research such as Massey et al.'s (1987) and Rouse's (1991) on the connections developed between Mexican migrants in the United States and their homeland led to the emergence of transnationalism as a concept, as well as a shift toward "new assimilation" perspectives.

In terms of the latter, Alba and Nee (1997) suggest that both migrants and societies change and that paths of assimilation can be multiple. As such, "segmented assimilation" occurs where migrants can be assimilated into some aspects of society and not into others and is crosscut by the contexts in the country of departure and destination, and the characteristics of migrants (Portes and Zhou 1993). While this "new assimilation" work focused on the United States, there were also important contributions based on the European case such as Brubaker's (2001) comparison of the United States, France, and Germany.

An important element in the multidimensionality of "new assimilation" is the diversity of transnational linkages that migrants maintain with their homelands. The classic definition of transnationalism by Basch, Glick-Schiller, and Szanton-Blanc (1994, 7) based on their study of Grenadians, Haitians, and Filipinos refers to it as "the processes by which immigrants forge and sustain multi-stranded social relations that link together their societies of origin and settlement". Transnational migration has thus been conceptualized as occurring within fluid social spaces that are multisited, multilocal, and multilayered (Levitt and Jaworsky 2007, 131). These social formations crucially challenge the notion of the nation-bound conceptualizations of class, ethnicity, race, and nation (Glick-Schiller, Basch, and Szanton-Blanc 1995), issues that emerge as central to many of the cases discussed in the current collection (see Bermúdez; Escrivá and Diaz-Gorfinkiel; Herrera; Però; McIlwaine and Carlisle; and Wright in particular).

However, there have also been a plethora of criticisms of this early transnational work that revolve around whether transnationalism is new or whether the scale of transnational ties are large enough to be important (Waldinger and Fitzgerald 2004). Also challenged has been the assertion that the importance of the nation-state and state sovereignty has diminished in an era of transnational migration (Levitt and Jaworsky 2007). Instead, many argue that the state regulation of migration regimes remains crucial in influencing the dynamics of international migration globally, as the cases of Latin American migration to Europe outlined in the chapters of this book attest (see Bailey and Mas Giralt, Escrivá and Diaz-Gorfinkiel, and Herrera in particular). In addition, national borders remain important even if it is now recognized that "border crossing" is no longer a singular, physical, and linear journey, but rather one that entails the creation of a range of transnational practices that operate in tangible and intangible ways (Goldring 2002).

Related to this is the question of whether transnational practices are important in terms of how many migrants engage in them. Some scholars such as Portes, Haller, and Guamizo (2002) have suggested that the active involvement in transnational activism among migrants in their research was as low as 10 to 15 percent among Dominicans, Salvadorans, and Mexicans in the United States. However, their definition focuses on activities and occupations of individuals. There are others who suggest that transnationalism needs to be conceived in a much broader sense to account for those who do not travel or remit regularly. This is essential in the case of Europe, where unlike the United States, is it very difficult to travel backward and forward across such long distances. Such an individualistic conceptualization has little resonance in this context, nor does it emerge as significant in any of the chapters in this collection (see also Cock 2009). Of much greater utility are the wider perspectives that delineate transnational "social fields" (Levitt and Glick-Schiller 2004) or "transnational social spaces" (Faist 2000) or "transnational social formations" (Guarnizo 1997). These broadly refer to social networks and relationships that function across borders and that entail the flow of people, goods, information, and ideas that affect those who move and those who do not.

I suggest that this latter conceptualization of transnationalism is more appropriate for examining the situation of Latin Americans in the European case. Various examples from the chapters in this collection outline the specific ways in which these social fields operate in different ways, such as how social ideologies, and especially gender ideologies, transform across borders (see Escrivá and Diaz-Gorfinkiel, Herrera, McIlwaine and Carlisle, Moser, Wright), as well as how youth identities change over time and space (Mas Giralt, Wright). However, this is not to say that the transfer and exchange of more tangible goods are not important. Indeed, Faist (2000, 199) notes: "Cultural, political and economic processes in transnational social spaces involve the accumulation, use, and effects of various sorts of capital, their volume and convertibility" that include economic, human, and social capital including symbolic ties. This also encompasses fluidity back and forth across borders. As outlined in Moser's chapter on the transnational asset framework, it is essential to adopt this more holistic interpretation in the European case in order to acknowledge the material and nonmaterial ties. This is especially important in light of the fact that much migration from Latin America to Europe is predicated on the search for better economic opportunities and the need to send home financial remittances (see also McIlwaine this volume Section 2).

One other area of importance that is relevant in the current context is that recent debates have acknowledged that processes of transnationalism and integration in destination countries are not mutually exclusive. Indeed, the relationship is not clear-cut, with the type and level of transnational engagement not necessarily linked with factors such as length of residence in the destination or occupational status (Snel, Engbersen, and Leerkes 2006). This is relevant in several of the cases discussed here such as Cock's analysis of how Latin Americans in London use shopping centers.

Latin American Diasporas in the European Context

It is also important to mention the notion of diaspora, not least because scholars are increasingly referring to a "Latin American diaspora." For example, Pellegrino (2004, 5) suggests that "the existence of what is now a significant LAC *diaspora* in Europe may itself be a driving force for further migration, and flows are likely to continue to increase in the future." Several authors also refer to "diasporic identities" among Latin American migrants (Roman-Velasquez 2009). However, not only is there little agreement on what diaspora actually refers to (Cohen 2008; Safran 1991), but there is no agreement as to whether Latin Americans constitute a diaspora. Early definitions of diaspora originally referred to people who live outside their homelands as a result of collective trauma and displacement and who lived in exile, such as Jews, Africans, Palestinians, Armenians, and Kurds (Cohen 2008). Safran (1991) further suggested that a diasporic people should have a collective memory of their homeland, which is a place they and their children should strive to return to, and that they should maintain solidarity as a group through a continuous relationship with the homeland (p. 83–84). Importantly, Clifford (1994, 308) makes the point that a diaspora is not a transnational community per se, but that there may be diasporic elements within the community. He notes that diaspora is a "signifier, not simply of transnationality and movement, but of political struggles to define the locals, as a distinctive community, in historical contexts of displacement". From these perspectives, there are few Latin American groups who could be defined as a diaspora with the exception of Cubans and possibly some Colombians (see Berg, 2009).

Some broader definitions include migrant groups who have been displaced whether by economic or political forces as Tölölian (1991, 4–5) states: "Diasporas are the exemplary communities of the transnational moment . . . the term that once described Jewish, Greek, and Armenian dispersion now shares meanings with a larger semantic domain that includes words like immigrant, expatriate, refugees, guest workers, exile community, overseas community, ethnic community." However, the ambiguities surrounding this deeply contested term, as well as the fact that Latin Americans have very diverse migration trajectories to Europe that do not focus on exile and an almost mythical homeland to which they cannot return, mean that it has limited relevance in the current case. As such it is not widely used in this collection.

In summary then, the main conceptual foci of the chapters included here are the various dimensions of transnational migration, transnational practices, and integration that include both tangible and intangible elements of connections and connectivities. Some of the chapters address more explicitly than others the material flows between countries in terms of asset transfers (Moser), or specific types of labor (Escrivá and Diaz-Gorfinkiel), as well as ties based around families (Herrera, Bailey, and Mas Giralt). Political transnationalism is important in the chapter by Bermudez in very concrete terms in terms of the ways in which ties to the homeland are maintained, whereas Però focuses more explicitly on the ways in which Latin Americans are integrated in uneven ways into the political landscape of the UK. Integration is also important in the chapter by McIlwaine, who assesses the ways in which the debates on "superdiversity" intersect with those on integration. Cock's chapter on Latin American cultural identities in public spaces suggests that shopping centers play an important role in both maintaining transnational connections and ensuring integration. Religious transnationalism is explored by Sheringham among Brazilians in London and in Brazil through concrete and "spiritual ties." The chapters by McIlwaine and Carlisle, Wright, and Mas Giralt focus on how ideologies and identities transforms across borders in complex ways, with the chapter by Herrera on Ecuador highlighting how communities at home in Latin America are coping with such changes, especially in relation to social reproduction. It is hoped that the following chapters will elucidate in empirical and conceptual ways a hitherto neglected flow of migrants from Latin America to the UK, as well as provide a range of perspectives on the wider processes of Latin American migration to Europe.

Acknowledgments

I would like to thank Sarah Bradshaw for her comments on an earlier draft of this chapter.

Note

1. See http://www.ifad.org/remittances/maps/latin.htm (accessed September 23, 2010). In 2009, Colombia received $4.13 billion in remittances, Brazil, $4.75 billion, Ecuador $4.49 billion, Bolivia $1.02 billion, and Peru $2.66 billion (http://www.iadb.org/mif/remittances/lac/remesas_co.cfm) (accessed September 23, 2010).

References

Al-Ali, Nadje, , Richard Black, and Kalid K. Koser K.. 2001. "The Limits to 'Transnationalism': Bosnian and Eritrean Refugees in Europe as Emerging Transnational Communities. *Ethnic and Racial Studies* 24:579–600.

Alba, Richard, and Victor Nee. 1997. "Rethinking Assimilation Theory for a New Era of Immigration" *International Migration Review* 31 (4): 826-874

Basch, Linda, Nina Glick-Schiller, Cristina Szanton-Blanc. 1994. *Nations Unbound*. New York: Gordon and Breach.

Berg, Mette. 2009. "Homeland and Belonging among Cubans in Spain." *The Journal of Latin American and Caribbean Anthropology* 14 (2): 265–90.

Bermudez, Anastasia. 2010. "Transnational Political Practices of Colombians in Spain and the United Kingdom: Politics 'Here' and 'There.'" *Ethnic and Racial Studies* 33 (1): 75–91.

Boccagni, Paolo. 2011. "Migrants' Social Protection as a Transnational Process: Public Policies and Emigrant Initiative in the Case of Ecuador." *International Journal of Social Welfare* 20: 1–8.

Brea, Jorge A., 2003. "Population Dynamics in Latin America." *Population Bulletin* 58 (1): 1–38.

Brubaker, Rogers. 2001. "The Return of Assimilation? Changing Perspectives on Immigration and Its Sequels in France, Germany, and the United States." *Ethnic and Racial Studies* 24 (4): 531–48.

Caglar Ayse 2006. "Hometown Associations, the Rescaling of State Spatiality and Migrant Grassroots Transnationalism." *Global Networks* 6 (1): 1–22.

Carlisle, Frances. 2006. "Marginalisation and Ideas of Community among Latin American Migrants to the UK." *Gender and Development* 14 (2): 235–45.

Clifford, James. 1994. "Diasporas." *Cultural Anthropology* 9 (3): 302–38.

Cock, Juan Camilo. 2009. Colombian Migrants, Latin American Publics: Ethnicity and Transnational Practices amongst Colombian Migrants in London. PhD diss., London: Geography Department, Queen Mary University of London.

Cohen, Robin. 2008. *Global Diasporas: An Introduction* (second edition). Oxford: Routledge.

Cwerner, Saulo B. 2001. "The Times of Migration." *Journal of Ethnic and Migration Studies* 27:7–36.

Darder, Antonia, and Rodolfo D. Torres, eds. 1998. *The Latino Studies Reader.* Oxford: Blackwell.

Escrivá, Angeles. 2000. "The Position and Status of Migrant Women in Spain." In *Gender and Migration in Southern Europe: Women on the Move,* ed. Floya Anthias and Gabriela Lazaridis, 199–226, Oxford: Berg.

Escrivá, Angeles, Anastasia Bermudez, and Natalia Moraes, eds. 2009. *Migración y Participación Política.* Madrid: Consejo Superior de Investigaciones Científicas.

Evans, Yara, Jane Wills, Kavita Datta, Joanna Herbert, Cathy McIlwaine, Jon May, Father José Osvaldo de Araújo, Ana Carla França, and Ana Paula França. 2007. *Brazilians in London: A Report for the Strangers into Citizens Campaign.* London: School of Geography, Queen Mary, University of London.

Faist, Thomas. 2000. "Transnationalization in International migration: Implications for the Study of Citizenship and Culture." *Ethnic and Racial Studies* 23 (2): 189–222.

Feldman-Bianco, Bela. 2001. "Brazilians in Portugal, Portuguese in Brazil: Constructions of Sameness and Difference Identities, *Global Studies in Culture and Power* 89 (4): 607–50.

Glick-Schiller, Nina, Linda Basch, and Cristina Szanton-Blanc. 1995. "From Immigrant to Transmigrant: Theorizing Transnational Migration." *Anthropological Quarterly* 68 (1): 48–63.

Goldring, Luin. 2002. "The Mexican State and Transmigrant Organizations: Negotiating the Boundaries of Membership and Participation." *Latin American Research Review* 37:55–99.

Gracia, Jorge. E. 2008. *Latinos in America: Philosophy and Social Identity.* Malden, MA, and Oxford: Blackwell.

Grasmuck, Sherri, and Patricia Pessar. 1991. *Between Two Islands: Dominican International Migration.* Berkeley, CA: University of California Press.

Guarnizo, Luis E. 1997. "The Emergence of a Transnational Social Formation and the Mirage of Return Migration among Dominican Transmigrants." *Identities* 4:281–322.

———. 2008. *Londres Latina: la presencia Colombiana en la capital Británica.* Mexico DF: Universidad de Zacatecas and Miguel Angel Porrúa.

Guarnizo, Luis E., Alejandro Portes, and William Haller. 2003. "Assimilation and Transnationalism: Determinants of Transnational Political Action among Contemporary Migrants. *American Journal of Sociology* 108 (6): 1211–48.

Gwynne, Robert N., and Cristobal Kay. 2000. "Views from the Periphery: Futures of Neoliberalism in Latin America. *Third World Quarterly* 21 (1): 141–56.

Joppke, Christian, and Ewa T. Morawska, eds. 2003. *Towards Assimilation and Citizenship: Immigrants in Liberal NationStates.* Basingstoke, UK: Palgrave Macmillan.

King, Kendall, and Natalie Ganuza. 2005. "Language, Identity, Education, and Transmigration: Chilean Adolescents in Sweden." *Journal of Language, Identity and Education* 4 (3): 179–99.

Levitt, Peggy. 2001. *The Transnational Villagers.* Berkeley: University of California Press.

Levitt, Peggy, and Nina Glick-Schiller. 2004. "Conceptualizing Simultaneity: A Transnational Social Field Perspective on Society." *International Migration Review* 38:1002–39.

Levitt, Peggy, and Nadya B. Jaworsky. 2007. "Transnational Migration Studies: Past Developments and Future Trends." *Annual Review of Sociology* 33:129–56.

Linneker, Brian, and Cathy McIlwaine. 2011. *Estimating the Latin American Population of London from Official Statistics.* London: School of Geography, Queen Mary, University of London. (Available from: http://www.geog.qmul.ac.uk/docs/research/latinamerican/48640.pdf) (accessed May 2, 2011).

Margheritis, Ana. 2007. "State-Led Transnationalism and Migration: Reaching Out to the Argentine Community in Spain." *Global Networks* 7:87–106.

Martínez Pizarro, Jorge, and Miguel Villa. 2005. *International Migration in Latin America and the Caribbean: A Summary View of Trends and Patterns.* United Nations Expert Group Meeting on International Migration and Development. New York: UN Secretariat (available from http://www.un.org/esa/population/meetings/ittmigdev2005/P14_jmartinez_ECLAC.pdf) (accessed May 1, 2011).

Massey, Douglas, Rafael Alarcón, Jorge Durand, and Humberto González. 1987. *Return to Aztlan: The Social Process of International Migration from Western Mexico.* Berkeley: University of California Press.

McIlwaine, Cathy. 2010. "Migrant Machismos: Exploring Gender Ideologies and Practices among Latin American Migrants in London from a Multi-Scalar Perspective." *Gender, Place and Culture* 17 (3): 281–300.

McIlwaine, Cathy, Juan Camilo Cock, and Brian Linneker. 2011. *No Longer Invisible: The Latin American Community in London.* London: Trust for London. (Available from: http://www.geog.qmul.ac.uk/docs/research/latinamerican/48637.pdf) (accessed May 20, 2011).

Meins, Robert. 2009. *Remittances in Times of Financial Instability*. March. Washington, D.C.: Inter-American Development Bank (available at: http://idbdocs.iadb.org/wsdocs/getdocument.aspx?docnum=1913678) (accessed February 2, 2011).

Menjívar, Cecilia. 2000. *Fragmented Ties: Salvadoran Immigrant Networks in America*. Berkeley: University of California Press.

Moser, Caroline O. N., and Cathy McIlwaine. 2004. *Encounters with Violence in Latin America: Urban Poor Perceptions from Colombia and Guatemala*. London: Routledge.

Murphy, Arthur D., Colleen Blanchard, and Jamie A. Hill, eds. 2001. *Latino Workers in the Contemporary South*. Athens: University of Georgia Press.

Oboler, Suzanne, ed. 1995. *Ethnic Labels, Latino Lives: Identity and the Politics of (Re)presentation in the United States*. Minneapolis: University of Minnesota Press.

Oso, Laura. 2003. "The New Migratory Space in Southern Europe: The Case of Colombian Sex Workers in Spain." In *Crossing Borders and Shifting Boundaries: Gender on the Move*, ed. Umut Erel and Kyoko Shinozaki, 209–27. Opladen: Leske and Budrich.

Padilla, Beatriz and Joao Peixoto. 2007. *Latin American Immigration to Southern Europe*. Washington, D.C.: Migration Information Source (available from: http://www.migrationinformation.org/Feature/display.cfm?ID=609) (accessed May 3, 2011).

Pastor, Ana María Relaño, and Guillermo Alonso Meneses. 2005. "Latino Diaspora in Chula Vista, San Diego, and Ciutat Vella, Barcelona." In *Crossing Over: Comparing Recent Migration in the United States and Europe*, ed. Holger Henke, 257–333. Oxford: Lexington Books.

Peixoto, Joao. 2009. Back to the South: Social and Political Aspects of Latin American Migration to Southern Europe, *International Migration*: DOI: 10.1111/j.1468-2435.2009.00537.x.

Pellegrino, Adela. 2001. "Trends in Latin American Skilled Migration: 'Brain Drain' or 'Brain exchange'? *International Migration* 39 (5): 111–32.

———. 2004. *Migration from Latin America to Europe: Trends and Policy Challenges*. Migration Research Series, 16. International Organization for Migration (IOM) (available from: http://www.unhcr.org/refworld/docid/415c6fec4.html) (accessed December 15, 2010).

Poblete, Juan, ed. 2003. *Critical Latin American and Latino Studies*. Malden, MA, and Oxford: Blackwell.

Portes, Alejandro, and Josh DeWind, eds. 2007. *Rethinking Migration: New Theoretical and Empirical Perspectives*. Oxford and New York: Berghahn.

Portes, Alejandro, Cristina Escobar, and Alexandria Walton Radford. 2007. "Immigrant Transnational Organizations and Development: A Comparative Study." *International Migration Review* 41 (1): 242–81.

Portes, Alejandro, Luis E. Guarnizo, and Patricia Landolt. 1999. "The Study of Transnationalism: Pitfalls and Promise of an Emergent Research Field." *Ethnic and Racial Studies* 22:217–37.

Portes, Alejandro, William J. Haller, and Luis E. Guarnizo. 2002. "Transnational Entrepreneurs." *American Sociological Review* 67 (2): 278–98.

Portes, Alejandro, and Min Zhou. 1993. "The New Second Generation: Segmented Assimilation and Its Variants. *The Annals of the American Academy of Political and Social Science* 530 (1): 74–96.

Raijman, Rebeca, Silvina Schammah-Gesser, and Adriana. Kemp. 2003. "International Migration, Domestic Work, and Care Work: Undocumented Latina Migrants in Israel." *Gender and Society* 17:727–49.

Román-Velasquez, Patria. 1999. *The Making of Latin London: Salsa Music, Place, and Identity.* Aldershot, UK: Ashgate.

Roman-Velasquez, Patria. 2009. "Latin Americans in London and the Dynamics of Diasporic Identities." In *Comparing Postcolonial Diasporas*, ed. Michelle Keown, David Murphy, and James Proctor, 104–24. Basingstoke, UK: Palgrave Macmillan.

Rouse, Roger. 1991. "Mexican Migration and the Social Space of Postmodernism". *Diaspora* 1 (1): 8–23.

Safran, William. 1991. "Diasporas in Modern Societies: Myths of Homeland and Return." *Diaspora* 1 (1): 83–99.

Smith, Robert C., 2003. "Migrant Membership as an Instituted Process: Transnationalization, the State and the Extra-Territorial Conduct of Mexican Politics." *International Migration Review* 37 (2): 297–343.

Snel, Erik, Godfried Engbersen, and Arjen Leerkes. 2006. "Transnational Involvement and Social Integration." *Global Networks* 6 (3): 285–308.

Solé, Carlota, and Sonia Parella. 2005. "Immigrant Women in Domestic Service: The Care Crisis in the United States and Spain." In *Crossing Over: Comparing Recent Migration in the United States and Europe,* ed. Holger Henke, 235–56. Oxford: Lexington Books.

Solimano, Andres. 2003. "Globalization and International Migration: The Latin American Experience." *CEPAL Review* 80:53–69.

Soysal, Yasemin. N. 1994 *Limits of Citizenship. Migrants and Postnational Membership in Europe.* Chicago: University of Chicago Press.

Tölölian, Khachig. 1991. "The Nation State and Its Others: In Lieu of a Preface." *Diaspora* 1 (1): 3–7.

Vicente, Trinidad L. 2010. Latin American Immigration to Spain, Network Migration in Europe (available from: http://www.migrationeducation.org/48.1.html?&rid=162&cHash=96b3134cdb899a06a8ca6e12f41eafac) (accessed May 10, 2011).

Waldinger, Roger, and David Fitzgerald. 2004. "Transnationalism in Question." *American Journal of Sociology* 109:1177–95.

Wright, Katie. 2010. "'It's a Limited Kind of Happiness': Barriers to Achieving Human Well-being through International Migration: The Case of Peruvian Migrants in London and Madrid." *Bulletin of Latin American Research* 29 (3): 367–83.

Section I

Conceptual Understanding of Latin American Migration across Borders

Chapter 2

Transnational Theory and South American Immigration across Europe

Adrian J. Bailey and Rosa Mas Giralt

The South American population living in the UK and Europe has grown decisively over the past decade (Foreign and Commonwealth Office 2007, McIlwaine 2007).[1] With an increasing number of economic migrants, students, and family reunifiers supplementing the earlier flows of those moving to seek asylum and to participate in skilled labor markets, the community has greatly diversified. The fact that, like many immigrant populations, South Americans tend to concentrate in some areas and not others introduces further diversity between, in the UK, the South American communities in London and the North. Understanding how growing immigration and diverse communities affects British, European, and South American societies in interdependent ways is important to debates on citizenship, belonging, and multiculturalism (Yuval-Davis 2006), development and position of South America in the global economy (Munck 2009, Robinson 2004), and convergence and divergence across Europe (Koser and Lutz 1998; Pellegrino 2004).

This chapter joins scholarship that links the growth and diversification of immigration to processes of transnationalization (Faist 2000, 2004a, Hannerz 1996). As cross-border living has intensified and bound together the lives of many in origin and destination societies, processes concerned with identification (Anthias 2002), familyhood (Bryceson and Vuorela 2002), state influence (Glick Schiller 2005), and, most generally, the reproduction of space-time (Bailey 2002) have been interpreted in light of the relational networks they help constitute (Levitt 2009). As these readings unsettle naturalized isomorphisms involving, for example, national-belonging, patrilineal-family, and generation-by-generation assimilation, they offer a potentially productive window on how the growth and diversification of contemporary South American immigration in Europe might affect experiences of citizenship, global economy, and convergence. Furthermore, accounts of transnationalisation highlight the role of immigrants' dynamic social networks in economic and cultural reproduction, and offer a theoretical corrective to traditional accounts of European immigration that have been criticized for ignoring the role of families and social networks (Kofman 2004). Thus, the goal of the chapter is to apply transnational theory to better understand the growth and diversification of contemporary South American immigration to and across Europe.

Applying transnational theory leads the chapter in two connected directions. First, we outline the mutually dependent relationship between neoliberalism, immigration, and transnationalisation, arguing that families and social networks play crucial roles in connecting and reconnecting individuals, identities, institutions, and society. We argue that, under transnational conditions, the ability to coordinate everyday life across borders becomes increasingly fraught for South American immigrants who are simultaneously building geographically stretched social networks across and beyond Europe. This leads us to identify and draw on four processes generated from transnational family theory that help better understand how South American families organize themselves and reproduce diversity.

Transnationalization, Neoliberalism, and Immigration

This section summarizes how neoliberal conditions impinge upon the immigration of South Americans to Europe and the UK. By neoliberal we mean the continuing project of capitalist accumulation that has become simultaneously concerned with the economic, social, and cultural reproduction of society (Ong 2006). Accumulation is advanced through such means as the speeding up of obsolescence, the reduction of dwell time between investing capital and realizing surplus, the near instantaneous exploitation of spatial differences in potential profit, the integration of military and imperialistic regimes of governance, the reorganization of governance and membership to facilitate temporal and spatial fluidity (including open borders, differentiated controls on the movement of people, and variegated rights), and the expectation that individual workers, consumers, migrants, and so on will assume greater responsibility for their own fortunes through self-reliance and individualization (Bauman 2007, Beck 1992). Neoliberalism transforms landscapes of immigration through the restructuring of labor markets, through the conditions for entry and residence, and through the marketization and privatization of social and state institutions including families and welfare regimes (Castles 1998).

However, we know that migrants use diverse strategies and cultural practices to rework labor markets, social institutions, and patterns of settlement and belonging (Bauder 2006, Castles and Davidson 2000). Drawing on the growing empirical record of South American immigrant experiences in and across Europe (for example, Bermúdez Torres 2010, Cwerner 2001; Margheritis 2007; McIlwaine 2010), we interpret such activities as part of the deepening transnationalisation of Europe. Four themes emerge. First, the "savage" neoliberalism institutionalized across South and Central America during the 1990s and first decade of the twenty-first century caused inequality to increase while government support for the poor fell (Robinson 2004). The concurrent loss of jobs, loss of collective support, and increased care burden prompted by the demographic ageing that followed earlier declines in fertility all encouraged mass outmigration, from "traditional" source areas such as Ecuador and Colombia, and newer origins, including Bolivia. The increased immigration control measures introduced by the United States after the events of September 11, 2001, also contributed to Europe becoming a popular migration destination for Latin Americans (Pellegrino 2004). Thus, significant new streams of South American migrants sought work in unfamiliar destinations to provide essential resources for their origin communities.

Second, the conditions under which immigrants could enter and remain within Europe have been continuously transformed during the first decade of the twenty-first century. While it is widely acknowledged that political institutions influence migration, citizenship, and the daily lives of migrant community members through national and regional modes of governance (Fix et al. 2008), European supranationalism and uneven progress toward the project of a single European community complicates the ways in which governance works across multiple scales (Leitner 1997). For example, while European residents (including South Americans who have lived in Spain, Italy, or Portugal and have reclaimed citizenship status in these countries) have "internal" access to European labor markets (including those in the UK), the UK continues to retain sovereignty over such issues as immigration, asylum adjudication and dispersal, and social rights and benefits. Continued uncertainty about rights and responsibilities in new destinations lends rationality to migrants' ongoing connections with, and investments in, offshore and "home" community.

Third, potential and actual disconnects between levels of governance lead to a scalar politics over issues of immigration and belonging, with contrasting and sometimes contradictory discourses about the "idea of Europe" and the nature of membership to different communities. The complexity and ambiguity of Europe's variegated immigration regime has been deepened by the recent enlargement of Europe. When members of the so-called Accession 8 (A8) countries began moving to selected European destinations after 2004, including the UK, opportunities for "other" migrant workers (including South Americans, but also Africans) may have contracted. Moreover, media reports struggled to rework the traditional reading of "immigrant" as "external" in light of the European status and whiteness of A8 migrants. Such shifting demographics transmit further pressure upon an already fragile migration-citizenship regime, and fuel uncertainty and popular discontent about the role of immigration in European society. Two indicative UK examples include the political storm about the Sangatte refugee camp in northern France, and the Lindley oil refinery strike protesting the presence of Italian workers in labor markets resolutely constructed as "British." South Americans in the UK found themselves in a potentially uncomfortable position as the first significant cohort of non-Commonwealth overseas migrants. As above, their positionality is further complicated by the reality that many arrived in the UK from Spain, Italy, or Portugal and carried European rights with them. Furthermore, while the notion of any pan-European ideal of a single community is quite variable from one part of Europe to the next, the pace with which such an aspiration might be obtained is also variable, as recent discussions of multiculturalism demonstrate (Van de Vijver, et al. 2006). Fourth, the rights of non-European residents have been more tightly managed and, in some cases, restricted, as retrenchment of welfare provisions and the impacts of the recession of 2008–2009 unfolded across Europe. As Flynn (2005, 463) noted for the UK, "migration management is now intended to regulate wider aspects of the life of immigrants, including access to jobs, welfare services, family reunification, and ultimately integration and the acquisition of citizenship." This has increased the costs of housing, childcare, health, and, most significantly, reduced access to well-paid employment opportunities with benefits. For Young (2003, 449) the concentration of deprivation and isolation of some immigrant groups has a particular effect upon second-generation immigrants who may achieve citizenship status in legal terms but, because of social exclusion and lack of employment (diminished economic rights), experience unfairness and, in effect, have citizenship "thwarted."

The squeeze between the obligations to meet the needs of family and community members in South America and the daily encounter with a difficult and sometimes hostile reception context with dwindling access to scarce resources (Margheritis 2007) deepens the transnationalization experienced by South Americans across Europe. Cultural expectations of individualization and self-reliance—coupled with the real withdrawal of collective support—have led South American immigrants to take poorly paid, temporary, and precarious jobs, work long hours, and remit as much as possible to expectant kin offshore (McIlwaine 2007). Such everyday experiences have implications for how the connections between individuals, identities, institutions, and society might be theorized. In many cases immigrants become trapped in a cycle of impoverishment, struggling to keep up with remitting obligations, working several jobs often in unregulated conditions, and experiencing deskilling. Precarious employment also means there is less money for immediate family members in destinations, or less time to see them, which undermines delivery of traditional intergenerational resources, such as a sense of enduring familyhood, and respect. Such entrenched experiences of daily life can erode trust and social capital between migrants (Menjívar 2000), and pressurize relationships and normative gender roles (Hondagneu-Sotelo and Avila 1997; McIlwaine 2010). Indeed, such is the pressure to support overseas kin and community that Bernhard, Landolt, and Goldring (2009) report Latin American women have come "full circle" from patriarchal constraints in their home communities to a hope of reformed gender relations and social standing in Canada to a condition of isolation and poverty occasioned by attempting to meet simultaneous demands.

Ambiguous and at times prickly transnational realities potentially unsettle classic sociological theory on migration (Massey et al. 1987). On the one hand, we record evidence for family networks providing social insurance, financial collateral, facilitating employment introductions, and reducing housing costs for newly arriving migrants, and find that by creating and circulating social, cultural, and network capital, families are becoming part of the cumulative dynamics that reproduce transnational migration (Carlisle 2006). However, we concur that insufficient attention is given to how families operating under contemporary neoliberal and transnational conditions face and strategize a set of expectations for material and symbolic exchange that appear both instantaneously and across the less certain horizons of far-flung places (Cwerner 2001; Bernhard, Landolt, and Goldring 2009).

Transnational Families, Liquid Life Paths

To further develop an account of the diversity of South American immigration across Europe, we turn to recent advances in transnational family theory. Reflecting on the European context, Bailey and Boyle (2004, 233–34) identified six challenges for frameworks that purport to describe the realities of family migration across the "new" Europe: the rise of lifecourse migration connected with, for example, transitions into and away from education, training, marriage, divorce, and retirement; the diversifying structure of the family; changing provision of social support including for housing and unemployment; the emergence of new discourses about citizenship and belonging; new sets of rights and responsibilities associated with citizenship and denizenship; interdependencies between mobility and changing gender and ethnicity constructions. Here we respond to these challenges by introducing four sets of processes to which transnational family theory draws attention.

First, transnational familyhood is seen as a cultural practice of identification (Waters 2002). Drawing on European case-studies, Bryceson and Vuorela (2002, 3) understand transnational familyhood as organized around a long-term and networked vision of belonging: "Families that live some or most of their time separated from each other, yet hold together and create something that can be seen as a feeling of collective welfare and unity, namely 'familyhood,' even across national borders." They emphasize the importance of frontiering (negotiating everyday life under conditions of scarcity) and relativizing (the strategic switching on and off of relationships and other social ties) in building and reproducing familyhood (Herrera this volume). There is some evidence that these concepts illuminate contemporary South American experience in the European context. There are several reasons why South Americans find themselves in the conditions of social and economic sparsity that characterize frontiering situations. Low-skilled and poorly paid employment in London often means working long hours, in more than one job, and living in substandard accommodation, conditions that jeopardize the migrants' opportunities to develop stable social relationships; the socioeconomic diversity of the populations and their settlement circumstances also contribute to the fragmentation of the "communities" (for those who are undocumented, fears of being reported by fellow migrants lead them to maintain controlled social networks) (McIlwaine this volume Section 2); outside of the capital, the number of fellow migrants is much smaller (e.g., students based at universities around the country but also increasing numbers of all types of migrants), and this translates into a lack of spaces and opportunities to frontier.

Relativization also provides useful purchase on South American immigrant practices. For example, not all projects transacted in the name of building family are altruistic or volitional. The high incidence of domestic violence, family breakups, and social isolation reflects gendered pressures to conform to unrealistic role stereotypes (Menjívar and Salcido 2002; see also McIlwaine and Carlisle this volume). We also know that compulsion is behind the relationships of dependence and in extreme cases servitude between migrants and those who fund their migration (and, increasingly, those who service the debts that have been accrued from the act of migration). Elsewhere, gang membership is thought to have risen among a disaffected second and third generation of immigrants who feel disempowered in traditional family hierarchies, and disenfranchised by a lack of economic opportunity and stalled benefits of citizenship. However, relativizing also functions at the local level and in conditions of scarcity, as the dynamics of social networks are strongly affected by the diverse circumstances of migrants, who tend to connect or disconnect with people in terms of similar life cycle stages and background (e.g., with young children, class) or shared settlement circumstances (e.g., asylum seekers, Latino-British couples). More generally, intergenerational and interethnic exchanges presumed in social capital approaches may be undermined by the reality of the sudden diversification of South American streams (Pieke 2007 makes this point for the Chinese diaspora). In the UK, the older streams of Chileans and Colombians (some of whom were political refugees and many of whom arrived in the 1970s and 1980s) have quickly been supplanted by Andean circuits (Ecuador), Brazil, and Bolivia, with whom they may share little in common.

Second, there is growing recognition that a distinctive feature of transnational families is their experience of temporariness. Indeed, for Faist (2004b), an experience of temporariness is a key dimension along which diversity of social formations unfolds. Drawing on the experiences of Turkish guest workers in Germany, he argues that the nature of social and symbolic ties can help differentiate between transnational families and other forms of social networks (fields), which include diffusion spaces, advocacy networks, and religious groups. In his view, the degree of institutionalization (e.g., functioning of internal rule sets, state regulation, availability of communications infrastructure) and the nature of time-space compression (conditions of low longevity and high longevity) affect the form and reproduction of social networks. Accordingly, transnational families are character- ized as temporary formations with low longevity but high degrees of institutionalization.

However, characterizing transnational families as temporary both appears to run against South American practice (Schmalzbauer 2008) and misses the relativizing nature of transnational social fields. In the latter case, while Bailey and Boyle (2004, 239) drew attention to the diversification of space-times "as more families are formed and split between nations *within* the [European] Community," it should be noted that South American migrant families are being formed and split *across* the boundaries of "fortress Europe" as well as within the Community. Considering the greater costs of distance for South Americans compared to A8 migrants implies the former groups may stay split longer and need to be more creative in space- time assignments.

Indeed, there is sustained attention to better understanding the ways in which space-times underpin the diversity of social formations in transnational settings. Here we note how literatures concerned with embodiment and lifecourses have, respectively, drawn attention to a third and fourth set of processes. Thus, a third set of processes illuminate the role of space-time by considering the embodied and emotional experiences of daily transnational life (Svašek 2008; Dunn 2010). For Svašek and Skrbiš (2007, 370) the circulation of emotion through everyday interactions sustains social hierarchies, and is thus part of the transmission of power through social networks, includ- ing those that operate transnationally. While emotions arise and are learned in group-specific social settings, the stretching of groups and cultures across borders means: "the self [is] . . . a multiple relational process in which subjectivities are shaped and reshaped as individuals engage with past, present, and future experiences and environments" (Svašek and Skrbiš 2007, 371). Specifically, transnational social fields imply translocal subjectivities, described elsewhere as the "multiply- located senses of self amongst those who inhabit transnational social fields" (Conradson and McKay 2007, 168). The implication of tak- ing what Hochschild (1983) terms "emotional work" seriously is that transnational families are not only synchronizing webs of material and symbolic exchanges over social networks, they are doing this while also reflecting on their own multiple subject positions, that is, their multiple selves. Working relationally across social networks, discourses, and representations of memory and imagination help migrants synchronize multiple selves (Chamberlain and Leydesdorff 2004).

Again, while emotions such as ambiguity, pain, and guilt have been shown to circulate across the transnational networks connecting North Africa and Europe, the greater distance over which such emotions must circulate over South American social fields could generate greater ambiguity. The frequency of corporeal interaction, which is reduced due to higher costs, together with difficulties caused by coordinating activities across distant time zones all serve to intensify the uncertainty surrounding intended emotional meanings (Baldassar 2007), compromising the sense of self. Crucially, as memories and imaginations are socially mediated and shared through public commemorations and normalized rhythms, the emotional work transacted by transnational families reproduces space-times. Put another way, transnational theory suggests that the everyday acts and emotions of immigrants have resonance beyond the social back to the circulation of power and constitution of society.

Fourth, ongoing efforts to better integrate space-times into accounts of social networks and transnational families have led some researchers to explore further the temporality of everyday life through lifecourse concept. Drawing on earlier lifecourse-inspired research (Blank and Torrecilha 1998; Olwig 2003; Kobayashi and Preston 2007), Mas Giralt and Bailey (2010) start by considering how individual immigrants coordinate a series of projects over their lifetimes, and how material and symbolic links develop between individuals and institutions. Projects arise from and crosscut specific domains including work, housing, family life, leisure, and education. The authors introduce the idea of "synchronization" as a vulnerability arising from transnational expectations of simultaneity in everyday life. Transnational families face particular pressures when projects start and end because of the complexities of synchronization. Moreover, changes in one domain have implications for projects in other domains (e.g., immigration by a partner often changes family life). Such transitions and events assume meaning for individuals and for institutions, and acquire normative values related to their order and their timing (e.g., social expectations about the order and timing of nest-leaving, independence, family formation and so forth; Hareven 2000; Bailey 2009).

More broadly, lifecourse theory may be extended to interpret the experiences of temporality as interdependencies between individual (biographical) time, institutional times, and historical times. As such, everyday practices associate with space-times that reproduce structural conjunctures, including neoliberalism, and vice versa. This is significant because, according to the liquid modernity thesis (Bauman 2007), the collapse in authority of long-termism and other "neoliberal" temporalities can challenge the idea that life paths are linear or even corporeal. However, while "liquid life paths" might appear to reflect hegemonic neoliberal norms about the value of forgetting, nimbleness, and flexibility, careful attention to the transnational context reminds us that life paths are relational narratives through which social selves are able to "make sense" of punitive neoliberal discourses by retelling pasts and reimaging futures: "Liquid life paths constitute circuits of identification through the interdependencies of fluid spatial and temporal imaginaries" (Mas Giralt and Bailey 2010, 388).

Accordingly, the concept of liquid life path complicates the space-time basis of selfhood. In transnational contexts, such as we have argued characterize South American immigrants in Europe, liquid life paths reference processes of identification and becomings of selfhoods over borders. Here we contribute to an understanding of the range of such selfhood becomings by recognizing two "ideal types" each with liquid life paths underpinned by distinctive space-times. That is, first, the emergence of composite selfhoods organizes around a dominant and finite project that lends integrity (structure) to temporality while retaining a fluid spatiality. Put another way, such composite selfhoods may emerge when immigrant family members are split geographically, but united by the shared project of familyhood (i.e., a kind of temporary permanence). Second, the emergence of situated identities lends integrity to spatiality by claiming propinquity but lends fluidity to temporality by building selfhood without reference to a fixed time horizon (i.e., a kind of permanent temporariness).

We draw this section to a close by briefly reporting examples of composite selfhoods and situated identities that, taken together, hint at an intrinsic structure and integrity to liquid life paths. The first example comes from the work of Jason Pribilsky (2004) on split families from Ecuador. Composite selfhoods emerge from his account of how separated (also Ecuadorian) transnational family members dealt with hostile local discourses about the difficulties of lone parenting. Pribilsky found they narrated life paths that "integrate their individual gender dramas and imagine their lives as unfolding on the same stage" (2004, 324). A second example is drawn from the experiences of a young Ecuadorian mother whom the second author interviewed in London in 2004. Ana (a pseudonym) had left rural Ecuador when she separated from the father of her daughter and moved to London through Quito in 1999. For Ana the imagination and enactment of a territorially based familyhood underpinned her biography. What she narrated as the everyday and long running problems and opportunities appeared as such because of their relationship to this project. Problems included the set of factors keeping her from seeing her daughter, whom she had left behind in Ecuador with her mother five years before, and who Ana had not seen since. The separation was an ongoing source of unfairness to Ana, and a constant source of emotional pain, as she could not remember what it was like to brush her daughter's hair or to touch her. Ana's own feelings of guilt about separation were further heightened by the fact that different time zones meant that, for example, she could not imagine herself and Ana brushing their teeth at the same temporal moment. Additional constraints included lack of immigration status that trapped her inside the UK and reduced access to jobs forcing her to spend more time working at lower rates and have still less time (or extra cash beyond remitting) to build a social life in London. While her work as a carer was hard and precarious, this was not a key aspect of her experience in the UK or her selfhood. Instead, she identified changing legal status (the granting of the right to remain in the UK) as the key resource that enabled strategies to build contiguous familyhood. Specifically, she described how she could now work legally, save to visit Ecuador, potentially bring her daughter to London, and start meeting new friends. Indeed, she had just started a relationship with a fellow South American that could possibly lead to the kind of becoming she continued to imagine.

Ana's life path is an example of one oriented around a singular project: the entrapment caused by her legal status combined with gendered norms passed down by her mother, which she intended to pass to her own daughter, led Ana to organize strategies in pursuit of a single goal, despite the pain (separation), guilt (from her mother and daughter in Ecuador), and loneliness (no time) that she experienced on a daily basis for five years. It illustrates how states (through granting status) and institutions (family norms, gender norms) exert influence upon her life path alongside her own reworking of memory and aspiration. As it is jointly worked on in material and symbolic ways by Ana, by those in her social network, and by institutions, Ana's life path transcends her corporeal lifecourse. Were we to listen to Ana some time before, or some years afterward, we can expect to recover and narrate a different life path.

Bailey et al.'s (2002) work among largely undocumented Salvadorans in New Jersey attests to selfhoods that showed signs of situated identities. "Permanent temporariness" was flagged in many ways, with respondents telling field researchers that "I am here while I can" and acknowledging they held different aspirations for U.S. residence than their children, who were more committed to assimilation. Elsewhere, Salvadorans have admitted that memories of civil war in El Salvador were unhelpful concepts in reconstructing sense of self (one woman said she "would throw some forgetting" on her previous life outside the United States.

We believe that by carefully recovering such contingent life paths, at different moments, and looking for common strategies and common experiences, we may build from the bottom up productive accounts of not just the diversity of South American immigration, but the ways in which such diversity has commonality. Thus framed, the possibilities for patterns of social solidarity, membership, and politics can be appreciated.

Conclusions

The dependent relationship between neoliberalism and immigration deepens the transnationalization of the experiences of South American immigrants in Europe. In response to the lack of attention to how immigrant families negotiate these conditions, the chapter applies transnational family theory and highlights several processes in the European case. These include frontiering and relativizing, experiences of space-time that contradict the idea that South American families are temporary formations, and emotional experiences of transnational daily life including emotional difficulties due to synchronizing in different time zones and across greater distances in the case of South Americans in Europe. We argue that this experience connects with lifecourse research on the temporality of everyday life and can be read through the concept of liquid life paths. Liquid life paths are the ways in which immigrants make sense of neoliberal conditions by negotiating multiple projects relationally and through interactions with other individuals, objects, and discourses. In transnational conditions, liquid life paths make reference to the becoming of selfhoods over borders. These multiple selfhoods may be bundled together (situated identity, such as Ana) or reduced to a composite selfhood. We conclude that interrogating contingent and diverse life paths and considering their common strategies and experiences can help illuminate the diversity of South American immigration and appreciate the implications for patterns of social solidarity.

Note

1. Here we choose the term "South American" to refer to the geographic area that includes Argentina, Bolivia, Brazil, Chile, Colombia, Ecuador, Falkland Islands, French Guiana, Guyana, Paraguay, Peru, Suriname, Uruguay, and Venezuela. While research take as a term of reference "Latin America" to flag the historical and common links among the different Central and South American countries, we deploy "South American" to simultaneously acknowledge the "Latin" (Spanish, Portuguese, French), African, and Indian heritage across the region (Eakin 2007, 3).

References

Anthias, Floya. 2002. "Where Do I Belong?: Narrating Collective Identity and Translocational Positionality." *Ethnicities* 2:491–514.

Bailey, Adrian J. 2009. "Population Geography: Lifecourse Matters." *Progress in Human Geography* 33:407–18.

Bailey, Adrian J., and Paul Boyle. 2004. "Untying and Retying Family Migration in the New Europe." *Journal of Ethnic and Migration Studies* 30:229–42.

Bailey, Adrian J., Richard A. Wright, Ines M. Miyares, and Alison Mountz. 2002. "(Re)producing Salvadoran Transnational Geographies." *Annals of the Association of American Geographers* 92:125–44.

Baldassar, Loretta. 2007. "Transnational Families and the Provision of Moral and Emotional Support: The Relationship between Truth and Distance." *Identities* 14:385–409.

Bauder, Harald. 2006. *Labor Movement.* Oxford: Oxford University Press.

Bauman, Zygmunt. 2007. *Liquid Times.* Malden, MA: Polity Press.

Beck, Ulrich. 1992. *Risk Society.* London: Sage.

Bermúdez Torres, Anastasia. 2010. "The Transnational Political Practices of Colombians in Spain and the United Kingdom: Politics 'Here' and 'There.'" *Ethnic and Racial Studies* 33:75–91.

Bernhard, Judith K., Patricia Landolt, and Luin Goldring. 2009. "Transnationalizing Families: Canadian Immigration Policy and the Spatial Fragmentation of Care-Giving among Latin American Newcomers." *International Migration* 47:3–31.

Blank, Susan, and Ramon S. Torrecilha. 1998. "Understanding the Living Arrangements of Latino Immigrants: A Life Course Approach." *International Migration Review* 32:3–19.

Bryceson, Deborah, and Ulla Vuorela. eds. 2002. *The Transnational Family: New European Frontiers and Global Networks.* Oxford: Berg.

Carlisle, Frances. 2006. "Marginalization and Ideas of Community among Latin American Migrants to the UK." *Gender and Development* 14:235–45.

Castles, Stephen. 1998. "Globalization and Migration: Some Pressing Contradictions." *International Social Science Journal* 50:179–86.

Castles, Stephen, and Alastair Davidson. 2000. *Citizenship and Migration: Globalization and the Politics of Belonging.* New York: Routledge.

Chamberlain, Mary, and Selma Leydesdorff. 2004. "Transnational Families: Memories and Narratives." *Global Networks* 4:227–41.

Conradson, David, and Deirdre McKay. 2007. "Translocal Subjectivities: Mobility, Connection, Emotion." *Mobilities* 2:167–74.

Cwerner, Saulo B. 2001. "The Times of Migration." *Journal of Ethnic and Migration Studies* 27:7–36.

Dunn, Kevin. 2010. "Embodied Transnationalism: Bodies in Transnational Spaces." *Population Space and Place* 16:1–9.

Eakin, Marshall C. 2007. *The History of Latin America: Collision of Cultures.* Basingstoke, UK: Palgrave Macmillan.

Faist, Thomas. 2000. "Transnationalization in International Migration: Implications for the Study of Citizenship and Culture." *Ethnic and Racial Studies* 23:189–222.

———. 2004a. "Towards a Political Sociology of Transnationalization: The State of the Art in Migration Research." *European Journal of Sociology* 45:331–66.

———. 2004b. "The Border Crossing Expansion of Social Space: Concepts, Questions, and Topics." In *Transnational Social Spaces: Agents, Networks, and Institutions,* ed. Thomas Faist and Eyüp Özveren, 1–34. Aldershot, UK: Ashgate.

Fix, Michael, Margie McHugh, Aaron Matteo Terrazas, and Laureen Laglagaron. 2008. *Los Angeles on the Leading Edge.* Washington, D.C.: Migration Policy Institute.

Flynn, Don. 2005. "New Borders, New Management: The Dilemmas of Modern Immigration Policies." *Ethnic and Racial Studies* 28:463–90.

Foreign and Commonwealth Office. 2007. *Latin America to 2020: A UK Public Strategy Paper.* London: Foreign and Commonwealth Office.

Glick Schiller, Nina. 2005. "Transnational Social Fields and Imperialism: Bringing a Theory of Power to Transnational Studies. *Anthropological Theory* 5:439–61.

Hannerz, Ulf. 1996. *Transnational Connections: Culture, People and Places.* London: Routledge.

Hareven, Tamara K. 2000. *Families, History, and Social Life: Life Course and Cross-Cultural Perspectives.* Colorado: Westview Press.

Hochschild, Arlie Russell. 1983. *The Managed Heart: Commercialization of Human Feeling.* Berkeley: University of California Press.

Hondagneu-Sotelo, Pierrette, and Ernestine Avila. 1997. "'I'm Here, But I'm There': The Meanings of Latina Transnational Motherhood." *Gender and Society* 11:548–71.

Kobayashi, Audrey, and Valerie Preston. 2007. "Transnationalism through the Life Course: Hong Kong Immigrants in Canada." *Asia Pacific Viewpoint* 48:151–67.

Kofman, Eleonore. 2004. "Family-Related Migration: A Critical Review of European Studies." *Journal of Ethnic and Migration Studies* 30:243–62.

Koser, Khalid, and Helma Lutz, eds. 1998. *New Migration in Europe: Social Constructions and Social Realities*. Basingstoke, UK: Macmillan.

Leitner, Helga. 1997. "Reconfiguring the Spatiality of Power: The Construction of a Supranational Migration Framework for the European Union." *Political Geography* 16:123–43.

Levitt, Peggy. 2009. "Roots and Routes: Understanding the Lives of the Second Generation Transnationally." *Journal of Ethnic and Migration Studies* 35:1225–42.

Margheritis, Ana. 2007. "State-Led Transnationalism and Migration: Reaching out to the Argentine Community in Spain." *Global Networks* 7:87–106.

Mas Giralt, Rosa, and Adrian J. Bailey. 2010. "Transnational Familyhood and the Liquid Life Paths of South Americans in the UK." *Global Networks* 10:383–400.

Massey, Douglas, Rafael Alarcón, Jorge Durand, and Humberto González. 1987. *Return to Aztlan: The Social Process of International Migration from Western Mexico*. Berkeley and London: University of California Press

McIlwaine, Cathy. 2007. *Living in Latin London: How Latin American Migrants Survive in the City*. London: University of London, Queen Mary.. (Available from: http://www.geog.qmul.ac.uk/docs/staff/4400.pdf) (accessed May 5, 2011).

———. 2010. "Migrant Machismos: Exploring Gender Ideologies and Practices among Latin American Migrants in London from a Multi-Scalar Perspective." *Gender, Place and Culture*. 17: 281–300.

Menjívar, Cecilia. 2000. *Fragmented Ties: Salvadoran Immigrant Networks in America*. Berkeley and London: University of California Press.

Menjívar, Cecilia, and Olivia Salcido. 2002. "Immigrant Women and Domestic Violence: Common Experience in Different Countries." *Gender and Society* 16:898–920.

Munck, Gerardo L. 2009. "Democracy and Development in a Globalized World: Thinking about Latin America from Within." *Studies in Comparative International Development* 44:337–58.

Olwig, Karen Fog. 2003. "'Transnational' Socio-Cultural Systems and Ethnographic Research: Views from an Extended Field Site. *International Migration Review* 37:787–811.

Ong, Aihwa. 2006. *Neoliberalism as Exception: Mutations in Citizenship and Sovereignty*. London: Duke University Press.

Pellegrino, Adela. 2004. *Migration from Latin America to Europe: Trends and Policy Challenges*. Migration Research Series, 16. International Organization for Migration (IOM) (available from: http://www.unhcr.org/refworld/docid/415c6fec4.html (accessed October 15, 2007).

Pieke, Frank N. 2007. "The New Chinese Migration Order." *Population, Space and Place* 13:81–94.

Pribilsky, Jason. 2004. "Aprendemos a convivir: Conjugal Relations, Co-Parenting, and Family Life among Ecuadorian Transnational Migrants in New York City and the Ecuadorian Andes." *Global Networks* 4:313–34.

Robinson, William I. 2004. "Global Crisis and Latin America." *Bulletin of Latin American Research* 23:135–53.

Schmalzbauer, Leah. 2008. "Family Divided: The Class Formation of Honduran Transnational Families." *Global Networks* 8:329–46.

Svašek, Maruška. 2008. "Who Cares? Families and Feelings in Movement." *Journal of Intercultural Studies* 29:213–30.

Svašek, Maruška, and Zlatko Skrbiš. 2007. "Passions and Powers: Emotions and Globalisation." *Identities* 14:367–83.

Van de Vijver, Fons J. R., Saskia R. G. Schalk-Soekar, Judit Arends-Tóth, and Seger M. Breugelmans. 2006. "Cracks in the Wall of Multiculturalism? A Review of Attitudinal Studies in the Netherlands." *International Journal on Multicultural Societies* 8:102–18.

Waters, Johanna H. 2002. "'Flexible Families?': Astronaut Households and the Experiences of Lone Mothers in Vancouver, B.C." *Social and Cultural Geography* 3:117–34.

Young, Jock. 2003. "To These Wet and Windy Shores." *Punishment and Society* 5:449–62.

Yuval-Davis, Nira. 2006. "Belonging and the Politics of Belonging." *Patterns of Prejudice.* 40:197–214.

Chapter 3

A Transnational Asset Accumulation Framework for Researching Latin American Migration

Caroline Moser

This chapter outlines a framework of transnational asset accumulation and assesses its relevance for research with Latin American migrants in Europe. The framework differentiates between a transnational asset index as a conceptual approach for the diagnosis of the assets of migrants, and transnational asset accumulation policy as an operational tool for designing and implementing sustainable transnational asset accumulation interventions. The chapter draws on earlier work on asset accumulation policy (see Moser 2007, 2008, 2010), as well as asset-focused transnational migration studies (Orozco 2007; Cordero-Guzman and Quiroz-Becerra 2007; Gammage 2007) and adapts these to create a framework specifically relevant to transnational migrants. It focuses on both well-known tangible assets such as human, financial, natural, and productive capital as well as intangible assets such as household and community social capital, as well as civic and political capital relating to such issues as citizens' rights, democratic development, and institutional accountability.

The discussion draws on empirical research with Ecuadorian migrants from Guayaquil moving to Barcelona in Spain identifying the assets that migrants bring with them, those they accumulate while abroad, and finally, those that are transferred back, directly or indirectly, to their city of origin. In distinguishing between the strategies of first-and second-generation migrants, the chapter shows how the diversity of accumulation processes is influenced by such factors as gender, class, and ethnicity, as well as externalities relating to legalization processes and labor market opportunities. Conceptually, the chapter seeks to demonstrate the added value of an asset-based conceptual approach for better understanding transnational migration and for developing appropriate long-term migration-relevant asset accumulation solutions. The chapter first provides background information on the development of an asset accumulation framework, highlighting those assets of particular relevance in examining transnational migration; second, it applies the framework to the analysis of data on Ecuadorian migrants to Spain.

Defining the Asset Accumulation Framework

It is important to provide some background to the chapter in terms of summarizing the main characteristics of an asset accumulation framework.[1] First, it is necessary to define an asset. An asset is a "stock of financial, human, natural or social resources that can be acquired, developed, improved and transferred across generations. It generates flows or consumptions as well as additional stock" (Ford Foundation 2004). Assets are not simply resources that people use to build livelihoods. As Bebbington (1999) argues, assets give people the capability to be and act. Thus the acquisition of assets is not a passive act but one that creates agency and is linked to the empowerment of individuals and communities (Sen 1997). The concept of asset accumulation draws on theoretical and policy-focused literature on asset-based development approaches (see, for instance, Sherraden 1991; Carter and Barrett 2006).

The concept of asset or capital endowments includes both tangible and intangible assets. The most widely known assets are natural (the stock of environmentally provided assets), physical (the stock of plant, equipment, infrastructure, and other productive resources), social (the rules, norms, obligations, reciprocity, and trust embedded in social relations, social structures, and societies' institutional arrangements), financial (resources available to people, such as savings and credit), and human capital (health and education). Recently, researchers and practitioners have expanded the notion of assets to include a broader range of particular intangible assets such as aspirational, psychological, civic, and political assets. Assets can be both individual and collective in nature. This means they can be possessed by individuals, households, communities, or entire societies, depending on the asset type.

An asset accumulation framework has the following two components. The first is an asset index, which is an analytical and diagnostic tool for understanding poverty dynamics and mobility.

It quantitatively, or qualitatively, measures the accumulation or erosion of different assets over time and clarifies the interrelationship between different assets. This may, or may not, mirror changes in income or consumption poverty. The second is an asset accumulation policy. This is an associated operational approach that focuses directly on creating opportunities for poor people to accumulate and sustain complex asset portfolios. Asset accumulation policy is not a set of top-down interventions. Although it may include interventions that focus on strengthening individual assets, it is essentially a framework that provides an enabling environment with clear rules, norms, regulations, and support structures to allow households and communities to identify and take advantage of opportunities to accumulate assets.

To facilitate asset accumulation it is necessary to simultaneously address components at the following three interrelated levels. First, at the structural level, factors can have direct and indirect impacts on assets at the local level, demonstrating that development is not just a technocratic process but also a structural one. The process of accumulating assets involves complex political contestation, as well as the negotiation of social power relations as much as technocratic solutions. Asset accumulation does not occur in a vacuum. Opportunities are influenced by complex causal relationships between both external and internal structural factors and internal social processes—both of which require addressing. Second, at the institutional level, international, national and local public, private, and civil society organizations are critical in providing an "enabling environment" for the accumulation of assets. While the state establishes the normative and legal frameworks that can either block initiatives or provide incentives, private sector entities, including banks and microfinance institutions, support the opportunities and facilitate access to promote asset accumulation. Third, at the operational level, assets are not static. In a changing global political, socioeconomic, and environmental situation, it is important to recognize their constant revalorization, transformation, and renegotiation. In addition, the accumulation of one asset often results in the accumulation of others, while insecurity in one can also affect other assets. This means that at the operational level, an asset accumulation policy framework recognizes prioritization, sequencing, trade-offs, and negotiation potential, and combines a range of context-specific strategy options.

It is also important to distinguish different stages or "generations" of asset accumulation strategies. The first-generation asset accumulation strategy is by far the most widespread. This strategy is intended to access assets and focuses on the provision of "basic needs" including water, roads, electricity, housing plots, better heath care and education, and microfinance. Essential for getting out of poverty is this primary emphasis on human, physical, and financial capital.

Once provided it is assumed that individual well-being improves and "development" occurs. However, the conditions for accessing assets do not necessarily bring the expected development outcomes. Second-generation asset accumulation strategies are therefore intended to ensure their further consolidation and prevent erosion—including the intergenerational transfer of assets. Such strategies go beyond the provision of basic services to embrace a range of concerns relating to citizen rights and security, governance, and the accountability of institutions. Third-generation asset accumulation strategies, still very nascent, need to explore interventions that can maximize the linkages between different types of interdependent assets, thereby ensuring "added value" and long-term sustainability.

Finally, it is useful to identify those assets that have been most associated with the phenomenon of transnational migration to date. First, and of greatest importance, are the financial assets that migrants accumulate and send back home as remittances, with studies reflecting variations in impact according to the different social, cultural, and geographical context of the money-recipients.[2] The Inter-American Development Bank (IDB), for instance, estimates that between 2007 and 2010 remittances to Latin America and the Caribbean will grow from US$66.5 billion per year to US$100 billion a year. At the same time, within the region, there is considerable internal differentiation; while in countries such as Honduras and El Salvador, remittances represented 25 percent and 18 percent of Gross Domestic Product (GDP) respectively, in Argentina and Uruguay they only account for, approximately, 0.2 percent of the GDP.

The second capital asset of particular importance is human capital. This has tended to be associated with brain drain, with an important debate relating to more educated (post secondary level) migrants (Yeates 2008). Higher education qualifications obviously result in greater remunerations, but at the same time it is the countries of origin that have invested in the costs of education. A third asset, less widely identified is social capital. Here the work of Cordero-Guzmán and Quiroz-Becerra (2007) is noteworthy in terms of their focus on the "collective" benefit of remittances. They have shown that countries such as Mexico have benefited from projects that the hometown associations (anchored in the receiving countries) have carried out in their places of origin.

Finally, it is useful to mention two intangible assets, as yet not fully theorized, but of relevance to transnational migration. These are civic and political capital. Civic capital is defined as a resource to promote the well-being and cohesion of the society.[3] Political capital, in turn refers to individuals' capabilities to influence political decisions and power relations. This includes their ability to affect changes in the political structures and the way they connect with the citizens (Bourdieu 1991; Ferguson, Moser, and Norton 2007; Ginieniewicz 2009).[4] The following section provides empirical evidence relating to those capital assets of importance in the lived reality of migrants.

The Transnational Asset Framework: The Case of Ecuadorian Migrants to Spain

This case study comes from a longitudinal study undertaken in a poor community called Indio Guayas in Guayaquil, Ecuador, between 1978 and 2004 on the complexities of intergenerational asset accumulation and poverty reduction strategies of local households (see Moser 2009).[5] The study used an asset index to measure the different capital assets that households accumulated—physical, social, financial, and human capital. It also examined the intergenerational transfer of household assets, and their impact on the economic and social mobility of the second generation—the children of the original households. Data were gathered over a twenty-five-year period using anthropological and sociological research methods while I was living intermittently in the same poor urban community. This included six rounds of qualitative research, a household panel data set that covers three phases of the research between 1978 and 2004, and surveys of the children of the original households that the panel data set provides—both those still living in other areas of Guayaquil as well as a group of twenty-one migrants living in Barcelona, Spain. The research was intended to contribute to current debates relating to poverty reduction, social protection, and asset accumulation policy and to the (re)definition of longitudinal, as against short-term, asset-based poverty reduction strategies.

In the study, international migration was identified as an important factor that affected the capacity of some Indio Guayas households to escape poverty, while remittances played an important role in helping some families either stay out of poverty or escape it between 1992 and 2004. This microlevel experience coincided with national level data. According to the Central Bank of Ecuador, remittances went up from US$643 million in 1997 to US$1.41 billion in 2001

(Jokisch and Pribilsky 2002). In macroeconomic terms these flows supported consumption and construction, contributing both to the survival of families and to the expansion of business and employment (Acosta, López, and Villamar 2004). Within the study, the analytical framework on transnational migrants focused on a range of assets during three stages of the migrant process. These include assets that migrants transfer with them when they migrate, those accumulated while in Barcelona, and those consolidated assets that directly or indirectly are taken back to Guayaquil.

Assets Transferred from Guayaquil

Migrants from Guayaquil to Barcelona did not arrive empty-handed as is often thought to be the case. Even if they lacked financial capital, over and above the statutory US$2,000 required to enter the country, they brought two critical assets with them. These were the human capital relating to education and health status enabling them to rapidly enter the labor market, and social capital at both the household and community level. While the latter was absolutely critical for their integration into Barcelona, the former, namely, a strong culture of household social capital, influenced the decisions they made as they settled into a new culture and lifestyle. Indeed, it explained why such a large number of people from the same street, or surrounding area, came to Barcelona. In a classic chain migration pattern, social capital provided the crucial start-up support structures for food, housing, and job contacts—with almost everyone assisted by a friend or family member upon arrival.

On arrival in Barcelona, both men and women did not stay on their own long but very quickly found partners from Indio Guayas itself or from nearby. The extreme loneliness they experienced related to the fact that they were not socialized to live on their own. In Indio Guayas it was customary to live in large, often extended households reflecting strong household social capital. Therefore, regardless of their marital status in Guayaquil, almost all migrants soon established a relationship with a partner in Barcelona. Most migrant men had live-in partners or wives rather than girlfriends. Partners met through parties organized by relatives or friends from home, at the innumerable Latino discothèques where many went on Saturday nights, or at the Parque Centenario where Ecuadorians gathered on Sundays.

The second reason for quickly forming a partnership in Barcelona was economic, relating to the necessity to share expenses. Living with another person was not only cheaper, it also reduced loneliness.

But such quickly formed relationships could also be fragile, particularly if the family was not known. As one young woman commented, "Couples here are less stable than in Ecuador because we don't know each other well. You can't get to know each other in one night, and a few weeks later you are living with that person. Later on each one's faults begin to surface, and you don't like each other so much."

Migrants to Barcelona also brought with them human capital assets associated with their educational achievements. While sons who remained in Guayaquil were better educated than their fathers, half of male migrants had completed secondary school. Indeed, many considered that the type of work opportunities available in Guayaquil were not commensurate with one's level of education. Daughters in Guayaquil were better educated than both their mothers and their brothers, and those migrating to Barcelona were better educated than men in general. All had completed high school while an additional small proportion had acquired some postsecondary education. Because the motive behind migration was to earn an income, very few migrants used the opportunity of being in Barcelona to seek further education.

Assets Accumulated in Barcelona

While assets transferred from Guayaquil were important, those accumulated while in Barcelona undoubtedly made a critical difference, not only economically but also in terms of associated social mobility. First, were the financial-productive assets associated with work opportunities in Barcelona. Ironically, the fact that Guayaquil migrants had not completed tertiary education meant that the jobs they found were those that other migrant groups were unwilling to do. Although these were similar to those of their parents and peers in Guayaquil, they were better paid, offering the possibility of accumulating financial capital. Migration was not an answer to unemployment but rather a response to low salaries, economic precariousness, and limited social mobility (CEPLAES 2005). The average income for the second generation from Indio Guayas varied considerably, from US$820.66 a month for those who migrated to Barcelona to US$67.97 for those that moved out of the plot but remained in Ecuador and US$60.24 for those that remained living with their parents.

In Barcelona, job options changed over time. On arrival, without work papers and "street sense," both men and women had real problems finding jobs, and when they did, they were often exploited. Some employers underpaid while others did not pay at all, situations that produced unhappiness as well as insecurity. Migrants agreed that women found work more easily than men, while the location of men's work made it more risky for them. Men often had to work in construction and so were visible on the street, whereas women found work in domestic service inside houses where they could not be spotted by the police. In this way women could hide their illegal employment from the authorities while men were far more exposed.

The importance and potential of getting legal residence documentation meant that both male and female migrants rapidly acquired the requisite knowledge about Spain's complex migration policy. In fact, the massive Ecuadorian migration flows of the late 1990s were initially facilitated by a 1963 Hispano-Ecuadorian agreement that allowed migrants with US$2,000 to enter Spain for ninety days as tourists without a visa and subsequently to look for a job as a first step toward obtaining a work permit. However, as migrant numbers grew, Spain revised its policy and amended the legal framework and regulations (Jokisch and Pribilsky 2002). Of particular importance were the amnesties that provided opportunities for legalized status in 1999 and then 2005 when some 130,000 Ecuadorians applied (CEPLAES 2005); the increased pressure put on employers to normalize their employee situations, which improved the likelihood that migrants could obtain residency through employment; and finally, an extension from two to five years in the temporary work permit period required for residence eligibility. This group of migrants benefited especially from the 2005 amnesty, and most had legalized their residency, while some were applying for citizenship.

Both men and women filled niche labor markets for which there was a specific demand for foreign labor. Like their contemporaries in Guayaquil, one in four men worked in the construction sector, but unlike in Guayaquil, many others continued in the same skilled crafts that their fathers did, such as carpentry, soldering, and furniture making. All were jobs requiring craft apprenticeship training rather than formal education qualifications, and many of the men had acquired such skills from their fathers or other male relatives in Guayaquil. The dramatic difference between male employment in Guayaquil as against Barcelona was in the higher proportion employed in better-paid factory manufacturing work in Barcelona. Unlike in Guayaquil, however, there were apparently no opportunities for men in the transportation and retail trade sectors in Barcelona, while service sector jobs such as factory cleaners and household workers were better paid and regulated. Gender roles were not as rigid as in Guayaquil: both men and women cleaned and looked after the elderly, sick, and infirm, most of which was relatively well-paid compared to back home when they secured their legal status.

After the long working hours in Guayaquil, the eight-hour work-day, along with the wage differential, presented a new and challenging work culture for many young men. Two brothers, for instance, complemented their eight-hour day jobs in a tire factory by setting up their own small enterprise specializing in apartment repairs and upgrading. While fixed work hours required changes in work behavior, it also demanded new levels of responsibility, which increased self-esteem. As one noted, "My life has taken a ninety-degree turn. In Barcelona you have to be punctual; you have to get to work on time. If you're an outsider, you have to adapt to the laws and punctuality." The brothers' self-esteem increased due to a combination of factors; not only were they the only Ecuadorians working in the tire factory, but also they got work quickly, held down more than one job, and did not experience the kind of exploitation that occurred in Guayaquil, with its customary nonobservance of labor laws.

Like men, women took up the same or even less skilled jobs than in Guayaquil, but they were better paid, obtained documentation papers, and were recipients of social security. Women worked in a range of domestic or cleaning jobs inside houses (including multiple cleaning jobs, full-time domestic servants, and live-in care for elderly women), or as chambermaids in hotels, while the remainder worked as shop cashiers, as seamstresses in small workshops, or as part-time legal auxiliaries. More than one in three augmented their work with a second job, generally as cleaners. Back in Guayaquil, slightly more of those surveyed were factory workers or owned their own shop, but their earnings were much lower. Although some women were better paid than men, they worked longer hours and were not protected to the same extent by labor laws that affected formal sector male employment.

As was true of Ecuadorian women in Spain generally, most of the women from Indio Guayas were working below their qualifications, thus deskilling. Despite their educational level, they were mostly restricted to domestic work. So, although women found it easier to get work, men generally earned more. Nevertheless, women still earned more than they would in Guayaquil, and many gained greater independence (Herrera this volume; Ruíz 2002). An older woman from Indio Guayas had a full-time live-in job in Barcelona and saved the most amount of money among the migrants surveyed. She worked as a care provider twenty-four hours a day, six days a week, tending to the needs of a ninety-three-year-old woman with Alzheimer's disease, living in her client's apartment in Barceloneta. In just under four years, she had saved US$20,000, and unlike her fellow migrants, had no interest in a relationship in Barcelona. She remitted almost all her monthly salary to rebuild her house for her children.

In Barcelona, migrants not only accumulated financial capital but also had the opportunity to accumulate the physical capital asset of housing. Most male migrants adopted such a strategy; they rented rooms until they had acquired their documents and then purchased a flat with a mortgage of up to 100 percent. As many rooms as possible were sublet or rented out in order to pay either rent or mortgage. As in Indio Guayas, lots of people lived in a small space, sharing a communal kitchen and sitting-dining room. The difference was that in Barcelona they were buying apartments whereas in Guayaquil their brothers and sisters were still living on the family plot or beginning the self-help housing process on the city's periphery.

While the transfer of a "culture" of household social capital meant migrants quickly established relationships in Barcelona, the nature of such capital itself was fragile and also could be rapidly transformed. The economic necessity for both partners to work, as well as cultural and legal influences, had implications for intrahousehold roles and responsibilities, and the associated empowerment of women. The economic rationale behind migration to Barcelona meant that both partners wanted to work. With no extended family to pick up domestic tasks, the most important change within many households was the increased domestic responsibility taken on by male partners, even if, as one woman migrant commented, "The change in role is more an economic necessity than a voluntary one." This related especially to cooking, with meals being simpler than in Ecuador, and shopping done by both partners weekly rather than daily (see also McIlwaine 2010). In working out strategies to balance productive and reproductive work, behavior changes occurred. As one young man noted:

> "The typical Ecuadorian male is very macho. When I had a girlfriend there [in Ecuador], I expected her to do everything. I've learned to do things here. Women here liberate themselves. We share the housework; if she cleans, I tidy up the room, clean the sink, or do the groceries. I don't expect her to do all the work. It's a total change, even she notices it."

Only when there was considerable trust between a couple, however, did they have joint bank accounts combining both salaries.

Generally, men tended to be more transparent than women, who often hid resources because of a lack of trust in long-term relationships. The independence of Spanish women was seen as a critical influence. Equally, not all Ecuadorian women totally agreed with the new "liberating" opportunities that Spain offered to women. Nevertheless their lifestyles reflected the changes Ecuadorian women made in Barcelona; they dressed more informally in jeans and T-shirts, wore flat shoes, rather than high heels, when traveling on the metros and buses, and wore less makeup and costume jewelry. Increased control over fertility and an associated decline in the number of children related once again to the lack of extended household members to provide assistance. As a migrant wife coping with the logistics of one small son, said, "Both women and men want fewer children here. In Guayaquil you do not think when you are going to have children because there is someone who can look after them. Here there is no one to look after them. Here you either work or have children."

Accompanying the changes in household social capital was the acquisition of what has been identified above as civic capital—that comprises civic understanding and tolerance, and the capability to contest and claim rights as well as to fulfill responsibilities. The recollections of three young Guayaquileño men in Barcelona all reflected this. One summed up the differences between Barcelona and Guayaquil as follows: "Laws are stricter here; life is more controlled, less wild. Politics works here better. You can see it in the streets—they're clean—and people are honest and kind." For his brother, citizen identity was associated with greater opportunities for upward socioeconomic mobility in a more inclusive society. This increased his awareness of class-bound constraints in Guayaquil, an important realization: "The structure of society in Guayaquil is more demarcated. Nobody goes to a good restaurant, as they 'feel bad.' In contrast, here there is more social liberty. I can go into any restaurant and get served."

For a third young migrant man, associated with the benefits that such a society could offer was also increased awareness of citizen responsibilities. As he commented:

> "Here you can't hit your child because someone may report you. Not to mention [hitting] your partner. If you try to beat her, the police will take you away. There's more respect here. You get used to the discipline here . . . The police officers treat you well. They ask you to show them your documents, and they thank you and even apologize

for bothering you. It's very different in Ecuador, where they ask you to
show your ID, and they beat you right away."

Enhanced understanding about the protection against domestic abuse
that a functioning democracy with accountable institutions provided
meant that Ecuadorian women became far more assertive about their
rights (see also McIlwaine and Carlisle this volume).

Assets Transferred Back to Guayaquil

The strong linkages back home in Guayaquil meant that an important part of most migrants' strategies while abroad was the transfer
of a range of accumulated assets back to their families and community. These included not only financial remittances but also intangible assets. The economic support embedded within household
social capital provided the basis for remittances, the most visible asset
transferred to families back home. With more than three out of four
migrants remitting, the amount sent home depended on numerous
factors. Migrants supported their families back in Guayaquil with an
average remittance of US$143 a month; this compared with an aver-
age of US$7.75 a month support from children living off the plot but
still in Guayaquil.

Nevertheless, such remittances might ultimately be time bound.
While women who had left children behind in Guayaquil were likely
to be more reliable remitters, over time, as men with families in
Guayaquil brought them to Barcelona, they were less likely to remit
to remaining family members, particularly once their parents had
died. Whereas support for children still living in Guayaquil tended to
be provided at time intervals ranging from daily to annually, four out
of five remitters from Barcelona (both male and female) did so on a
regular monthly basis. It was not only the amounts of remittances but
also the reliability that was critical in keeping Indio Guayas families
out of poverty.

Remittance financial capital was used for short-term crises as well
as longer-term consumption. Thus, while one male migrant bailed
out his brother from prison by sending US$2,000, he was also send-
ing money on a monthly basis to enable his father to pay for medical bills. Another young woman sent remittances to her mother for
maintenance expenses relating to the food, clothing, and education of her two children. In contrast, an older woman's remittances
illustrated how, with older children and less demand to meet daily
needs, it was possible to invest in assets such as housing. For men,

money transfers also were often linked to power and identity back in Indio Guayas—whether it was manifested through building a bigger house, generally for one's mother, or holding fiestas when one came home for a visit.

Remittances, however, were also the financial manifestation of complex familial relationships and acted as a mechanism that redefined or ruptured social relations (see also Datta et al. 2007). For wives left behind in Guayaquil, their husbands' failure to send remittances indicated abandonment. When one migrant man acquired a partner in Barcelona and stopped sending money home, it caused criticism among friends. Concern for children left behind often resulted in serious stress and depression for their mothers. But this was not straightforward. While women wanted to bring their children to Barcelona, they could not cope with the complexities of child care in the city. In addition, over time they often became accustomed to living freer lives without the encumbrances of children, and to earning decent wages. So they felt guilty and justified separation from their children in terms of the culturally acceptable practice in Guayaquil that children can be raised by other kin, particularly mothers and sisters (see Herrera this volume).

Returning to Guayaquil was a critical rite of passage for migrants living in Barcelona. The dates and costs of trips home were much discussed. Yet, when migrants visited, it was not always an easy transition. Political, spatial, and environmental issues had a profound impact. One young man, for instance, said that when he went back after seven years, he could not stand the lack of order and the fact that everything was chaotic. For young adult migrants, the dynamics of their marital relationship were particularly affected by the transnational context. Partnerships formed in Barcelona often were perceived as specific institutions that had nothing to do with what happened in the barrio. In these relationships formed without family approval, the tension between two separate worlds surfaced when families returned to visit Guayaquil, with conflicts often occurring even among married couples.

If women who had left children behind in Guayaquil worried about the likelihood of being judged about their new partners, those who brought children with them were beginning to experience the complexities of multiple identities, particularly in terms of the next generation. Parents who had given birth to children in Barcelona accepted that their children would be Spanish. For this generation, Ecuador would become the place to visit to discover roots rather than to maintain social capital. As a male migrant reflected, "I'm

Ecuadorian and my new granddaughter is Spanish, of Ecuadorian descent. My grandchildren will grow up here and live their lives here. If they go to Ecuador at all, it will be to visit the place where their grandparents and parents were born."

Conclusion

Analysis of the experiences of migrants from Guayaquil to Barcelona in terms of an asset framework shows the importance of a range of transnational assets and not just financial remittances. The experience of living in Barcelona resulted not only in the accumulation of financial and productive capital but also in social and civic capital, associated with identity and shifts in power relations. For men, this related more to the wider society in which they lived, and with their increased awareness of their rights came a growing recognition that the persistent inequality in Guayaquil constrained them both as citizens and as workers. For women, the migrant experience meant some release from the trap of patriarchal gender inequalities. Thus, they gave much greater priority than men did to renegotiating gender relations (see also McIlwaine 2010). For all migrants, however, of considerable importance were the links and reinforcement of trust and social capital back home, at both the household and the community level. As a male migrant commented, "Guayaquil is your home, but you do not want to go back and live there. You know what the situation is there."

Notes

1. This section summarizes detailed descriptions of the asset framework developed by Caroline Moser (2007;, 2009).
2. See Orozco (2007) for the identification of four transnational spending and/or investment practices, namely, family remittance transfers, demand for services, capital investment, and charitable donations. Orozco argues that, while important for both host and recipient country, they do not automatically promote asset accumulation.
3. The components of civic capital include levels of awareness and respect for "the other,", including levels of tolerance (perception about minority rights), a sense of belonging, expressed through participation in community organizations, NGOs, school boards and volunteer work, and levels of environmental and human rights awareness.
4. The components of political capital include exercising the right to vote and to participate in formal political structures such as political parties and unions, as well as an understanding of political issues and the procedural system.
5. This section draws on Chapter 9 in Moser (2009).

References

Acosta, Alberto, Susana López, and David Villamar. 2004. "Ecuador: oportunidades y amenazas económicas de la emigración." In *Migraciones: un juego con cartas marcadas*, ed. Francisco Hidalgo, 259–302. Quito: Abya-Yala/Instituto Latinoamericano de Investigaciones Sociales (ILDIS).

Bebbington, Anthony. 1999. "Capitals and Capabilities: A Framework for Analyzing Peasant Viability, Rural Livelihoods and Poverty." *World Development* 27 (12): 2021–44.

Bourdieu, Pierre. 1991. "Political Representation: Elements for a Theory of the Political Field." In *Language and Symbolic Power,* ed. Pierre Bourdieu, 171–202. Cambridge: Polity Press.

Carter, Michael R., and Christopher B. Barrett. 2006. "The Economics of Poverty Traps and Persistent Poverty: An Asset-Based Approach." *Journal of Development Studies* 42 (2): 178–99.

Centro de Planificación y Estudios Sociales (CEPLAES). 2005. "Migraciones internacionales: principales implicaciones de las migraciones para el desarrollo del Ecuador." Quito: Fondo de Desarrollo de las Naciones Unidas para la Mujer.

Cordero-Guzmán, Héctor, and Victoria Quiroz-Becerra. 2007. "Transnational Communities of the United States and Latin America." In *Reducing Global Poverty: The Case for Asset Accumulation,* ed. Caroline O. N., 239–54. Washington, D.C.: Brookings Institution Press.

Datta, Kavita, Cathy McIlwaine, Jane Wills, Yara Evans, Joanna Herbert, and Jon May. 2007. "The New Development Finance or Exploiting Migrant Labour? Remittance Sending among Low-Paid Migrant Workers in London." *International Development Planning Review* 29:43–67.

Ferguson, Claire, Caroline Moser, and Andy Norton. 2007. "Claiming Rights: Citizenship and the Politics of Asset Distribution." In *Reducing Global Poverty: The Case for Asset Accumulation*, ed. Caroline O. N. Moser, 273–88. Washington, D.C.: Brookings Institution Press.

Ford Foundation. 2004. *Building Assets to Reduce Poverty and Injustice.* New York: Ford Foundation.

Gammage, Sarah. 2007. "Gender and Transnational Asset Accumulation." In *Reducing global Poverty: The Case for Asset Accumulation*, ed. Caroline O. N. Moser, 255–72. Washington, D.C.: Brookings Institution Press.

Ginieniewicz, Jorge. 2009. "The Accumulation and Transfer of Civic and Political Assets by Argentinean Migrants to Spain." Global Urban Research Centre Working Paper 2, Global Urban Research Centre, Manchester: University of Manchester.

Jokisch, Brad D., and Jason Pribilsky. 2002. "The Panic to Leave: Economic Crisis and the 'new emigration' from Ecuador." *International Migration* 40 (4): 75–101.

McIlwaine, Cathy. 2010. "Migrant Machismos: Exploring Gender Ideologies and Practices among Latin American Migrants in London from a Multi-Scalar Perspective." *Gender, Place and Culture.* 17:281–300.

Moser, Caroline O. N., ed. 2007. *Reducing Global Poverty: The Case for Asset Accumulation.* Washington, D.C.: Brookings Institution Press.

———. 2008. "Assets and Livelihoods: A Framework for Asset-Based Social Policy." In *Assets, Livelihoods and Social Policy,* ed. Caroline Moser and Anis Dani, 43–81. Washington, D.C.: World Bank.

———. 2009. *Ordinary Families, Extraordinary Lives: Assets and Poverty Reduction in Guayquil, 1978–2004.* Washington: Brookings Press.

———. 2010. "Safety, Gender Mainstreaming and Gender-Based programmes." In *Women in the City: On Violence and Rights,* ed. Ana Falu, 1–15. Santiago: Ediciones SUR.

Orozco, Manuel. 2007. "Migrant Foreign Savings and Asset Accumulation." In *Reducing Global Poverty: The Case for Asset Accumulation,* ed. Caroline O. N. Moser, 225–38. Washington, D.C.: Brookings Institution Press.

Ruiz, Marta Cecilia. 2002. "Ni sueño ni pesadilla: diversidad y paradojas en el proceso migratorio." *Iconos: Revista de Ciencias Sociales* 14:88–97.

Sen, Amartya. 1997. "Editorial: Human Capital and Human Capability." *World Development* 25 (12): 1959–61.

Sherraden, Michael W. 1991. *Assets and the Poor: A New American Welfare Policy.* Armonk, NY: M. E. Sharpe.

Yeates, Nicola. 2008. "Transnationalism, Social Reproduction, and Social Policy: International Migration of Care Workers." In *Assets, Livelihoods, and Social Policy,* ed. Caroline O. N. Moser, 149–68. Washington, D.C.: Brookings Institution Press.

Chapter 4

Rethinking the Family through Migration: Gender Ideologies and Practices of Care in Ecuador

Gioconda Herrera

Over the last ten years the geography and composition of international migration from Latin America has been transformed. Europe, and Spain and Italy in particular, have become major destinations. In addition, the traditional pattern of rural masculine migration has been changed by an important flow of impoverished women from urban areas. From 1960 to the mid-1990s, the United States was the most common destination for migrants from the Andean Region; Europe was mostly seen as the place for students, artists, or political refugees. Beginning with the migration of Peruvian women to Italy in the early 1990s, the massive arrival of Ecuadorian men and women to Spain occurred at the turn of the century, followed by Colombians and more recently by Bolivians, the majority as economic migrants. While the presence of Argentinean and Uruguayan migrants has also been significant, the social composition of this flow, its labor insertion, and the types of transnational ties they build are different from those of the Andean countries.

This chapter examines the effects of such international migration patterns on those families left behind in Ecuador as well as the ways in which transnational ties contribute to the well-being of these families. The chapter argues for the need to challenge the stereotypical notions of families of international migrants in public discourses as either "broken" or "vulnerable." It suggests that the reality, both historically and on the ground in contemporary times, is more complex and that families of migrants left behind develop "non-traditional" patterns of caring and reproduction.

More specifically, the rapid increase of Andean migration to Europe and its female-dominated pattern have been widely analyzed through a combination of different factors that relate a structural crisis of care in the countries of destination with crises of social reproduction in the countries of origin. First, a pronounced aging of the population in Spain and Italy, the countries with the highest rates in Europe, provided important niches for jobs related to the care of the elderly. Indeed, familialist welfare states did not guarantee services of social protection for this growing segment of the population, and put the responsibility for managing their needs in the hands of women and families. At the same time, an increasing number of women entered the labor force without adequate childcare services. This has resulted in a privatization or informalization of care services in the hands of newcomers—mostly women from Asia and Latin America (Bakker and Silvey 2008; Hondagneu-Sotelo 2001). Recent patterns of female migration are related with how caregiving activities have been distributed and redistributed in the international system. This is a system in which the immigrant workforce provides care in destination countries, through domestic labor, in many cases to the detriment of care and social protection of populations in the countries of origin (Ehrenreich and Hochschild 2003; Hondagneu-Sotelo 2001; Hondagneu-Sotelo and Ávila 1997; Salazar Parreñas 2001).

At the same time, during the 1980s and 1990s, Latin American economies and societies underwent several rounds of neoliberal policy that accentuated the concentration of wealth and social inequalities. In addition to increased poverty, this phenomenon produced a crisis of expectations for intergenerational social reproduction among poor and impoverished families. Migration became an alternative and southern Europe a desired destination for many of these families (Herrera 2008a; Hinojosa 2009).

Within this structural framework, the migration of Andean women to Europe has also raised questions about the motivations and causes of migration from the perspective of women's subjectivities and has shown that women migrate for different reasons than men (Herrera 2008b; Hinojosa 2009;Wagner 2008). In addition to economic exclusion, gender, sexual, or ethnic discrimination pushes women to decide to migrate. The experience of migration as a liberating transit, an argument prevailing in some of the literature on gender and migration has also been interrogated. Some works speak rather of a series of paradoxes between the attainment of economic autonomy from family and partners and the social exclusion and discrimination faced in the labor market, public spaces, neighborhoods, and so on

(Herrera 2008a; McIlwaine 2010; McIlwaine and Carlisle this volume). While the exit, the journey, and some of the issues regarding the integration and exclusion of women in destination countries have been addressed, the social experience of migration among the members of migrant families at home has been much less analyzed.

This chapter focuses on this microworld of origin, and examines the transformations as well as continuities at stake in the dynamics of migrant families at home. Many women who migrate leave partners, children, and parents behind. After ten or more years, some have followed the path of their spouses, mothers, and daughters, but others have not. I examine how gender and family relations have been reconfigured in these dynamics, and particularly, the role of gender ideologies in the way social arrangements of care take place at home. In what way is the family rationalized among migrants and in public discourse? On what gender hierarchies are these conceptions built? What are the cultural and social presuppositions that sustain the practices and ties of transnational families? Are these conceptions coherent with hegemonic views on the family? Or rather, are there any conceptions of the family in dispute? What has been the role of female migration in unleashing these disputes regarding the meaning of families? How does this affect care practices?

I focus on the case of Ecuador and ground my analysis in two research projects among transnational families in two settings with high migration rates: an urban community in Quito, the capital, with pronounced migration to Spain, and a rural community with traditional US-directed migration. The first project was conducted in 2005 among teenagers in rural and urban contexts and examined their perceptions about their parent's migration project as well as the resulting arrangements of care within their families (see Herrera and Carillo 2009). The second project sought to reconstruct the practices of care among transnational families and their relationship with institutional settings of social protection and political discourse about migrant families and social disintegration.[1] This latter research looked at both origin and destination, and focused on the practices of the caregivers.

Drawing on the findings of these two projects, I argue that by looking at the social organization of care among transnational families through the context of departures, one can better understand the way in which social processes of global inequality encounter historical experiences of domination ingrained in local ideologies of gender, race, and class. At the same time, these family and gender ideologies are shaken by the way in which transnational families experience migration and deal with care. Transnational practices of care take place within these encounters between geographies of inequality and histories of gender domination. Through them, migration renders visible a series of transformations surrounding the conceptions of family, gender, and care in societies of origin affected by migration.

In order to address the questions mentioned above, I outline the historical context in which female migration to Europe took place, highlighting the long history of the feminization of migration in intraregional and internal migration in Latin America. This shows that transnational families, separation among the members of migrant households, motherhood at a distance, and diverse notions of care are not necessarily new phenomena; rather, there exists an historical experience of mobility among families that has not been covered by hegemonic notions of the family. By contrast, many of these notions presuppose a static family structure.

In the second section, I examine hegemonic views of the family as they appear in contemporary political discourse, as well as social policy, and the way they contribute to an understanding of the migrant family as a disintegrated body, hiding what has been the historical experience of many migrant families before the recent, massive migration to Europe.

Finally, I assess some of the social practices around care found in transnational families in order to show how, together with precariousness, they express contradictory ways of thinking about the family, gender, and social reproduction. For this analysis, I draw on a feminist political economy perspective to visualize the different forms of gender and class inequality and exclusion present in transnational social reproduction strategies. Inequality is understood as a structural dimension of globalization with concrete expressions at the regional, local, family, and subjective scales, and these can be examined through social reproduction practices. Following Bakker and Gil (2003), the latter are understood as the transformation of social processes and the mechanisms, institutions, and practices necessary for the sustenance of communities. This implies, fundamentally but not exclusively, the social organization of caregiving, in addition to the more general process of life sustenance. Feminists thus propose recovering in analyses of globalization aspects related to social reproduction and the sustainability of life at its various scales, that is, both at the places of arrival and in the reorganization of the departure contexts. Within this general framework, the concept of global care chains allows for an analysis of the different nodes of this global social reproduction, and especially of societies from where migration departs. In addition,

unequal practices of social reproduction are ingrained in gender ideologies of family and care that circulate through public discourse and
are also heard locally among neighbors, public servants, and family
members. Thus, following Pribilsky (2007), analysis of the migrant
family has to go beyond economic and social reproduction strategies
and investigate the meanings, tensions, and contradictions that arise
from these practices for members of both transnational homes and
communities.

The Migrant Family in Historical Perspective: Internal, Intraregional, and Transcontinental Migration of Women in Latin America

Women's mobility in Latin America is not a new phenomenon. During
the colonial era, many women from rural areas went to the cities
mainly as domestic workers, as permanent, temporary, or circular
migrants (Burkett 1975; Kusnesof 1989). Women were also an important part of the rural-urban flows that prevailed during the nineteenth
and twentieth centuries in Latin America (Ariza 2000; Pellegrino
2003). Indeed, migration was often the mechanism through which
many poor Latin American women entered the paid labor force for
the first time, again, usually as domestic workers (Ariza 2000, 17).
The vast majority of these women were young and unmarried and
often transgressed gender roles and ideologies through their migration. In addition, mothering at distance is also part of the migration
history of women in Latin America. The nurturing and reproduction
of children and the elderly through their work in the cities or abroad
also occurred in the rural areas of many places in Latin America as
women sought to fund their education or support illegitimate children (Kusnesof 1989). Studies on women's internal migration in
Ecuador and the Andean Region testify to the fact that in the absence
of mothers and fathers, different family arrangements were deployed
locally, not without the arousal of some tensions and an overload
of work for both the women who stayed behind and the ones that
moved (Poeschel 1986). However, paternity at a distance, rather than
maternity, was more commonly and socially accepted in both rural
and urban environments with the result that migration of men was
more accepted than that of women (Herrera 2010). In the second half
of the twentieth century, female mobility between neighboring countries became an extension of internal migration for many poor women.
Argentina and Venezuela became important destinations for men and
women from the Andean countries: the migration of Colombian

women to Venezuela and Paraguayan women to Argentina started in the 1950s and continues today. According to Lipszyc (2001), in Argentina, Paraguayan and Bolivian female migration kept the cost of domestic work accessible to wide sectors of Buenos Aires' middle class. By 1960, there were 80 Paraguayan men for every 100 women in Argentina. From 1980 on, this niche was populated by Bolivian and Peruvian women.

The rapid increase of women's migration to Europe occurred at the end of the 1990s. As mentioned above, after the arrival of Peruvian women to Italy in the early 1990s, at the turn of the century Ecuadorians became the first Latin American nationality to settle in Spain in large numbers. Not only did Ecuadorians make an important contribution to the transformation of Spain, but it also became the second most important immigrant receiving country (after the United States). Different motivations underpin this migration flow from the Andean Region. In the case of Ecuador, most interpretations point to the economic crisis of 1999 as the main explanation for the exodus of around 1,000,000 people in ten years (Acosta 2005; Ramirez and Ramirez 2006). In the case of Colombia, it was the internal political conflict that pushed more and more Colombians not only to Europe and particularly to the United Kingdom, but also to several other countries, including other Latin American countries (see McIlwaine this volume). For Bolivians, the latecomers, both a previous tradition to migrate to Argentina together with economic reasons account for the sudden increase of migrants in Italy and Spain (Hinojosa 2009). In all cases, the structural crisis of care created a demand for informal activities of care for immigrant women and the feminization of these flows.

From 2000 on, paralleling the important increase of transcontinental migration to Europe, intraregional migration also grew considerably. According to Cerrutti (2009), between 1960 and 2000 women's migration within Latin America rose from 44.7 percent to 50.5 percent in 2000, which was particularly important for some countries. For instance, Peruvian women in Argentina increased from 33.5 percent in 1980 to 59.3 percent in 2000. Similarly, in Chile, Peruvian women represented 48 percent in 1980 and 60 percent in 2000. The conditions of these migrant women indicate that their situation combines very precarious labor insertion with ethnic and racial discrimination, highlighting how class and race reinforce gender inequalities, deepening conditions of social exclusion (Stefoni 2002). In most of these cases, proximity to their country of origin enables these women to maintain strong reproductive ties with their families and communities when they migrate alone.

In the case of Ecuador, the rapid increase in migration by the turn of the twentieth century was basically directed to Europe and, as mentioned above, was pioneered by women, who were joined by their husbands, and then their children. Indeed, family reunification was facilitated by Spanish legislation (and was actively discouraged by laws in the United States) (Herrera 2009). However, not everyone chose to bring their family to join them or was able to do so. Recently, official data shows that 38 percent of migrant fathers and 34 percent of migrant mothers have left at least one child under 18 years old in Ecuador (INEC 2007). This reality implies that many migrant families have to deal not only with emotional separation but with the practical and material issues at stake when dealing with social reproduction at a distance, including the management of remittances and care arrangements.

Regarding the latter, while the majority of women in charge of care activities among nonmigrant families in Ecuador are aged from 25 to 35, the majority of those who take care of children left behind by international migrants are women aged between 46 and 65 (INEC 2007). In addition, the members of migrant families aged under 18 years spent more time in care activities than their nonmigrant counterparts (ibid.). Thus, apparently both grandparents and young people share migrant children's care. The migration of women, and particularly of mothers, has elicited different reactions, to which the discussion now turns.

The Construction of Migrant Families in Public Discourse

This section explores the ways in which social policies construct migrant families and migrant women in Ecuador, especially in relation to how certain gender configurations are legitimized, while others are not. I consider the authorized discourses on the migrant family within the realm of political discourse and public policies, and how alternative constructions of the migrant family are helping to dispute gender norms and gender relations. I assess how the migrant family is constructed by certain public policies in relation to how the state is an organizational structure that regulates social practices. By doing so, it exerts a formative action of durable dispositions (Bourdieu 1997 23). According to Bourdieu (2005, 96), the state has the power to produce and to impose categories of thought, acting in the domain of symbolic domination: "When the state describes, at the same time, it prescribes." In consequence, by examining the migrant family as an object of social intervention, I interrogate the preconceptions inscribed in reality, and look at the origin of certain evaluative and cognitive structures, that are converted into principles of classification. By doing so, I seek to recognize the constructed character of these notions, and thus, their potential for transformation.

In addition, I take Scott's (1996) emphasis on the significance of gender in power relations to analyze how certain institutions, such as the state or the family, organize what is legitimate for men and women in society and what is not. That is, the constitution of a gender order based on the construction of a series of "commonsense" categories such as the "disintegrated family," the "abandoned child," the "bad mother." According to Elizabeth Dore (2000), state policies transform a series of gender relations into norms through a set of social and political institutions. What society considers acceptable in terms of masculine and feminine norms will vary according to class and many other dimensions of inequality. However, states construct gender regimes that regulate social life, including sexuality and family.

Bearing in mind these considerations, I argue that international migration has rendered visible the family as an object of intervention. We witness the emergence of a rhetorical narrative among state institutions, in which traditional constructions of motherhood and care, grounded in the idea of a fixed family and a rigid gender division of labor among men and women, prevail. At the same time, the migration of women has allowed the marginal circulation of alternative representations of the family in which social ties at a distance redefine the notions of family and care. These representations that circulate in microspaces, such as neighborhoods and communities, are gradually permeating the realm of public policies as well. In what follows, I examine two kinds of family representations: the disintegrated family and the vulnerable family.

The Broken Family

The "broken family" has been a frequently used metaphor both in Ecuadorian political discourse and by the media over the last ten years. On several occasions, President Rafael Correa spoke of the broken family as associated with international migration and the country's social and economic crisis, although this image was not new in that Ecuadorian politicians in the 1990s had already used it to name the negative consequences of migration (Eguiguren 2010). This metaphor has a double function. On the one hand, it legitimates the perception of international migration as a national tragedy, most of time related to the country "that Ecuadorians need to leave behind." On the other hand, it sustains the implementation of policies grounded in psychological rather than social dimensions: broken families produce pathologies, particularly among the youth, that need to be healed.

The image of the broken family is part of a new social problem within the realm of public policy—international migration. This results in the pathologization of the migrant family as a broken social organism that needs to be replaced or eliminated instead of recognizing the existence of different kinds of families. In this sense, the migrant family emerges as a "new" problem, while denying its existence in the lives of Ecuadorians over decades of international migration. The image channeled by political discourse is that this problem will be solved with the return of migrant mothers and fathers to the country and family reunification.[2] Such representation is reflected in the main social program put in place by the secretary of migration called "The Welcome Home Program," which promotes migrant return through different mechanisms.[3] In other words, the transnational family and the social ties that these families have maintained over time are not recognized. There is a contradiction between the visibility of remittances and the invisibility of the actors at both ends of the transactions who are mainly transnational families. Economic relations are separated from social and emotional transnational ties, making it difficult to assess the complexity of the relations at stake in extraterritorial family practices. The next step, within the discourse of public policy, will be to relate this broken family with problems of social cohesion and vulnerability.

The Vulnerable Family

The migrant family as a vulnerable entity is also frequently represented, this time in the narratives of social programs and public servants. Both the entities in charge of the families left behind, as well as the programs oriented to childhood welfare and the youth, conceive the migrant family as an entity that needs to be assisted in order to prevent problems of social integration with the main protagonists being children and youth. The risks to which they are exposed are gangs in the case of young men, and teenage pregnancy for young women. While these social phenomena are quite prevalent in Ecuador, they are not necessarily related to the migration of parents. However, social policies directly link migration with the vulnerability of families and children. By doing so, they ignore the social organization of care, as well as the strategies deployed by migrant families to cope with the care of children and the elderly in contexts of departure.

Indeed, social programs oriented toward the children of migrant families are legally sustained by Article 193 of the *Código de la Niñez y Adolescencia* that prescribes protection policies toward children in situations of vulnerability. Under this article, children's vulnerability is defined as follows: "sexual exploitation, economic and labor exploitation, the smuggling of children, lost children, children with parents in jail, son and daughters of migrant families, refugees, pregnant teenagers" Such a way of classifying the sons and daughters of migrant families contrasts with a much more complex reality in which the migration of parents and the construction of ties and bonds between transnational families do not always mean underprotection and vulnerability.

In addition, given that such discourse privileges the situation of the children, only one side of the care relation is taken into account—the person in need of care. Therefore, what emerges is a rhetoric that reinforces an idea of "care deficit" and renders invisible the role of the caregiver. This deficit is not associated with structural conditions, such as the privatization of social reproduction or social inequalities related to the migration of women. On the contrary, it hides the transnational bonds established by migrant families in order to guarantee, not only everyday care activities but also the social reproduction of later generations. The deficit discourse expresses a notion of care based on a static mother-child bond. Such a conception is ingrained historically in the public imagination of social protection and has to do with what Maxine Molyneux (2000) calls social maternalism: an ideology that naturalizes the role of mothers in families as caregivers and extrapolates such practices to the relationship of women with the state. Women are conceived as the intermediaries of the welfare of the nation, rather that the subjects of rights and citizenship. This mother-child dyad has been present in Ecuadorian social policies since the 1930s through health and social protection policies directed toward poor mothers implemented by the state (Clark 2001).

International migration of mothers is interpreted by state institutions within this historically constructed framework that places children as the main subjects of policies and mothers as the intermediaries of their welfare. Thus, their absence through migration is translated automatically into a deficit of care. Local and transnational networks of care activated by absent mothers with their relatives and the social organization of care put in place before and during the migration process in the communities of origin both surpass the notions of care involved in the mother-child dyad.

However, a different discourse is emerging, paralleling the broken family and the vulnerable family discourses, but still quite peripheral to the mainstream idea of the static family that prevail in social protection policies. I refer to the notion present in the new Constitution of 2008 (Third section, Third Chapter, article 40) that acknowledges the existence of particular rights pertaining to members of transnational families and poses that the state should protect these families and the rights of their members. Such a notion is taken by the *Plan Nacional de Desarrollo Humano para las Migraciones 2007–2010* (National Plan for Human Development for Migration), a public policy document that guides the actions of the national secretary of migration (SENAMI). In this document, the second main objective of the plan is defined as "to generate and to consolidate social ties between the migrant person and its family, and with the country" and states two specific policies for this: to promote family reunification, and to help in reinforcing transnational families. In other words, the institution in charge of migration policies has a different vision from the sustained by social welfare institutions.

In both cases, the Constitution and SENAMI's plan, the discourse on the transnational family is the result of previous political processes of lobbying undertaken by migrant organizations of civil society over the last ten years that have been working in Ecuador, particularly at the local and community level, to change traditional notions of families. This is the case of the organizations of the Pastoral de Movilidad Humana (Human Mobility Group) in southern Ecuador, a series of community-based organizations, that after many years of work among the youth, mothers, grandmothers, and returned migrants are promoting the idea of family diversity as part of the agenda of migrant human rights. Although this is still a tentative discourse within the state, its legitimacy in the Constitution is an important step to challenge the meanings and representations around the family and the migrant families within public policies.

Transnational Arrangements of Care: Toward the Construction of the Transnational Family

Discourses on the vulnerable and broken family are present within migrant families and their communities as well. A 2005 study conducted in Quito and Guayaquil showed that this hegemonic discourse is deeply ingrained in the ways migrant families at home, particularly adults, conceive and judge their migrant female relatives (Herrera and Carrillo 2009). This social discourse stands in contrast with many of the actual practices deployed by these families to cope with the care of children and the elderly. Such practices show an active concern on the part of migrant members abroad to maintain sustainable links with their dependants in origin, and a series of strategies by family members at home, to make possible care activities of social reproduction within families that stay in Ecuador.

Indeed, practices of care among these migrant families are part the transnational forms of social reproduction from below that workers and families establish through their migration experience. Together with remittances for everyday consumption, or transnational political and cultural links between communities in sending and receiving countries, transnational arrangements of care are important ways in which families reproduce themselves across borders. Moreover, this social reproduction from below occurs in a context in which these links and connections at a distance have been intensified as compared with previous migration flows due to globalization facilitating better communications.

But this also occurs in a context of structural inequality. Many of these links and connections established by migrant families intersect through labor markets segmented by race, gender, and class, by segregated societies that classify people by this same trilogy in both sending and receiving countries, and states that are not working on redistributive policies to mend these inequalities. In the context of such intense connections, the social agents involved in migrant family arrangements of care are both determined by these structural inequalities, which usually locate them in lower social and economic positions, but also by the historical reproduction of systems of social classification in their countries of origin.

Thus, social arrangements of care in the countries of origin are crossed by different dimensions of inequality especially gender, age, and class. From this perspective, relations of power based on gender and age among members of the migrant family, as well as their structural class position within the country of origin, are important to identify the kind of social arrangements that take place and, above all, the different degrees to which these arrangements reproduce or transgress these forms of inequality.

Here I draw on the findings of the study carried out among urban communities of migrant families in Ecuador in 2005 and examine the social arrangements of care deployed by these families. Despite the wide variety of situations, four findings sum up the social organization of care among these families. First, it is clearly a female activity. Indeed, the study examined four situations—the migration of the father, the mother, both parents, and the migration of mothers when they were the head of household. In every case, one or more women were in charge of primary care, education and health issues, housing investments, and bureaucratic paperwork for their migrant relatives, among other activities. Thus, migration rarely alters the gender division of labor within households, although, in the case of migrant mothers, they have usually become both caregivers and economic providers. Masculine figures usually intervene very little in everyday activities but have a significant symbolic presence. While care is covered by women from different ages and kin position, children and particularly teenagers state that their father was very important for them, even if they did not see him frequently. Thus, fathers were not part of the social organization of care, but maintained a significant presence in the lives of teenagers left behind. In contrast, in most of the cases, the migrant mother is in charge of the management of care activities at a distance and also acts as an important provider for the family. Communication, remittances, and exceptional visits home on special occasions, such as graduation, are combined to make transnational motherhood a new form of mothering.

Second, as a derivation of this perpetuation of the gender division of labor, when the mother migrates, care activities go from concentration to dispersion. While social policies tend to look exclusively at one side of the care relationship, the one potentially lacking care (the child), in practice, the caregiver has multiple faces: grandmothers, grandfathers, aunts, elder sisters, domestic workers, neighbors. Care activities, once concentrated on the present and nonmobile mother, are reorganized into multiple figures once she is abroad. This occurs with or without the presence of the father. This sort of dispersion of care activities has several implications for both caregivers and care receivers. On the one hand, more than one person (female) is in charge of the diversity of activities ensuring the social reproduction of the minors. Consequently, the size of the female kin network put in place in order to take care of the children is crucial—the bigger the network, the better the possibilities of structuring an adequate informal system of care. Vulnerability is linked with scarcity of female relatives or neighbors, and can only be compensated with paid domestic work. However, a 2009 study of these communities shows that paid domestic work is the last priority in the use of remittances by migrant families after food, education, housing, and other material consumption and goods (Herrera 2010). Thus, care activities are not considered a significant part of the migration project at home. On the other hand, when care is in the hands of two or more carers, authority difficulties may emerge especially when the relationship of children and teenagers involves a wide intergenerational gap.

The third finding is that independently of family structure or the size of the kin network, the younger relatives, usually the sons and daughters of the migrant parents, are overloaded with domestic and care work. Although the formal caring figure of the dependants at home is usually one or two grandparents, it is the teenage grand-daughters who are often playing the role of caregivers for younger brothers and sisters or elderly relatives. Often, particularly when the relationship is between a granddaughter and a grandmother, the difference between the caregiver and the care receiver becomes irrelevant or may simply disappear. This creates confusion over the roles fulfilled by each member of the family and, most importantly, it postpones the teenagers' own life project.

Finally, the role of communication among these families is important in determining social arrangements of care. Contrary to public discourses of family disintegration and abandoned children, communication among transnational families is quite frequent, especially between parents and children. Nonetheless, they tend to weaken over time, and we found cases where communication and the sending of remittances stopped altogether. However, when communication is stable and regular, it plays an essential role in reproducing transnational ties. It also helps guarantee successful transnational arrangements of care and makes it possible for family members, not only to ensure social reproduction, but to share expectations among its different members and to think about building common projects for the future. This is why the use and quality of communication technologies such as the Internet and video-calls can become important for reinforcing transnational ties. When calls and messages are not only related to the management of remittances but also inquire into details of everyday life, the parents' presence in the life of the children is more deeply ingrained, and emotional ties acquire certain stability. Communication also accompanies the fulfillment of other family rituals that usually involve the migrant parents' visit at home, such as baptisms, wedding anniversaries, and fifteen-year-old birthday celebrations, that contribute to the recreation of family ties through the ritual and symbolic representations of the unity of the family at home.

In summary, social arrangements of care at home are connected transnationally with at least one of the migrant parents. Moreover, this transnational tie is usually a condition for the success of the reproduction of care at home and translates into remittances, communication, and the building of common projects. By looking at practices of care among migrant families on the ground, it is possible to challenge representations of migrant families either as broken, and disintegrated, or as transnational entities that establish smooth relations among their members. Both the construction of transnational ties and the social organization of care at home are complex processes that are not free from tensions. Gender and age are signifiers of important inequalities that are usually hidden under the rubric of family cohesion and unity and will vary according to the evolution of the migrant project.

Conclusions

While international migration has a long tradition in Ecuador and the Andean Region, the intercontinental migration of women is more recent and has had a greater impact than former flows. Several factors converge, from the weight of remittances in a small economy such as the Ecuadorian, to the ways in which families reorganize themselves to cope with social reproduction. This chapter shows that ideological constructions of gender and family play an important role in both the way in which public discourses represent and construct social policies for migrant families and the way these families organize their social reproduction and deploy their strategies transnationally. When contrasting public discourse with actual migrant practices around care several distortions emerge. On one hand, the role of transnational families in the social organization of care is scarcely recognized by families and communities and is even less acknowledged in public policy. In addition, the existence of different types of families is hidden. On the other, social arrangements of care are embedded in familial and gender ideologies and produce severe inequalities among family members that contradict the hegemonic representation of the family. All these aspects seem to be related to the absence and invisibility of migrant women's experiences in public policy-making and political discourse. It is as if the figure of the fixed mother, so ingrained in the social construction surrounding the family and the nation and in the cultural imagination of social protection, prevents the experience of female migration and transnational motherhood from being narrated, and from existing legitimately in public discourse. Therefore, the tentative appearance of transnational families in the state discourse under an article of the 2008 Constitution that recognizes transnational families as part of the diversity of family forms creates an opportunity to dispute the meanings around care, maternity, and the migrant family in the terrain of state policies but also in the realm of public opinion.

Transnational practices and discourse revolving around the social organization of care among migrant families may constitute open channels to transform the fixed ideologies of gender and care that still permeate the hegemonic ways in which the migration experience of women is interpreted in Ecuador. In this sense, the sudden increase in women's migration in the last ten years in Ecuador is not only influencing migrant families and communities, it is also shaking some of the ideological constructions of gender and the family that are interrogated through the migrant experience.

Notes

1. This second study was part of a broader project that includes the analysis of other flows from Latin America to Spain and to Chile, such as Peru and Bolivia and was funded by INSTRAW, the Institute for the Training and Research of Women (UN). The project was entitled "Latin American Women in the Global Chains of Care."
2. "My family, along with of hundreds of thousands of Ecuadorians, was also broken by migration. Like many of you I experienced the great pain of farewells and separations from my loved ones. I know very well the problems and necessity of the people who have to migrate to build a life of dignity, and I know the pain of the ones who have stayed behind . . . we are going to make possible the encounter among families . . . this citizen revolution will persecute those responsible of this national tragedy called migration" (Correa: Letter on the day of the Absent Ecuadorian, July 25, 2006, presidential campaign).
3. This program started in 2008 and constitutes the main policy implemented by the secretary of migration toward its diaspora.

References

Acosta Alberto, Susana López O. and David Villamar. 2005. "Las Remesas y su Aporte para la Economía Ecuatoriana." In *La Migración Ecuatoriana: Transnacionalismo, Redes e Identidade*s. eds. Gioconda Herrera, Maria Cristina Carrillo, and Alicia Torres, 227-252, Quito, Ecuador: FLACSO.

Ariza, Marina. 2000. *Ya no soy la que dejé atrás . . . mujeres migrantes en República Dominicana*. México: Instituto de Investigaciones Sociales. Editorial Plaza y Valdés.

Bakker, Isabella, and Stephen Gill. 2003. *Power, Production and Social Reproduction. Human Insecurity in the Global Political Economy.* Toronto: Palgrave MacMillan.

Bakker, Isabella, and Rachel Silvey. 2008. *Beyond States and Markets. Essays in Social Reproduction.* Abingdon and Oxon, UK, and New York: Routledge.

Bourdieu, Pierre. 1997. "Espíritu de estado. Génesis y estructura del campo burocrático." In *Razones prácticas. Sobre la teoría de la acción*, ed. Pierre Bourdieu, 45–56. Barcelona: Anagrama.

————. 2005. "El misterio del ministerio: de las voluntades particulares a la 'voluntad general.'" In *El misterio del ministerio: Pierre Bourdieu y la política democratic,* ed. Loic Wacquant, 230–45. Barcelona: GEDISA.

Burkett, Elinor. 1975. "Indian Women and White Society: The Case of 16th Century Peru." In *Latin American Women: Historical Perspectives,* ed. Asunción Lavrin, 108–28. Westport, CT: Greenwood Press.

Cerrutti, Marcela. 2009. *Gender and Intra-Regional Migration in South America.* New York: UNDP Human Development Reports Research Paper 2009/12.

Clark, Kim. 2001. "Género, raza y nación: la protección de la infancia en el Ecuador (1910–1945)." In *Antología de estudios de género,* ed. Gioconda Herrera. Quito: FLACSO-Sede Ecuador.

Dore, Elizabeth. 2000. "One Step Further, Two Steps Back: Gender and the State in the Long Nineteenth Century. In *Hidden Histories of Gender and the State in Latin America,* ed. Elizabeth Dore and Maxine Molyneux, 3–32, London: Duke University Press.

Eguiguren, María Mercedes 2010. "Sujeto migrante, crisis y tutela estatal. Construcción de la migración y modos de intervención desde el Estado ecuatoriano.".Masters dissertation in Sociology. Quito: FLACSO.

Ehrenreich, Barbara, and Arlie Russell Hochschild. 2003. *Global Woman: Nannies, Maids and Sex Workers in the New Economy.* New York: Henry Holt and Company.

Herrera, Gioconda. 2008a. "Mujeres ecuatorianas en el trabajo doméstico en Madrid. Estrategias de inclusión y exclusión." In *Ciudadanía y exclusion: Ecuador y España frente al espejo,* eds Víctor Bretón, Francisco García, and María José Vilalta, 279–99, Madrid: Catarata.

————. 2008b. "States, Work, and Social Reproduction through the Lens of Migrant Experience: Ecuadorian Domestic Workers in Madrid. In *Beyond States and Markets: The Challenges of Social Reproduction,* ed. Isabella Bakker and Rachel Silvey, 93–107. Abingdon and Oxon, UK, and New York: Routledge.

————. 2009. La Migración de Los que se Quedan: Género, OrganizaciónSocial del Cuidado y Familias Transnacionales. Research Report. Quito:FLACSO-INSTRAW.

————. 2010. "Stratified Workers/Stratified Mothers. Migration Policies and Citizenship among Ecuadorian Immigrant Women. In *The Globalization of Motherhood: Deconstructions and Reconstructions of Biology and Care,* ed. Wendy Chavkin and Jane Maree Maher, 55–76. Abingdon and Oxon, UK, and New York: Routledge.

Herrera, Gioconda, and M. Cristina Carrillo. 2009. "Transformaciones familiares en la experiencia migratoria ecuatoriana. Una mirada desde los contextos de salida." In *Dossier Dialogues Transatlantiques autour des migrations latino-américaines en Espagne* 39 (1): 97–114.

Hinojosa, Alfonso. 2009. *"Buscando la vida: familias bolivianas transnacionales en España."* La Paz: CLACSO, Fundación PIEB.

Hondagneu-Sotelo, Pierrette. 2001. *Doméstica*. Los Angeles: University of California Press.

Hondagneu-Sotelo, Pierrette, and Ernestine Avila. 1997. "'I'm Here, But I'm There' The Meanings of Latina Transnational Motherhood." *Gender and Society* 11 (5): 548–71.

Instituto Nacional de Estadística y Censos [INEC]. 2007. *Encuesta de empleo, desempleo y subempleo.* Quito: ENEMDU.

Kusnesof, Elizabeth. 1989. "A History of Domestic Service in Spanish America, 1492–1980." In *Muchachas No More. Household Workers in Latin America and the Caribbean,* ed. Elsa Chaney and Mary Castro, 17–36. Philadelphia: Temple University Press.

Lipszyc, Cecilia, 2001. Mujeres Migrantes en la Argentina Contemporánea. Especial Enfasis en Bolivia, Paraguay y Perú. Report prepared for the UN Conference on Racism, Racial Discrimination and Xenophobia. Instituto Nacional contra la Discriminación (INADI). Cape Town, South Africa.

McIlwaine, Cathy. 2010. "Migrant machismos: exploring gender ideologies and practices among Latin American migrants in London from a multi-scalar perspective." *Gender, Place and Culture* 17 (3): 281–300.

Molyneux, Maxine. 2000. "Twentieth Century State Formations in Latin America." In *Hidden Histories of Gender and the State in Latin America*, ed. Elizabeth Dore and Maxine Molyneux, 33–84. London: Duke University Press

Pellegrino, Adela. 2003. "La migración internacional en América Latina y El Caribe: tendencias y perfiles de los migrantes." *Serie Poblacion y Desarrollo* 35. Santiago: CELADE, División de Cepal.

Poeschel, Ursula. 1986. *La mujer Salasaca. Transformaciones socio culturales.* Quito: Abya Yala.

Pribilsky, Jason———. 2007. *La Chulla Vida. Gender, Migration and the Family in Andean Ecuador and New York City.* Syracuse, NY: Syracuse University Press.

Ramirez, Franklin, and Jacques Ramirez. 2004. *La Estampida Migratoria.* Quito: Abya Yala.

Salazar Parreñas, Rhacel. 2001. *Servants of Globalization: Women, Migration and Domestic Work.* Stanford,CA: Stanford University Press.

Scott, Joan. 1996. "El género: una categoría útil para el análisis historic." In *El Género: La Construcción Cultural de la Diferencia Sexual, ed.* Marta Lamas, 265–302. México DF: PUEG-UNAM.

Stefoni, Carolina. 2002. "Mujeres inmigrantes peruanas en Chile." *Papeles de Población* 33:118–45.

Wagner, Heike. 2008, "Maternidad Transnacional: Discursos, Estereotipos, Prácticas." In *América Latina Migrante: Estado, Familia, Identidades. Ed.* Gioconda Herrera Gioconda and Jacques Ramirez, 325-340. Quito: FLACSO.

Chapter 5

Latin American Domestic Workers Abroad: Perspectives from Spain

Ángeles Escrivá and Magdalena Díaz-Gorfinkiel

Latin America has a long history of servitude and a more recent record of paid domestic and care work, both inside the region and overseas. While some continuity in the sector between periods and locations can be observed, other features of the activity have been changing over the years, affecting the national and international dynamics of the sector as well as the social processes linked to them. In this chapter, we analyze the presence of Latin American domestic workers abroad, with a focus on Spain. This country has been a main destination for Latin American domestic workers since the late 1980s. A combination of historical conditions with more recent push and pull factors has shaped this migration corridor. In the following sections, we outline a profile of Latin American domestic workers, emphasizing their diversity in origins and trajectories. The characteristics of the context of labor incorporation are also addressed, including a typology of job modalities, the legislative framework, and the working and living conditions often related with them. Specific points are highlighted in relation to the relevance of the care market for the elderly, taking into account both live-in and live-out domestic employment in which Latin Americans concentrate. In addition, other related topics such as the presence of the state and other social agents in facilitating the reconciliation of work and family, and the gender and class relations that domestic work involves, are discussed throughout the analysis. A brief historical overview of domestic work in Latin America precedes this discussion. The chapter argues that it is essential to take into account the historical context of how domestic service has emerged and been configured over time in the context of

Latin America as well as the ways in which class and race intersect to shape the nature of the profession over time.

A Historical Overview of Domestic Work in Latin America

Latin America has a long tradition of domestic employment, and although migration for work abroad captures most attention nowadays, other trajectories were, and are still, present. Before the twentieth century, the American continent was a destination for European and non-European domestic workers in the form of slavery, patronage, life-long servitude, or temporary work contracts. In a few countries, European immigration continued well after the Second World War (Moya 1998). Since the twentieth century, however, increasing numbers of internal migrants moving from rural areas to urban settings provided a native workforce, which in turn, replaced foreign labor. This demographic shift has also been part of wider social and ideological transformations (Hojman 1989). Later, the impoverishment of Latin American economies and the rising demand for paid domestic labor from wealthier countries have led to a new trend: the emigration of Latin Americans to serve in private households abroad.

The vast majority of Latin American domestic workers, both abroad and in the region, are women. However, the gender composition of this workforce has changed over time and has come to depend, among other things, on the characteristics of the employment. In the preindustrial age, servants included men and women, especially the young and those from rural backgrounds (Sarti 2008). With industrial modernization, the value assigned to household tasks decreased and gender ideologies that praised women's place as unpaid homemakers and providers of care were challenged, contributing to the racialization and feminization of the domestic workforce (Kuznesof 1989). Today, men are employed as domestic workers for specific tasks—as gardeners, chauffeurs, and caretakers of heavy patients. In overseas migration, this often responds to their need to be eligible for inclusion in regularization processes.[1] Beyond this, however, their labor incorporation in this sector has to conform to masculine imaginaries, and therefore it is justified on the basis of changing cultural norms and unexpected circumstances (McIlwaine 2010; Sarti 2008). Yet, we are still not witnessing a masculinization of domestic employment in Latin America. On the contrary, the ongoing depreciation of domestic service in the realm of collective subjectivities, and an ever-growing supply of female labor from all continents contribute to keep the idea that domestic work is for female rather than male hands (Moya 2007).

Another point of comparison between former and contemporary domestic workers relates to the age of servants. As in the case of pre-industrial Europe, in Latin America live-in domestic workers originating from internal migration have been mainly girls and young women who have secured jobs in homes in the absence of factory employment (Potthast 2006). The terms "*criada*" in Spanish and "maid" in English refer to the young age and minor status of servants, who moved out or were sent by their families in rural areas to the cities to reduce economic burdens and to improve their educational and work opportunities. On the contrary, in the age of the so-called imperialistic servants, the average age of domestic workers was not that low. Recalling British historical patterns, research shows that it was common for single, mature women and widows to find domestic employment overseas (Horn 1975). Likewise today, people from all ages compose the international domestic workforce moving from Latin America, including young people and mothers who have left their children behind, as well as those in an advanced age. The latter will probably constitute a growing category in the decades to come, enrolling in paid domestic work, either to secure an income for themselves or to aid their grown-up children, grandchildren and even very old parents, as reported among Latin Americans in Spain (Escrivá and Skinner 2006) or Eastern Europeans all over Western Europe. For these mature domestic workers, Ralitza Soultanova (2007) uses the expression "end career migrants" to highlight that they enter into domestic employment at a later stage in their lives, after widespread experience of employment in another sector or having been housewives.

Racist hierarchies have commonly helped to legitimate the immutable position of servants. This has had a special impact in Latin America. The racist stance of Spanish as well as British and other imperialisms, that identified certain people's phenotypical features with inferior capacities, permeated in the colonies and has survived until the present day (Radcliffe 1999). Persistent social organization based on flagrant ethno-racial and gender hierarchies has kept domestic workers in particular in the lower end of the labor market, resulting in poor working conditions and an undervaluing of their jobs in Latin America and in countries where they migrate. It is therefore no wonder that when moving abroad, many middle-class Latin Americans perceive their new jobs in household services as highly exploitative. Following similar paths to many others before, the medium-term strategy is to move out of domestic work, especially from live-in to live-out regimes, and search for other "better" occupations (Escrivá and Skinner 2008; Hondagneu-Sotelo and Avila 1997).

In summary, domestic work offers a fruitful terrain for analyzing the social structures and relations between individuals and groups in different historical periods and parts of the world. In Latin America, as elsewhere, domestic work can be viewed as much as a form of slave labor or servitude, as an apprenticeship for later family formation, or in a more modern version of capitalist free-market transaction, as the embodiment of the servant-master through an employee-employer relationship. All these forms are based on unequal economic and social relations, where gender, age, race, origin, and citizenship status have served to create deep disparities (Anthias and Lazaridis 2000; Oliveira and Ariza 1998; Young 1987). This uneven relationship at the microlevel reflects broader patterns of uneven global development within and between nations.

Although domestic servants have been viewed as dominated subjects, they have historically also been active agents as purveyors of ideologies. Because of their direct intrusion in private family life, domestic workers have often acquired certain civilizing or moralizing roles, directly promoted by states, intermediaries (such as religious congregations) or employers, or even by the employees themselves. Rafaella Sarti (2008) summarizes the different roles that subsequent flows of overseas domestics moving from the metropolis to the colonies and vice versa have played through the centuries. Examples of this are the Spanish "imperialistic" and "colonialist servants" who were the ones responsible for carrying the language and habits of the country of origin to the employers' household, with their move to the Latin American colonies viewed as having a "civilizing" effect on the region as a whole. Similarly, contemporary "servants of globalization," a term coined by Rachel Parreñas (2001) to refer mainly to Latin American or South Asian women, are moving from the peripheries of the world's economies to the private homes of the economic centers. Consciously or unconsciously, they are instrumental in meeting certain aims; first, in maintaining prevailing gender ideologies and dissolving conflicts between couples, which, in turn, means that men are not required to participate more fully in domestic chores (Tobío and Díaz 2007); second, in controlling and reinforcing religious values, when maids are recruited by religious organizations (Wagner 2010); and third, in encouraging the gain or regain of some political/linguistic equilibrium in a given setting.[2]

A final point is that most knowledge about the characteristics and conditions of domestic work and workers in Latin America in the preemigratory period was created by feminist research in the 1970s and 1980s (Jelin 1976; Young 1987). At that time, consciousness and claims of domestic workers and their organizations was strengthened across the region (Chaney and Garcia 1989). In parallel, European and North American feminist researchers were widely engaged in the study of the persistent gendering of domestic work and the low value attributed to it, despite major societal advances (Bock and Duden 1977, cited in Lutz 2007, 187).

Historical accounts inform us how during much of the twentieth century paid domestic work decreased dramatically in Anglo-Saxon and other industrialized European nations (Sarti 2005), whereas in other countries it increased internally and became an exported commodity. Academic, as well as literary and film, work depicts the lives of many Spanish, Portuguese, or Italian women of poorer rural regions moving to the more urbanized areas in the postwar period up until recently (Oso 2004; Sarasúa 1994).

Yet, although there was a temporary decrease in paid domestic work in some of these Organization for Economic Cooperation and Development (OECD) countries, and a long tradition of migration for domestic work in others, since the end of the twentieth century all of them became net importers of maids especially coming from Latin America in the cases of the United States and Spain.

Diversity of Origins and Trajectories of Migrant Domestic Workers from Latin America

Domestic work has become an important economic activity in Latin America, given that it amounted to an average of 7 percent of the total urban employment for the region in 2003 (ILO 2005). Internal and international migrants make up a large proportion of those working as domestic workers. Within Latin America, people tended to migrate first to neighboring countries if they were wealthier. Venezuela, for example, became a destination country for Dominicans, Colombians, and even Peruvians, from the 1960s to the 1980s (Torrealba 1992). Today, Chile and Argentina attract women searching for domestic jobs from Peru, Bolivia, and Paraguay (Stefoni 2008), while in Central America, Costa Rica receives mainly Nicaraguan migrant women (ILO 2002). In the United States, Mexicans and Puerto Ricans tended to substitute for the partial retreat of African American women from domestic service (Glenn 2007). Nevertheless, from the late 1980s onward, other more distant countries became accessible to Latin American women who were in search of work abroad, either independently or following their male partners, or together with the families for whom they had been employed in the country of origin.

In Angeles Escrivá's (1999) research on Peruvian domestic workers in Barcelona, she encountered several pioneer women who had arrived in Spain in the 1970s and 1980s, working for the same families as in Lima. This path is even more visible in the United Kingdom, following the history of returning expatriate British families, or in the United States, as noted by Hondagneu-Sotelo (2001) when talking about her mother who as a young woman moved from Chile to the United States following the American family she had been working for.

Concerning the diversity of migration and occupational trajectories, Safa (1984) pointed out more than two decades ago that the labor incorporation of migrant women to receiving countries like the United States follows very diverse patterns. Among the trajectories related to domestic work, we highlight the following processes as key to understanding international domestic work from Latin America to Spain. First, in many cases, given that it is not the poorest who migrate in the first instance, those searching for domestic employment do not initially have experience of paid domestic work; instead, they are often employers of other lower-status women back home (Restrepo 2006). Second, in other cases, migrant women obtain experience of domestic work on their way to a final destination, following a path from countryside to an urban setting, and from there to a middle-income country until arriving in a higher-income country. This is the case of Peruvians interviewed by Escrivá (1999), who had a background of migration from the highlands to the coast, then to Argentina/Chile, later to Spain or Italy, and much later to another European country such as the UK. Third, and in a similar manner, previous internal migrants directly migrate to perform the same job for new employers abroad, being replaced by their daughters later on. For example, many Dominicans from the rural south-west province of Barahona who settled in Madrid in the late 1980s and early 1990s followed this path (Gregorio 1998, Sørensen 2005). Fourth, there is evidence that sometimes migrants with families in receiving countries call upon someone from their home town or neighborhood to migrate in order to help them with household chores on a paid or unpaid basis (Escrivá and Skinner 2008). Finally, some agencies and in-origin recruitment programs sponsored by the state are increasingly searching for experienced domestic workers, nurses, and professional caretakers in source countries.

The key issue, however, is that many Latin Americans are employed as domestic workers at least for some time during their life abroad whatever the woman's background and trajectory, and whether this work was planned or not before migrating (McIlwaine 2010; Menjívar

2003; Oso 2007). This experience of paid domestic work includes a range of different regimes, usually differentiated on a live-in or live-out basis, and in the latter case, jobs are divided into full-time or part-time or per hour jobs, which may entail being employed in different households. Live-in employment is more available to newly arrived and undocumented migrants and is increasingly common in Spain (Parella 2003). The tasks requested of domestic workers in households may also differ substantially, from caretaking of dependants and pets and gardening, to cooking, cleaning, or general housekeeping. Sometimes domestic workers are given household management responsibilities such as budgeting and shopping. This requires employees having a good command of the language and knowledge of the social norms in place.

Employment of Live-In and Live-Out Domestic Caretakers in Spain

Not only do Latin American domestic workers abroad reflect a strong diversity in nationality origins and employment trajectories, but the receiving contexts offer great variations in terms of immigration legislation, demographic structures, and family and institutional arrangements. These variables clearly affect the practice of employing domestic workers in different contexts.

Researchers argue that migrant women's incorporation into household services is high where all or some of the following conditions exist: a strong tradition of domestic servitude, familialism, weak industrial economies with less supportive welfare states, and high rates of female incorporation into full-time paid employment. This is the case all around Latin America, and in many parts of Europe and the United States (Ehrenreich and Hochschild 2003; Williams and Gavanas 2008). However, other factors influence the greater popularity in certain societies for employing live-in helpers than in others. On one hand, it makes a difference whether the job is just for cleaning, cooking, and general domestic tasks, or entails caring work for babies, the sick, and the elderly at home, the latter requiring more intensive working days. On the other hand, employing someone on a live-in basis requires a certain attitude or predisposition from the employer's side, who has to address and marry her own needs and desires with social expectations and norms that relate to wider "cultures of care" (Finch 1989; Tobío 2005). Expectations and desires with regard to eldercare may diverge among generations and depend on previous life experience. While coping with the constant presence of a domestic worker may be easier for individuals who have been living more independently and have been less reliant on their extended family or other networks, in Spain care work is still mainly provided by the family and only when absolutely necessary other sources of help are sought (Martínez 2010). Therefore, many elderly are quite often against having someone strange in their house and avoid it as long as they can. Finally, their adult children are the ones who have to make the decision to employ a domestic care worker, sometimes against their older parents' will (Colectivo Ioé 2005).

Complementary explanations of the persistence and even increase in paid domestic and care work relates to changing demographic circumstances (including population aging and growing inflows of migrant women accepting especially live-in jobs); the cutback in state expenditures in caring and the privatization of personal services; and housing arrangements and attitudes toward being at home among employers' families. In particular, when home ownership is widespread and when the elderly do not wish to be put in nursing/ elder homes when they become fragile, the number of live-in domestic workers is much higher. All three factors are interrelated in the Spanish case (Berjano, Simó, and Ariño 2005; Escrivá and Skinner 2008; Rodríguez et al. 2010).

Therefore, the new trend in domestic service is the increasing demand on elder care. Research in Spain analyzes the physical, mental, and emotional effort that domestic caring work for elderly people involves (Escrivá 2004; Vega 2009; Martínez 2010). These authors have argued that characteristics now required of domestic workers, such as being able to conduct a wide range of household chores, as well as being a good nurse and a companion, and to show respect and affection for the elderly, make (in principle) Latin American women especially suitable for eldercare in Spain because of linguistic and cultural proximity.

In accordance, Martinez (2010) has noted that daughters who employ Latin American workers to care for their elderly parents prefer warmth over technical knowledge (professionalism), since they expect them to behave as if they were their own daughters, far from the cold and distant treatment one may receive from medical staff. Yet, apart from emotional care, elderly people with poor physical and mental health have to receive constant medications and treatments. This necessarily begs the question as to what training nonprofessional care workers should follow to look after the sick and disabled (Cangiano et al. 2009; Colectivo Ioé 2005).

The intimate proximity sought in the relationship between the caretaker and the elderly person differs from the distant relationship pointed out by Anderson (2000) in some au pair and domestic arrangements. For some of Anderson's interviewees, the domestic helper was thought to be "one of the family," which in turn was used as a justification for putting loved ones in somebody else's hands in a position that requires a lot of trust and empathy. For others, there was a desire to maintain distance with their employees in order to control their activities and avoid coming into competition for their children's affection, so that proximity was not confused with intimacy, thus contributing to the social alienation of the foreign worker in the domestic sphere (Mundlak and Shamir 2008).

Finally, because of the real or perceived suitability of certain workers to specific tasks, in most societies a hierarchy of positions and jobs by nationality (reflected in language, skin color and body appearance, religion, or "cultural proximity") emerges (Anderson 2000; Cox 1999). This is a social order that fellow migrant women usually defend and thus contribute to reinforce, as is the case among Latin American domestic workers (Tamagno 2002; Vega 2009). Not only does such a hierarchy mean that women of a certain background will have limited chance to get other jobs than those attributed to their kind, but also that the best jobs (best paid, valued, and most gratifying) are confined to the same, more advantaged groups.

Legal Frameworks and Policies toward Domestic Work and Overseas Immigration

Social preferences for certain migrant domestic and care workers have been translated into legal measures in order to select specific groups and allow them to enjoy more favorable conditions in destination countries. This preferential treatment has applied to Latin Americans in Spain in a comparable way to Commonwealth citizens in the United Kingdom. Legal differences have included advantages in professional recognition, in-origin recruitment, and access to citizenship rights such as voting and naturalization thanks to bilateral agreements.[3] Apart from these measures, the Spanish government has been less reluctant to limit Latin American migration, which has resulted in higher rates of success in regularization processes and family reunification procedures. Except for a few cases where the United States has been more open to certain Latin American groups (such as refugees from Cuba or citizens of the associated State of Puerto Rico), there has been little favoritism toward Latin Americans working as domestics. On the contrary, Mexicans and Central Americans are especially discriminated against (Hondagneu-Sotelo 2001).

Migrant domestic workers' legal status has consequences for their living and working conditions, but also beyond the immediate and the individual. On the one hand, while in the United States many domestic workers remain undocumented for years, in Spain they have systematically been able to obtain work permits through amnesties and in-origin recruitment. On the contrary, in the UK, foreign household helpers usually work while holding statuses not (or not fully) designed for that purpose (students, au pairs, asylum seekers, and spouses of legal residents). As a result of fewer legal constraints until now, Latin Americans have been more able to reunite with their loved and dependent people in the short run, as well as to move out of the domestic service in Spain than in other countries (Ozyegin and Hondagneu-Sotelo 2008). This procedure, although publicized as a policy favoring human rights, has been criticized by others for entailing a call effect (a pull factor), given that a continuous substitution of those leaving the sector (due to poor conditions and status change) is required. Nonetheless, a high turnover has also helped to keep salaries low and to introduce a more exploitable labor force. Yet, in order to avoid high turnover and permanent settlement of care workers, the Spanish government could be tempted to implement, similarly to countries like the UK, stricter controls in order to facilitate the formal migration of nurses and caretakers from overseas with short-term visas, limited to a single employer, and with no family reunification rights (Galloti 2009).

On the other hand, even if holding a valid work permit, as domestic employees, Latin American women continue to suffer comparatively worse occupational status than all other registered workers. In Spain, waged domestic work is still included in a special labor regime that assigns lower social benefits, more flexible and long working hours, no career advancement, nonstandardized labor conditions, and lack of control over employers' observance of the law (Colectivo Ioé 2001). Nowadays, in a period of high unemployment, migrant women have no access to public subsidies, while their male fellow countrymen who work in construction do. Even less protected are domestic workers in the United States (Ariza 2008). Social rights such as paid vacations, annual bonuses, and holiday cover are nonexistent, and live-in domestic workers as well as personal attendants dedicated primarily to care work remain excluded from federal regulations concerning minimum salaries, weekly working hours, and overtime payments. State initiatives undertaken by regional governments such as those of New York and California have modified these general federal regulations and improved domestic workers conditions, most commonly following pressure exercised by domestic workers and their representatives (DWU & D 2006; Delp and Quan 2002).

Collective Action and Organization of Latin American Domestic Workers

Individual and collective action at different levels and the alliance of different governmental and nongovernmental actors are common ingredients of any attempt to address the abuses and the inferior labor status of domestic workers. First, we need a thorough understanding of the many different constraints faced by domestic workers. As women's domestic work is performed in private domains and is often unregistered, this activity is generally not visible nor considered a true labor relation. The fact that domestic work is regarded as a private labor relation, or what Anderson (2007) refers to as "a very private business," underpins the possibilities of recognition and enforcement of work-related social rights. Second, Lautier (2003) affirms that the predisposition of domestic workers is an important barrier to collective action. He notes how women are often more interested in negotiating individually their relationships with employers or *patronas*, given their isolation and the very nature of the master-servant relation, than trying to change labor conditions collectively. This is referred to as a kind of "false conscience," since these women see their condition as temporary and try to hide it when outside the employer's home. Third, social agents such as trade unions in Spain have traditionally discarded domestic service as a priority, and have been mainly active launching information and awareness campaigns (Peterson 2007). Religious groups have tended to maintain the status quo by emphasizing modesty and sacrifice, thereby avoiding confronting political actors and the better-off members of their parishes. This has been the case in Italy or Spain, where nuns have played a very important role recruiting and placing domestic workers in Catholic households, as well as negotiating the conflicts between employers and employees, usually tipping the balance in the employer's favor (Andall 2000; Escrivá 2003). Yet, in the United States (Hondagneu-Sotelo 2008) and other countries, some Christian leaders have been extremely active in claiming and supporting actions for immigrants' rights more generally. In so doing, they have helped immigrant domestic women to fulfill their needs, and to organize for labor, civil, and immigrant rights.

Far from a victimization and passive perspective, our final focus is on how domestic workers have taken several collective actions in different and distant locations, with or without the support of established trade unions and other social actors, to improve their condition.

In Spain, there was an attempt promoted by solidarity organizations, trade unions, and domestic workers associations to remove the special labor regime of domestic service workers and incorporate them into the general labor regime between 2004 and 2006. However, this initiative got stuck in the legislative process (León 2010). In addition, politicians have been waiting for transformations in the homecare sector after the implementation of the so-called dependency law starting in 2007, although public funding cuts since 2008 due to the economic crisis have ruined any prospects of this becoming a reality.

More recently, the United Nations International Research and Training Institute for the Advancement of Women (INSTRAW), now a part of UN-WOMEN, with financial support from the Spanish International Cooperation Agency (AECI), launched an action-research project aimed at mobilizing the social actors involved and pushing the process toward better social recognition of the value of domestic work as well as assessing the personal costs to migrant workers. This project involved meetings among different organizations that have been, but in a separate manner, claiming for the improvements of the sector such as Territorio Doméstico, Precarias a la Deriva and Servicio Doméstico Activo (SEDOAC), and a march on the annual day for domestic workers (March 28, 2010). Interestingly, this initiative has a transnational stance, involving action-research in Spain and countries of Latin America (Ecuador, Peru, Bolivia, and Chile) with the aim of including national and international bodies and nonstate actors based in all these places.

Transnational campaigns and cooperation have indeed proved to be more effective in addressing the issues that affect people everywhere and represent a more serious turn than solely national efforts (Galloti 2009). Long and intense national and international campaigning to raise awareness and lobby for better conditions for all and especially migrant domestic workers has finally led to the decision to create the International Convention on Decent Work for Domestic Workers that was launched in 2011.

Conclusions

Under the generic term of Latin American domestic workers in European and North American countries, there are a diversity of peoples and trajectories, based on the characteristics of different groups and contexts of reception. Prevailing care and gender regimes in sending and receiving societies shape the domestic employment for Latin Americans, and other migrant women. Accordingly, the demand for female migrant labor suggests continuity with the demand for domestic work that was previously provided by local and internal migrant women, but a change in relation to the sector of work where there is growing demand of care work for the elderly (Andall 2005). Migration regimes add complexity to the picture, often condemning waged domestic work to irregularity and devaluation.

Even though the sector offers opportunities for the workers, there is some consensus on the need to improve the conditions and regulations governing paid domestic and care work. Although some steps have been taken in this direction, as Anderson (2010) describes for the UK policy, this is a "one step forward, two steps back" process. The "dependency law" passed in 2007 in Spain, which also aimed to help to improve the status and conditions of informal migrant care workers, has been poorly implemented with recent funding cuts likely to undermine it further. The negotiations between the state-trade unions-employers' organizations at the end of 2010, to restore the Spanish economy with changes on the labor market under EU pressures, have been another lost opportunity to move into the inclusion of domestic workers in the general workers regime.

In general terms, where the state is subsidizing eldercare, and care workers are employed by external organizations instead of by families, their labor conditions seem to be better guaranteed. This makes the inclusion of domestic workers in the general workers regime important, giving them more chances to unionize and make their working conditions more accountable. A better balance between the genders with regard to paid and unpaid work would also help to avoid employing large numbers of nannies and housekeepers. However, immigrant domestic work has tended to be excluded from a debate that has focused mainly on gender inequalities in unpaid domestic work (Peterson 2007).

Yet, as people live longer, an aged population poses new challenges for families, societies, and states. An increasing demand for care workers is expected in the years and decades to come, to be met by immigrant women. However, the implementation of restrictive norms for immigrant domestic and care workers poses new questions about whether it will be morally sustainable (taking into account all international civil and human rights charters) to restrict people's mobility between territories independently of nationality and immigration status, or to condemn them to lifelong servitude. Finally, yet importantly, is the question of how sending societies in Latin America will manage to protect their younger and older generations when their own middle generations have disappeared abroad.

Acknowledgments

The authors wish to thank Cathy McIlwaine for her comments and editing of the chapter.

Notes

1. This has been the case in countries like Spain or Italy. In Italy, the "*bandanti*" (domestic workers and caretakers) are in fact almost the only category under which immigrants can obtain a residence and work permit. That explains why Andall (2000) reports that in 1992, for example, male migrants constituted 61 percent of domestic workers in Sicily. In Spain, quotas have been open to different sectors, and although numbers did not reach that level, 7 percent of all those registered in the domestic workers labor regime in 2008 in Spain were men, according to data from the Instituto Nacional de Estadística (INE).
2. This could be the case of countries where subnational or indigenous tongues compete with an official and more worldwide-spread language. In Spain, a way to counteract Catalan advance in Catalonia would be opening the door to the employment of Spanish-speaking migrants by Catalan-speaking families.
3. Nationals from Latin American countries (and of Andorra, Equatorial Guinea, the Philippines, Portugal and Sephardic origins) can apply for Spanish citizenship after only two years legal residence in Spain, while migrants from other national origins need to prove at least ten years of legal residence.

References

Andall, Jacqueline. 2000. "Organizing Domestic Workers in Italy: The Challenges of Gender, Class and Ethnicity. In *Gender and Migration in Southern Europe. Women on the Move*, ed. Anthias, Floya, and Gabriella Lazaridis, 145–71. Oxford: Berg.
———. 2005. "Change and Continuity in the Italian Domestic Work Sector." Paper presented at the international conference on Migration and Domestic Work in Global Perspective, May 26–29, in Wassenaar, The Netherlands.
Anderson, Bridget. 2000. *Doing the Dirty Work? The Global Politics of Domestic Labour.* London: Zed.
———. 2007. "A Very Private Business. Exploring the Demand for Migrant Domestic Workers." *European Journal of Women's Studies* 14 (3): 247–64.

————. 2010. "Mobilizing Migrants, Making Citizens: Migrant Domestic Workers as Political Agents." *Ethnic and Racial Studies* 33 (1): 60–74.

Anthias, Floya, and Gabriella Lazaridis. 2000. "Introduction: Women on the Move in Southern Europe." In *Gender and Migration in Southern Europe: Women on the Move*, ed. Floya Anthias and Gabriella Lazaridis, 1–14. Oxford: Berg.

Ariza, Marina. 2008. "Migration and Female Labor Markets in the Context of Globalization: Latina Domestic Workers in Madrid and New York." Paper presented at the European Population Association Congress, July 9–12, Barcelona, Spain.

Berjano, Enrique, Carles Simó, and Antonio Ariño. 2005. "Condicionantes de la aparición del fenómeno social 'inmigrantes que cuidan a mayores.'" In *Cuidado a la dependencia e inmigración*. Informe de resultados, ed. IMSERSO, 21–121. Madrid: Instituto de Mayores y Servicios Sociales.

Cangiano, Alessio, Isabel Shutes, Sarah Spencer, and George Leeson. 2009. "Migrant Care Workers in Ageing Societies." Research findings in the United Kingdom. Oxford: COMPAS.

Chaney, Elsa, and Maria Garcia .1989. *Muchachas No More. Household Workers in Latin America and the Caribbean*. Philadelphia: Temple University Press.

Colectivo Ioé. 2001. *Mujer, trabajo y migración*. Madrid: Ministerio de Trabajo y Seguridad Social.

————. 2005. "El cuidado de personas mayores dependientes realizado por ciudadanos inmigrantes en la Comunidad de Madrid." In *Cuidado a la dependencia e inmigración*. Informe de resultados, ed. IMSERSO, 233–370. Madrid: Instituto de Mayores y Servicios Sociales.

Cox, Rosie. 1999. "The Role of Ethnicity in Shaping the Domestic Employment in Britain." In *Gender, Migration and Domestic Work*, ed. Janet H. Momsen, 134–47. Oxford: Routledge.

Delp, Linda, and Katie Quan. 2002. "Homecare Worker Organizing in California: An Analysis of a Successful Strategy." *Labor Studies Journal* 27 (1): 1–23.

Domestic Workers United & Datacenter. 2006. "Home is Where the Work Is: Inside New York Domestic Industry." http://www.datacenter.org /wpcontent/uploads/homeiswherethe workis.pdf (accessed January 23, 2011).

Ehrenreich, Barbara, and Arlie R. Hochschild. 2003. *Global Woman. Nannies, Maids and Sex Workers in the New Economy*. New York: Metropolitan Books.

Escrivá, Angeles. 1999. "Mujeres peruanas del servicio doméstico en Barcelona: trayectorias sociolaborales." Doctoral thesis. Barcelona: Universitat Autònoma de Barcelona.

————. 2003. "Latinoamericanos en España: iglesias e integración social." In *Las Iglesias y la Migración*. Actas de las Jornadas celebradas del 25 al 26 de abril. Consejo Evangélico de Madrid, Seminario Teológico, Madrid: UEBE.

Escrivá, Angeles. 2004. "Securing the Care and Welfare of Dependants Transnationally: Peruvians and Spaniards in Spain." Working paper. Oxford: Oxford Institute of Ageing.

Escrivá, Angeles and Emmeline Skinner. 2006. "Moving to Spain at an Advanced Age." *Generations Review* 16:8–15.

————. 2008. "Domestic Work and Transnational Care Chains in Spain." In *Migration and Domestic Work. A European Perspective on a Global Theme*, ed. Helma Lutz, 113–26. Aldershot, UK: Ashgate.

Finch, Janet. 1989. *Family Obligation and Social Change*. Cambridge: Polity Press.

Galloti, María. 2009. "The Gender Dimension of Domestic Work in Western Europe." *International Migration Papers 96*. Geneva: ILO.

Glenn, Evelyn Nakano. 2007. "Caring and Inequality." In *Women's Labor in the Global Economy. Speaking in Multiple Voices*, ed. Sharon Harley, 46–61. New Brunswick, NJ: Rutgers University Press.

Gregorio, Carmen. 1998. *Migración Femenina: Su Impacto en Las Relaciones de género*. Madrid: Narcea.

Hojman, David. 1989. Land Reform, Female Migration and the Market for Domestic service in Chile. *Journal of Latin American Studies* 21 (1):105–32.

Hondagneu-Sotelo, Pierrette, and Ernestine Avila. 1997. "'I'm here, but I'm there' the meanings of Latina transnational motherhood." *Gender and Society* 11 (5): 548–71.

Hondagneu-Sotelo, Pierrette, 2001. *Doméstica. Immigrant Workers Cleaning and Caring in the Shadows of Affluence*. Berkeley and Los Angeles: University of California Press.

————. 2008. *God's Heart Has No Borders. How Religious Activists are Working for Immigrant Rights*. Berkeley and Los Angeles: University of California Press.

Horn, Pamela. 1975. *The Rise and Fall of the Victorian Servant*. Dublin: Gill and New York: Macmillan and St. Martin's Press.

International Labor Organization. 2002. *Estudio de Hogares de Mujeres Nicaragüenses Emigrantes en Costa Rica*. Managua: ILO.

————. 2005. *Panorama Laboral de América Latina*. Lima: ILO.

Jelin, Elizabeth. 1976. Labor Migration and Female Labor Participation in Latin America: The Case of Domestic Servants in the Cities. *Signs* 3 (1): 129–41.

Kuznesof, Elizabeth. 1989. "A History of Domestic Service in Spanish America, 1492–1980." In *Muchachas No More. Household Workers in Latin America and the Caribbean*, ed. Elsa Chaney and Maria Garcia, 17–35. Philadelphia: Temple University Press.

Lautier, Bruno. 2003. "Las empleadas domésticas y la sociología del trabajo." *Revista Mexicana de Sociología* 65 (4): 789–814.

León, Margarita. 2010. "Migration and Care Work in Spain: The Domestic Service Revisited." *Social Policy and Society* 9 (3): 409–418.

Lutz, Helma. 2007. "Editorial: Domestic Work." *European Journal of Women's Studies* 14 (3): 187-192.

Martínez, Raquel. 2010. *Bienestar y Cuidados: El Oficio del Cariño. Mujeres Inmigrantes y Mayores Nativos*. Madrid: CSIC.

McIlwaine, Cathy. 2010. "Migrant Machismos: Exploring Gender Ideologies and Practices among Latin American Migrants in London from a Multi-Scalar Perspective." *Gender, Place and Culture* 17 (3): 281–300.

Menjívar, Cecilia. 2003. "The Intersection of Work and Gender. Central American Immigrant Women and Employment in California." In *Gender and US Immigration. Contemporary Trends*, ed. Pierrette Hondagneu-Sotelo, 101–26. Berkeley: University of California Press.

Moya, José. 1998. *Cousins and Strangers: Spanish Immigrants in Buenos Aires, 1850–1930*. Berkeley: University of California Press.

———. 2007. "Domestic Service in Global Perspective: Gender, Migration, and Ethnic Niches. *Journal of Ethnic and Migration Studies* 33 (4): 559–79.

Mundlak, Guy, and Hila Shamir. 2008. "Between Intimacy and Alienage: The Legal Construction of Domestic and Carework in the Welfare State." In *Migration and Domestic Work. A European Perspective on a Global Theme*, ed. Helma Lutz, 161–76. Aldershot, UK: Ashgate.

Oliveira, Orlandina, and Marina Ariza. 1998. "Terciarización, feminización de la fuerza de trabajo y precariedad laboral en México." In *Género y Pobreza. Nuevas dimensiones*, ed. Irma Arriagada and Carmen Torres, 111–17. Santiago de Chile: Isis Internacional Ediciones de las Mujeres.

Oso, Laura. 2004. *Españolas en París. Estrategias de Ahorro y Consumo en las migraciones internacionales*. Barcelona: Edicions Bellaterra.

———. 2007. La inserción laboral de la población latinoamericana en España: el protagonismo de las mujeres. In *Nuevas Migraciones Latinoamericanas a Europa: Balances y Desafíos*, ed. Isabel Yépez and Gioconda Herrera, 453–79. Flacso-Obreal-UCL-UB.

Ozyegin, Gul, and Pierette Hondagneu-Sotelo. 2008. "Conclusion: Domestic Work, Migration and the New Gender Order in Contemporary Europe." In *Migration and Domestic Work. A European Perspective on a Global Theme*, ed. Helma Lutz, 195–208. Aldershot, UK: Ashgate.

Parella, Sonia. 2003. "Immigrant Women in Paid Domestic Service. The Case of Spain and Italy." *Transfer: European Review of Labour and Research* 9 (3): 503–17.

Parreñas, Rachel. 2001. *Servants of Globalization: Women, Migration and Domestic Work*. Palo Alto, CA: Stanford University Press.

Peterson, Elin. 2007. "The Invisible Carers: Framing Domestic Work(ers) in Gender Equality Policies in Spain. *European Journal of Women's Studies* 14 (3): 265–80.

Potthast, Barbara. 2006. "Mujeres inmigrantes en América Latina: una perspectiva histórica". In *Un Continente en Movimiento: Migraciones en América Latina*, ed. Ingrid Wehr, 111–30. Madrid: Editorial Iberoamericana/Vervuert.

Radcliffe, Sarah. 1999. "Race and Domestic Service. Migration and Identity in Ecuador." In *Gender, Migration and Domestic Work*, ed. Janet H. Momsen, 83–97. Oxon: Routledge.

Restrepo, Ofelia. 2006. *Mujeres Colombianas en España. Historias, Inmigración y Refugio.* Bogotá: editorial Pontificia Universidad Javeriana.

Rodríguez, Vicente, Eva Martín, Silvia Marcu, Santiago Ramos, Fermina Rojo, Gloria Fernández-Mayorales, Raúl Lardies, and Jesús Rogero. 2010. Inmigración y cuidados de mayores en los hogares de la Comunidad de Madrid. *Informes Portal Mayores*, 102.

Safa, Helen. 1984. "The Differential Incorporation of Hispanic Women Migrants into the U.S. Labor Force." In *Women on the Move. Contemporary Changes in Family and Society,* 159–73. Paris: UNESCO.

Sarasúa, Carmen. 1994. *Criados, Nodrizas y Amos.* Madrid: Siglo XXI.

Sarti, Raffaella. 2005. "Conclusion: Domestic service and European identity. Final Report of *the Servant Project.*" Brussels: European Commission.

———. 2008. "The Globalisation of Domestic Service. An Historical Perspective." In *Migration and Domestic Work. A European Perspective on a Global Theme,* ed. Helma Lutz, 77–97. Aldershot, UK: Ashgate.

Sørensen, Nina. 2005. "Narratives of Longing, Belonging and Caring in the Dominican Diaspora." In *Caribbean Narratives,* ed. Jean Besson and Karen F. Olwig, 222–43. London: Macmillan.

Soultanova, Ralitza. 2007. "La migration de fin de carrière. Le cas des femmes bulgares à Madrid." In *Vivre ensemble au XXIème siecle.* Actes du colloque international de l'Institut de Sociologie, ed. Institut de Sociologie, 471–86. Brussels: Université Libre de Bruxelles.

Stefoni, Carolina. 2008. "Migración, Género y Servicio Doméstico. Mujeres Peruanas en Chile." In *Trabajo Doméstico y Equidad de Género en Latinoamérica: Desafíos para el Trabajo Decente,* ed. Claudia Mora and María Elena Valenzuela. Santiago: ILO.

Tamagno, Carla. 2002. "'You Must Win Their Affection.' Migrant's Social and Cultural Practices between Peru and Italy. In *Work and Migration: Life and Livelihoods in a Globalizing World,* ed. Karen Fog Olwig and Nina Sørensen, 106–26. London: Routledge.

Tobío, Constanza. 2005. *Madres que Trabajan. Dilemas y Estrategias.* Madrid: Cátedra.

Tobío, Constanza, and Magdalena Díaz. 2007. "New Gendered Relationships in Spain: The 'Other' in the Care Triangle. *International Journal of Iberian Studies* 20 (1): 41–63.

Torrealba, Ricardo. 1992. *Trabajadoras Migrantes en el Servicio Doméstico en Venezuela,* Documento de Trabajo: Migración y Población. Geneva: OIT.

Vega, Cristina. 2009. *Culturas del cuidado en transición. Espacios, sujetos e imaginarios en una sociedad de migración.* Barcelona: Editorial UOC.

Wagner, Heike. 2010. *Dasein für Andere—Dasein als Andere in Europa. Ecuadorianische Hausarbeiterinnen in Privathaushalten und Katholischen Gemeinden Madrids.* Wiesbaden: VS Verlag für Sozialwissenschaft.

Williams, Fiona, and Anna Gavanas. 2008. "The Intersection of Childcare Regimes and Migration Regimes: A Three-Country Study." In *Migration and Domestic Work. A European Perspective on a Global Theme*, ed. Helma Lutz, 13–28. Aldershot, UK: Ashgate.

Young, Grace Esther. 1987. "The Myth of Being 'Like a Daughter.'" *Latin American Perspectives* 14 (3): 365–80.

Section 2

Understanding Latin American Migration to the United Kingdom

Chapter 6

Super-Diversity, Multiculturalism, and Integration: An Overview of the Latin American Population in London, UK

Cathy McIlwaine

It is now widely acknowledged that international migration flows have increased and diversified in recent years, presenting a series of challenges for conceptualizing mobility (Faist 2004, 2009). Transnationality has become a central element of this diversity as people live increasingly complex lives that cross borders, with ramifications for social and economic livelihoods, identity formations, and political allegiances. However, public policy and public service provision have struggled to deal with this diversification in migration, which has in part fuelled the debates on the relevance, or not, of multiculturalism in destination countries (Kymlicka 2010; Vertovec 2010). While this diversification has occurred globally, it has been especially marked within Europe. London in particular has been singled out as one of the cities where this diversity, or what Vertovec (2007) refers to as "super-diversity" is most obviously manifested. In London, there has been a shift away from large-scale migration from Commonwealth countries toward smaller groups of migrants who are more transient, ethnically and linguistically diverse, from a wider range of countries with no previous ties with the UK, who have a wide range of different immigration statuses, and who maintain a wide range of different transnational linkages (see also Wills et al. 2010).

In this chapter, I suggest that the presence and growth of the Latin American population in London is a clear manifestation of one of the "new migrant" groups that are contributing to the super-diversity of the city. However, until recently, Latin Americans have been largely invisible as a migrant group in the city. The chapter therefore provides an overview of the population, highlighting the main types of diversity that exist among them and also providing an important foundation for the subsequent chapters focusing on the UK, most of which are on London. Conceptually, the discussion highlights the need to challenge the utility of multicultural and integration perspectives for understanding Latin American migrants in UK and other new migrant groups more generally when analyzed in conjunction with the notion of "super-diversity." It also suggests that it is important to recognize the "super-diversity" within "new migrant groups" and not just between them.

Super-Diversity, Multiculturalism, and Integration

The issues of diversity and multiculturalism are not new, with some suggesting that both Roman and Ottoman empires struggled with the governance of peoples from different cultural and linguistic backgrounds (Vertovec 2010). However, they have been most debated in the second half of the twentieth century as the scale of immigration has increased globally. In particular, since the end of the 1960s, the importance of promoting cultural pluralism has been recognized in contrast to previous assimilation approaches to migration (Brubaker 2001). This accommodation of diversity was enshrined through conceptualizations and policies of multiculturalism that were taken up in various ways in different countries. Schuster and Solomos (2002, 39) suggest that debates about multiculturalism in advanced industrial societies revolve around "the struggle for equality by minorities who are excluded from equal inclusion in society, and (2) the affirmation of cultural difference through claims to ethnic and racial authenticity." These minorities can be indigenous peoples, national minorities such as Basques or Catalans in Spain, and immigrant groups (Kymlicka 2007). However, it is not just cultural recognition that is important, but also economic and political participation, especially in relation to citizenship (Kymlicka 2010). The complexity of these processes of incorporation and the lack of clarity around conceptualizations of multiculturalism have led to confusion. Indeed, Vertovec (2010) notes that there are eight or nine different kinds of multiculturalism cited in the literature.

Not surprisingly, such contestation has meant that different countries have interpreted multiculturalism in varied ways both conceptually and in terms of the policies they have implemented around issues of equal rights, recognition, and citizenship with respect to migrants

(Joppke 1996). Indeed, while France has emphasized assimilation of migrants, Germany has tended to focus on temporary guest workers who are expected to return to their home countries after their visas expire. The UK has adopted a more fluid and potentially contradictory interpretation that has combined reducing racial tensions and encouraging cultural diversity, while promoting the notion of British national unity (Favell 2001). This created what some have termed "reluctant multiculturalism" in the UK (Wills et al. 2010, 10), accompanied by "managing migration" through greater immigration restrictions; it has been recognized the migrant labor in particular is necessary, but also that only certain types of migrants are deemed to be welcome (usually highly skilled).

In recent years, multiculturalism has been questioned in the UK and beyond (Bauböck 2008; Kymlicka 2010). Although some argue that multiculturalism and assimilation are not necessarily different as modes of incorporation (Kivisto 2001), there has been a marked shift since the turn of the century in the UK toward integration. Critics have argued that multiculturalism reifies communities, ignores internal tensions and diversity within groups, and gives too much power to ethnic leaders (Anthias and Yuval-Davies 1992). This retreat has also been fuelled by concerns that accommodation of diversity has gone too far and that community cohesion has been undermined, as well as by fears over home grown terrorism (Wills et al. 2010). Instead, migrants in the UK are now expected to integrate through a range of English language requirements, citizenship tests, and ceremonies, as the managed migration regime makes it ever more difficult for non-EU migrants in particular to enter and settle (ibid.).

While some suggest that this signals a return to assimilation approaches, it also reflects how increasing diversification of migration in countries such as the UK require that integration policies need to be reworked (Vertovec 2010). For instance, the British integration approach toward community cohesion is based on citizenship and ethnicity, despite the fact that many recent migrants do not plan to settle or are irregular (Wills et al. 2010). However, Vertovec (2010, 91) suggests that the current British integration approach reflects "post-multiculturalism" rather than assimilation, because, "despite a strong emphasis on conformity, cohesion, national identity and dominant cultural values, in practically all the contexts in which such new policies are being implemented an acceptance of the significance and value of diversity is voiced and institutionally embedded."

For these reasons, there has been a concerted effort to try and delineate the issue of diversity in more coherent and conceptual forms, with Vertovec's (2007) notion of "super-diversity" gaining most currency. This term refers to a multidimensional interpretation of diversity that moves beyond ethnicity to highlight huge variations in the country of origin of migrants, together with language, religion, migration channels, and immigration statuses of individuals. The last in particular has created a stratified system of rights and entitlements that fundamentally affect the experiences of migrants (McIlwaine 2009). These are intersected by gender, age, residency, and a diverse range of transnational linkages, all of which vary between and within one nationality group or set of groups, often referred to as "new migrant groups" (Vertovec 2007). In particular, the relationships between transnationalism and integration have been widely interrogated in recent years to highlight that they are mutually reinforcing processes and that high levels of interaction among migrants between home and destination countries does not necessarily mean that they are less integrated (Snel, Engbersen, and Leerkes 2006), although this varies according to the nature of transnational engagement and the integration philosophies and policies in destination countries (Morawska 2003). Indeed, Faist (2009, 172) suggests that the notion of super-diversity is especially helpful in delineating the "new medievalism," which refers to "an expression of a partial, successive disaggregation of territory, political control, and cultural practices." However, while work on super-diversity has provided a useful framework at the level of the city, there is little research on the ways in which this notion can be used to examine a given migrant community. Indeed, Vertovec (2010, 89) also notes that a shift toward recognizing diversity in public policy and conceptually "must begin with gathering basic information on the new diversity." The remainder of this chapter therefore addresses the various axes of diversity among Latin Americans in London. It shows how this is an important yet underresearched community, yet one that is internally differentiated in terms of nationality, class position, and occupational status.

Setting the Scene: Background and Methods in Researching Latin Americans in London

Although research on Latin Americans in the UK is growing, much of it focuses on one nationality group, such as Colombians (Guarnizo 2008), or is relatively small-scale qualitatively (Bermudez 2010; Carlisle 2006; Wright 2010), with few attempts to consider more than one nationality group at a time (however, see Carlisle 2006;

McIlwaine 2007; Peró 2008; Roman-Velasquez 1999). This is partly because Latin Americans are a relatively newly established group in the city. They have also remained largely invisible until recently partly because many have EU passports or are irregular.

Historically, Latin Americans have had a presence in London since the days of independence for the territories of Spanish America, with the city giving refuge to leaders of the liberation struggles. Throughout the nineteenth century London remained the primary source of investment loans for Latin America, with diplomats, commercial envoys, and political exiles resident in the city. During the second half of the nineteenth century, the elites of Latin America nations began to travel to London for leisure and studies (Decho and Diamond 1998).

It was not until the 1970s that significant numbers of Latin Americans began to arrive in London. These included political refugees, mainly Chileans fleeing after the military overthrow of the Allende government by Augusto Pinochet, as well as others from Uruguay, Argentina, and Colombia. The other major flow was Colombians, who arrived with work permits to work in hotels and restaurants and as cleaners in public buildings. While the work permit scheme was reduced in 1979, effectively closing this route, Latin Americans continued to arrive throughout the 1980s for family reunion, as students, and in some cases as refugees (McIlwaine, Cock, and Linneker 2011). Community organizations were also formed at this time, with some undertaking solidarity work and others providing social welfare and immigration assistance for Latin Americans in the city (Cock 2009).

In the late 1990s and the first decade of the twenty-first century, the Latin American population in London grew significantly with most migrants coming from Colombia, Ecuador, and Bolivia in response to complex political and economic upheavals during this decade, and to the United States tightening its border. Colombians and Ecuadorians in particular applied for asylum during this period, many of whom were eventually granted permanent residence status through processes of regularization such as the family amnesty exercise in the UK in 2003. It was primarily political upheavals in their countries that gave them grounds to claim asylum.

Since 2000, another important flow of migrants from Latin America has been the arrival of Brazilians, who have become the largest nationality group among Latin Americans as a whole.

A second trend is that the proportion of students and professional migrants has increased among the Latin American community. This reflects the increase of border controls and the introduction of managed migration policies that favor highly skilled migrants (see Wills et al. 2010, who note that this pattern has been replicated among other groups in London).

Despite comprising a wide range of nationalities, ethnicities, and cultures, Latin Americans are generally referred to as a community. However, it is important to emphasize that this is a "community" in a sense of denoting people from the same continent, sharing a language (with the exception of Brazilians) and a very loose cultural affinity. It is not one based on homogeneity and social cohesion (see Kivisto 2001).

Perhaps because of the diversity and lack of cohesion, the size of the Latin American "community" in London has been the subject of considerable debate. This is mainly because of the inadequacy of the data, but also because many Latin Americans are invisible because of underrecording, due to their European Union (EU) or irregular migration status. Until recently, unsubstantiated estimates derived mainly from the opinions of community leaders range from 50,000 to one million. The research on which this chapter is based attempted to estimate the size of the population using the Annual Population Survey (APS). Acknowledging the difficulties with existing data sources, we combined figures for the regular population from the APS together with a figure based on the irregular and second-generation Latin Americans (the latter referring to people born in the UK with at least one parent born in a Latin American country). This produced a central estimate of 113,578, of which 79,296 were regular, 17,100 were irregular, and 17,182 were second generation. This is only slightly smaller than the Polish population of London (122,000 in 2010) and similar to the Chinese ethnic group (111,500 in 2006). A less robust figure was calculated for the UK as a whole, with a central estimate in 2008 of 186,469, suggesting that 61 percent of the UK Latin American population resides in London. The largest nationality group is Brazilian followed by Colombian (Linneker and McIlwaine 2011; McIlwaine, Cock, and Linneker 2011).

The study also used primary research to explore the characteristics of migrants through questionnaires, and the diversity of experiences through qualitative interviews. More specifically, the research was based on a long questionnaire survey with 453 Latin Americans, as well as a short questionnaire with a further 509 individuals conducted between 2009 and 2010. A further survey of 52 second-generation Latin Americans was also carried out to try and assess whether there were any changes over time and to explore the degree to which the children of migrants had managed to improve their lives (a total of

1,014 people).[1] In order to add depth and insight, qualitative interviews were conducted with 50 people who had already been interviewed in the survey, together with four focus groups, and 15 interviews with representatives from organizations working with Latin Americans, the latter in order to assess the needs of the population.

The survey included people from all socioeconomic backgrounds and nationalities and was based on purposive sampling and sought to broadly represent the proportions identified in official statistics and with discussions with community leaders. Therefore, it included 249 Colombians and 234 Brazilians as the two largest groups, with a further 182 Ecuadorians, 116 Bolivians, and 71 Peruvians, as well as the inclusion of other smaller nationalities. Slightly more women were interviewed than men (53 percent and 47 percent).

Characteristics of Latin Americans in London

Despite the diversity of sending countries in London, different nationalities are not geographically concentrated and, indeed, Latin Americans in general are residentially dispersed. However, there are some concentrations in certain boroughs such as Southwark (15 percent of respondents), Lambeth (14 percent), Newham (8 percent), Haringey (7 percent), Islington (6 percent), Hackney (6 percent), and Tower Hamlets (5.5 percent) (see figure 6.1). These concentrations are also reflected in the location of a series of Latin American shopping areas in Elephant and Castle (in Southwark) and its environs in the south and in Seven Sisters (in Haringey) in the north.

The average age of those interviewed was 36 years (acknowledging that only those aged 16 and over were included). As such, Latin Americans were concentrated in the economically active age groups with more than one-third (37 percent) aged between 30 and 39. They were mostly very well-educated, the majority (70 percent) having some form of education beyond secondary level, with 13 percent attaining a technical education while the rest achieved undergraduate and postgraduate qualifications. Despite high education levels, nearly one-third (29 percent) were able to understand very little English or none at all, and less than half (41 percent) were able to speak, read, and write English very well. One-third of Latin Americans were single, whereas 40 percent were married.

Acknowledging that social class is open to wide variations in interpretation between Latin America and the UK and among different countries, more than half identified their social class position in London as lower middle class (20.5 percent) or working class (34.5

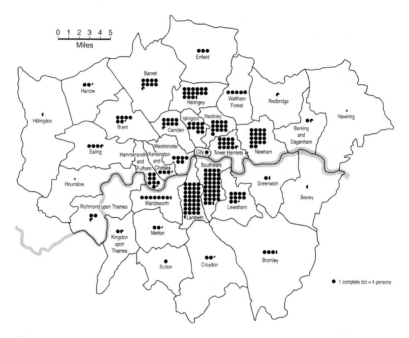

Figure 6.1   Map of the distribution of the Latin American population in London

percent). Officially, Latin Americans are not an ethnic group in the UK although there have been recent campaigns to lobby for such recognition revolving around the Iberian American Alliance (AIA, *Alianza Ibero-Americana*), who are calling for the term "Iberian American" to be included in all official data recording, and the Latin American Recognition Campaign (LARC), who advocate "Latin American" as an ethnic classification. Bearing in mind similar caveats, more than 40 percent of people identified their racial and ethnic origin as mestizo (mixed race) with white and Latin American emerging as important (29 percent and 17 percent, respectively); only 0.4 percent identified themselves as Iberian American.

Migration Experiences of Latin Americans in London

The reasons why Latin Americans leave their home countries are hugely diverse and influenced by when they migrated, their nationalities, and their class status in their home countries. However, more than 40 percent identified either lack of economic or professional opportunities at home and/or the prospect of better opportunities abroad as the primary reason for migrating. This was especially marked among recent migrants, with more than half of Brazilians (57 percent) citing economic motivations. Those working in elementary jobs were also more likely to cite economic factors than professional and managerial workers, the latter who were more likely to identify educational reasons (34 percent of this group). Women tended to be more likely to mention social and family factors than men (19 percent compared with 12 percent).

Vertovec (2007) identifies the experience of secondary migration movements within Europe as a characteristic of a super-diverse migrant group. Among Latin Americans, more than a third (36.5 percent) moved first to Spain and then to the UK. This was especially important for Ecuadorian and Colombian migrants; almost three-quarters of Ecuadorians and half of Colombians who had resided elsewhere before arriving in London had lived in Spain beforehand. This has been a recent phenomenon with more than half of those who had taken this route arriving in the UK since 2000. The recent global economic recession that has hit Spain especially hard has been partly responsible for the recent upsurge, although this process was already established as people moved in search of higher paid jobs and in order to escape racism in Spain (see also McIlwaine 2011).

Turning to the attraction of London, the existence of friends or family already living in the city (40 percent) was the main factor, reflecting a classic case of chain migration (see also Moser this volume). These contacts assist in providing initial accommodation and help with securing jobs. The case of Mercedes, who was 27 years old and from Bolivia, illustrates a range of the issues noted above. Mercedes had been studying agronomy at university. However, when her mother couldn't afford to continue to pay her fees, she decided to migrate to London in order to save money to be able to finish her studies. She chose London because she already had two sisters, a brother-in-law, three cousins, and a niece living in the city. After moving to Spain first for two weeks, she arrived in London on a tourist visa and stayed with one her sisters.

In terms of the actual process of entering the UK, the vast majority of Latin Americans come in with some sort of valid document; in the study only 3 percent entered with invalid documents. Almost two-thirds initially entered with a temporary visa, mainly tourist and student visas. One-fifth entered with documents that gave them the right to settle, with another 9 percent having documents that usually lead to settlement, such as work permits. Bolivians were the most like to enter as tourists or visitors, while Brazilians and Ecuadorians were the most likely to enter with EU passports.

However, the immigration status of Latin Americans is very dynamic with almost 70 percent entering the UK with a different immigration status to their current status, reflecting another core characteristic of a super-diverse population (see also McIlwaine 2009). Although two-thirds entered using a temporary visa, more than half ended up with a visa that allowed them to settle permanently. More specifically, a quarter had British citizenship, one-fifth had an EU passport (mainly Spanish, Italian, and Portuguese), and 12 percent had permanent residency (through Indefinite or Exceptional Leave to Remain). However, 19 percent had no valid documents. Within these broad categorizations, there were multiple visa types, including au pair visas, business visas, dependent visas, and so on. Brazilians and Bolivians were the most likely to be irregular (38 percent and 36.5 percent), while Peruvians and Colombians were most likely to hold British passports (38 percent and 37 percent), the former being the most recently arrived and the latter being the longest established. EU passport ownership was highest among Brazilians (31 percent), mainly Portuguese and Italian passports, partly reflecting stage migration as well as the ability to claim hereditary citizenship (from ancestors who had migrated to Brazil from Portugal and Italy). Women tended to be more likely than men to have British passports (30 percent and 20 percent), whereas men were more likely to be irregular (22 percent and 16 percent).[2]

Laboring Latin Americans: Experiences in London's Labor Market

Latin Americans have a very high employment rate with 85 percent in work, which is much higher than the overall rate for the London population as a whole and for those born overseas (see Wills et al. 2010). This is mainly related with the fact that many Latin Americans have migrated for economic reasons and many had no option but to work because making claims on the welfare state was not possible.

In terms of the types of jobs held by Latin Americans in London, while they worked in all spheres of the urban economy, almost half of all working Latin Americans were employed in elementary occupations (47 percent), which includes contract and domestic cleaners, kitchen assistants, porters, waiters and waitresses, chambermaids, and security guards. Indeed, almost one-third of all jobs carried out by working Latin Americans in London were in cleaning (either in subcontracted office cleaning or domestic cleaning in houses). Having said this, it is important to recognize that one-fifth of working Latin Americans were working in managerial and professional jobs in the city. These include accountants, investment bankers, lawyers, architects, and recruitment analysts. There were variations according to nationality, in that working Bolivians and Brazilians were the most likely to work in elementary jobs (57 percent and 55 percent), with Bolivians being the least likely to work in professional and managerial jobs (9 percent) and with Peruvians being the most likely (almost one-third). Again, this was related with the fact that the latter were more established in the city. In addition, 10 percent of Latin Americans ran their own businesses, mainly small shops and retail outlets serving the "community" (40 percent) or as professionals such as computer consultants (40 percent) (see figure 6.2). Overall, the more established nationalities in London were more likely to be professional or managerial workers and to own their own business.

It was rare for Latin Americans to be able to work in the professions or sectors they had been in back home, with migration engendering a severe decline in occupational status and deskilling for the vast majority. A very small proportion worked in elementary jobs in their home countries (3.3 percent), yet this increased to almost 70 percent in London on first arrival; in turn, this fell to 40 percent at

Figure 6.2   Latin American butcher's shop, Brixton, London (photo by Juan Camilo Cock)

the time of survey. At the upper end of the labor market, there was a similar pattern with more than a third working in professional and managerial jobs in Latin America, yet this reduced to only 6 percent on arrival in London and 17 percent at the time of survey. Therefore, only a minority managed to transfer from one professional job back home to a similar one in London. This was the case of Alonso, who was 48 years old and from Venezuela, where he worked as an oil engineer before he migrated in 2002. Alonso left because of the nationalization of the oil industry and managed to secure a job with British Petroleum also as an engineer earning a salary of over £100,000. This was rare, and even if people managed to obtain a job similar to the one they held at home, it was usually after several years of working in much lower-status occupations. The concentrations in the lower echelons of London's labor market were reflected in the average wage levels earned by Latin Americans. They earned a median hourly rate of pay of £7.07, which is higher than the National Minimum Wage (NMW) at the time of survey of £5.73. However, this is lower than the London Living Wage (LLW) at the time of £7.60—which is the rate that is required to lift people out of poverty in London. Indeed, 44 percent earned between the NMW and the LLW, with 11 percent earning less than the statutory minimum.

These low wages are also reflected in the fact that almost 40 percent of working Latin Americans reported that they had experienced problems at work. These were mainly not getting paid for work they had done as well as verbal abuse and were most prevalent among those working in skilled jobs, as machine operatives and in elementary occupations. Irregular migrants were especially vulnerable to exploitation by supervisors and managers including other Latin Americans. Alberto's case was typical; he was a 40-year-old from Ecuador where he had been an art teacher. After migrating first to Spain but not being able to find work, he moved to London where he had no immigration papers. He had always worked in cleaning jobs, usually from between 12 and 14 hours a day. Alberto had had several experiences of exploitation:

> There is exploitation by Latinos to other Latinos, that's what you see. For people with no papers, the supervisors and managers take away their papers and after a period of time they tell them that their papers are no good and they can't pay them for all the work they have done.

However, it is also important to reiterate that Latin Americans also work in the upper echelons of London's labor market as well, even though there is little contact between those at the top and those at the bottom. Indeed, 45 percent earned more than the LLW, with professional workers earning a median of £15 per hour and a mean of £25.53. For example, Andres was a 30-year-old Mexican from Mexico City who had been living in London since 2000. He had worked in an estate agency back home, and after working as a waiter for three years in London, he had managed to get a job in property management for a large company. He had been doing this for six years and had also managed to start up his own company in Mexico, where he bought houses and rented them out. He did this with his savings of £2,000 per month (his earnings were over £5,000).

Latin American Lifestyles in London

While the lifestyles of Latin Americans are diverse, for the significant proportion that works in manual and low-paid jobs, their living conditions are precarious. In terms of housing, they were concentrated in the private rented accommodation (40 percent) with high levels of subletting (20 percent). Brazilians were the most likely to be living in private rented housing (81 percent) along with irregular migrants (93 percent). Overcrowding was also prevalent with almost a third sharing their home with other families (with an average of two other families—usually other Latin Americans). Such overcrowding was most common among those on low incomes, working in elementary jobs and with no legal immigration status, with marked concentrations among Bolivians (57 percent lived with other families). Thirty-seven-year-old Marisol from Bolivia, who arrived in London in 2003, lived with her two children in a shared house with four other Bolivian families in south London. Each family had one room, where they lived, cooked, and slept, and they had to share a bathroom among all the families. She paid £50 per week for the room and could not afford any more from her wages working as a cleaner. It is perhaps not surprising that 45 percent of Latin Americans were not satisfied with the quality of their housing in London. However, 55 percent were satisfied, and there were several examples of people managing to improve their housing conditions. Ramiro, who was a 40-year-old dentist and entrepreneur from Ecuador, had been living in London since 1999 and had British nationality. Although he had lived with his brother when he first arrived, he eventually got a council house which he then bought:

> My brother told me that I could make an application so that the government give us a house which I did and after 6 months they gave me a home and I'm still living there. In this place I began by paying

a percentage of the rent, I paid full rent and after that I bought it.
I'm now paying a mortgage . . . It's really nice . . . I pay £500 per
month over 20 years.

Some has also bought a flat as an investment. For example, Javier,
who was a 37-year-old from Chile who worked as a kitchen supervisor
since he arrived in 2003, had bought a studio flat:

I have three and a half years left to pay on the mortgage. At the beginning it was 30 years, but with all my savings and everything that we
had we have been able to pay a lot of it. The flat is probably worth
£95,000 to £120,000.

However, among those Latin Americans living in conditions of hardship, they have developed invaluable networks of support. Formally,
these included accessing the services of migrant community organizations (32 percent), most of them oriented toward Latin Americans in
particular, such as Latin American Women's Rights Service (LAWRS)
and Indoamerican Refugee and Migration Organisation (IRMO).
These organizations provide key welfare and immigration advice,
especially for those excluded from mainstream services (see below).
The other more formalized source of support was the church, with
almost 70 percent attending church services. Two-thirds attended
Catholic services. The remainder were mainly Protestant Evangelical,
and the majority of these were services were specifically aimed at
Latin Americans (in Spanish and Portuguese).

As well as formal organizational support, there are also informal
support networks among Latin Americans in London that help to
ameliorate economic and emotional hardships. Friendship groups
were important although they were relatively small with people identifying a median of five friends. Half of migrants reported that these
friends were Latin Americans either from their own country or from
other Latin American countries (50 percent), with a further quarter
(24 percent) saying their friends were from Latin America or other
migrants; only 6 percent stated that none of their friends were Latin
American. Friendship networks provided both emotional and economic support, especially in providing small loans, and information
about accommodation and jobs. Indeed, for those working in low-
paid jobs, the majority secured them through other Latin American
friends and contacts. However, levels of trust among the population
varied, with just over half (53 percent) trusting other Latin Americans,
which is higher than is normally assumed (Bermudez 2010; also

Guarnizo, Sánchez, and Roach 1999). However, while people con-fided in their close friends, trust in the wider community was more limited, linked with jealousy and envy over immigration status. For example, Felicidade, a 44-year-old from Brazil noted:

> My circle of friends is quite closed, I have few friends. No, I don't trust people a lot, no. I'm afraid of being let down. Because I have heard cases of people—sometimes people from the same country have handed over other people to the authorities or they borrow money and don't pay it back.

In turn, those working in professional and managerial occupations were much more likely to trust other Latin Americans (70 percent) compared with those working in elementary jobs (45 percent), where the latter were more likely to experience poor working conditions and competition for jobs as well as irregularity. There were also some divi-sions among different nationalities, especially between Spanish- and Portuguese-speaking Latin Americans; only 44 percent of Brazilians identified as Latin American, compared with over 70 percent of Spanish-speakers. Among the latter, however, people tended to note that divisions were stronger within their own nationality group. Javier, from Chile, pointed out: "Within the same country there are divisions. For example, where I work [as a kitchen assistant], there are people from Medellín who won't speak to the people from Bogotá . . . Ecuadorians do it as well."

Having said this, participation levels in cultural events were high, with almost two-thirds attending the summer carnivals such as the Carnaval del Pueblo regardless of their occupational background or income (see figure 6.3). Also important was engaging with Latin American culture on an everyday basis through using Latin American services and shopping areas such as Elephant and Castle and Seven Sisters market; 85 percent used these markets in order to visit cafes or restaurants, buy food and ingredients, send money home, or use hairdressers. People often collected the free London-based Latin American newspapers in these markets, with readership levels at 77 percent (see Cock this volume).

This highlights how, on the one hand, Latin Americans tend to have relatively strong social networks that provide essential emotional and economic assistance. They also create and use the services of Latin American organizations as well as attend churches and other cultural events, and visit Latin American markets. On the other hand, how-ever, there are marked internal diversities and divisions within the

Figure 6.3   Stalls at the Carnaval del Pueblo, London (photo by Cathy McIlwaine)

"community." Also notable is that integration into the wider sociocultural life of London is quite limited, reflected in the fact that friendship groups are dominated by other Latin Americans, as are most of the leisure, religious, and social spaces that are most commonly frequented. However, class divisions emerged as significant in that professional Latin Americans were much less likely to engage with these specific "everyday" spaces, for example, Emilio, who was 36 years old and from Colombia. He had been living in London since 2007 after he was transferred by his Dutch-based bank after being promoted to vice president. Although he lived in west London in an area with no other Latin Americans, he made an effort to attend the carnivals as well as occasionally visit Elephant and Castle; this was not part of his daily, weekly, or monthly routine however. Indeed, Emilio had many choices and opportunities that other working-class Latin Americans did not have in terms of their use of community resources and places.

Relational Latin Americans: Linking London and Latin America

The vast majority of Latin Americans maintain strong contact with their friends and family back home (97 percent), mainly through landline telephones, e-mail, and Internet chat. This contact was very regular, with almost a quarter communicating every day. The regularity was usually highest when close family such as spouses and children were separated. For example, 54-year-old Jaime, for example, who had been living in London for seven years and whose wife and children still lived in Bolivia, spoke to his wife every day. He felt this had allowed him to strengthen his relationship.

These linkages were also material in the form of sending money and gifts (64 percent). Most of this was in remittances (90 percent) sent through Latin American money transfer agencies, although many also

Figure 6.4 A money transfer agency, London (photo by Cathy McIlwaine)

sent gifts, usually at Christmas or birthdays (see figure 6.4). Sending remittances was usually on a monthly basis, with a median of £2,000 sent home annually.[3] Overall, Latin Americans sent 12 percent of their personal weekly income in remittances, with Brazilians sending almost a quarter. Most migrants sent money to Latin America for family maintenance such as food, rent, and so on (60 percent), with education expenses and house building also important (one-fifth in each case). Most sent money for a range of different things depending on their circumstances. For example, Yaneth was a 33-year-old Colombian who had been in London since 2000 where she worked as a housekeeper for a wealthy Arab family and earned £1,000 per month. Although she was pregnant with her first child, she was still sending money to her mother to help her pay her bills (£1,000 per year). However, the previous year she had also bought land and built a house back home partly financed with her savings and supplemented with a bank loan she got in London.

Those with incomes between £1,000 and £3,000 sent the largest amounts of money home, with those earning more than £4,000 sending the least. In turn, professional and managerial workers sent the least in remittances, with those working in personal service jobs sending the most. This could suggest that those earning less tend to make major economic sacrifices to send money home. Indeed, there was widespread evidence of hardship in trying to send money home (see Datta et al. 2007). For example, 47-year-old Jesus from Bolivia supported his wife, father, and five children in Bolivia. In the previous year he had sent £12,000 back home from his two cleaning jobs, which was the equivalent of 60 percent of his income. As a result, the money that remained was spent entirely on his rent and transport. Therefore, while maintaining ties with home was essential for people to cope with living in London and to feel connected with their family and culture, it also entailed significant hardships. For others whose monthly incomes were much higher, remittance sending was less regular and tended to be sent to more distant family members. For instance, José, 47, from Colombia, who worked in the city, sent money every six months to an aunt whom he used to visit as a child and who was having financial worries; he said that his parents did not need the money.

Discrimination, Exclusion, and Inclusion among Latin Americans

The various dimensions of hardships outlined above were also reflected in the fact that almost 70 percent of Latin Americans in London perceived discrimination to be a problem, especially Bolivians, and those who were irregular. However, those with British passports were just as likely to say that they experienced discrimination, suggesting that exclusion is more multifaceted than simply attaining legal immigration status (De Genova 2002). The most frequently cited type of discrimination was workplace exploitation, followed by housing and accommodation, educational disadvantage, hostilities on the part of the police, and abuse in public places and on public transport. It is also telling that almost two-thirds of the second generation identified discrimination as an issue, again related with workplace abuses, educational racism, and police harassment, suggesting again that citizenship and language skills are only part of integration. Carlos, who was 20 years old and of Colombian origin but born in London, noted in relation to schooling:

> They put us in the bottom groups in college so that we don't get ahead. We are not an ethnic minority . . . My friends can all speak English, but in college we are always put in the lower end in the lower streams and they never advise us to go to university.

Part of this discrimination also involved negative stereotyping. Several people complained of Latin Americans being stereotyped as cleaners, and Colombians, in particular, suffered from a constant association with drugs. For example, 42-year-old Alba stated: "When you tell an English person you are from Colombia, all they say is, Colombia drugs, Colombia cocaine or Colombia drug traffickers."

In very practical terms, a significant proportion of Latin Americans were excluded from many basic services. For example, one in five had never been to a medical doctor in London and six out of ten had not used a dentist's services. Partly related with this but also fuelled with dissatisfaction with the National Health Service (NHS) and language barriers was that 40 percent had used private health services (half of whom were Latin American). Not surprisingly, irregular migrants and Brazilians and Bolivians were the most likely to be excluded. This also highlights the importance of recognizing exclusion as multidimensional in that even those who were not excluded from accessing the system felt excluded by their sociocultural expectations. For example, Maria José, 38, from Colombia, noted that she felt much more comfortable going to a private doctor not because of language, but because it is what she was accustomed to in Colombia where only the very poor used state healthcare; she worked as a recruitment consultant and so could afford the private charges.

None the less, processes of exclusion are strongly underpinned by difficulties with English language and irregular immigration status, both of which emerged as the most pressing problems identified by Latin Americans (by 58 percent and 25 percent, respectively). In terms of "papers," even though only one-fifth explicitly stated they were irregular, many had experienced irregularity at some point. While this led to economic exclusion in terms of work opportunities as well as poor living conditions and a lack of freedom to move around the city for fear of being detained by police, there were important psychosocial aspects around fear and anxiety that are often ignored. For example, Emilio, who was 40 years old and from Ecuador, stated:

> It's an oppression, you don't feel secure in anything, you can't be relaxed even at home, you can't do anything, you are like a type of ghost, you are not secure. Psychologically it affects you, you get depressed, you get stressed, you feel like you are being persecuted as if you were a delinquent.

There was a close relationship between language problems and immigration status because those with no "papers" were unlikely to be able or to afford to learn English. People were scared to go to classes in case they were reported to the authorities. For example, Aurelio, who was 40 and from Ecuador, noted:

> I haven't learnt English because I don't have papers, and they always ask you for them. If I was to have documents I would study English and I would dedicate my time to being a teacher [his profession in Ecuador].

However, while discrimination and exclusion were certainly extremely important among Latin Americans, the situation was actually more complex than a victimized population who were uniformly excluded from London life. For example, almost one-third did not think that discrimination was an issue in London, with several people in the qualitative research suggesting that discrimination had reduced over time. A Brazilian man from a focus group discussion noted:

> I think there was a lot more [discrimination] in the past, because in the past when you talked about Brazil, all women were sluts and men were thieves, tramps, they'd take advantage of you, steal from you. It is not like that now.

Exclusion, inclusion, and integration intersect in multiplex ways. On the one hand, several middle-class professional Latin Americans blamed working-class Latin Americans for their exclusion because of their separatism and a desire to create separate spaces in the city. For example, 33-year-old Reynaldo from Colombia, who worked for in human resources for a large multinational, said that he didn't feel much affinity with other Latin Americans, stating: "I think that, although it's difficult to generalise, Latin Americans close themselves in a lot. They will say, let's go here because there are other Latinos there." Because many Latin Americans find it difficult to secure decent jobs that match their qualifications and they end up working in low-paid jobs alongside others from the same backgrounds, which means they can't afford to live in adequate accommodation, their interactions with people beyond their Latin American networks are often limited. This is worse for those with temporary or insecure immigration status. In their search to "get by" in London, they are much more likely to frequent Latin American places and generate Latin American social networks, because, first, they have little choice and, second, participating in and engaging with churches, shops, and organizations oriented specifically toward them allows them to feel a sense of belonging in order to cope with other adversities (see also Wills et al. 2010). The class divisions are extremely important here in that middle and upper-class Latin Americans think of themselves as included and integrated into British life and were often disdainful of those who could not speak English and who frequent places such as Elephant and Castle. Therefore, Latin Americans have multiple experiences of inclusion and exclusion in London that depends on their immigration status, nationality, occupation, and class position (among other things).

Conclusions

This chapter has highlighted how Latin Americans epitomize one of London's "new migrant" groups that contribute to the city's super-diversity. However, the discussion has shown that they are not a homogenous community with uniform experiences in that they are themselves a super-diverse group. As a result, some have integrated more than others depending on their nationality, year of arrival, immigration status, and class positions. It appears that those who have managed to "integrate" according the British government's current conceptualization that entails citizenship and English language skills are those from professional backgrounds who have transferred their status to London as well as those who have been living in the city for a long time and have managed to regularize their status and establish themselves. Many of these groups, while still participating in Latin American cultural events and visiting commercial spaces, do so on a much less frequent basis and often with more ambivalence than their counterparts further down the social hierarchy (Cock this volume). For this group who are usually more recent arrivals, and especially Bolivians and Brazilians, and those with irregular or temporary status, the notion of this conceptualization of integration has little resonance. For them, their primary concern is often to find work that will pay their expenses and allow them to send money back home. They are more likely to participate in Latin American events and to use the services provided by Latin American organizations and businesses because their English will be limited and they do not expect to remain in the UK.

From the outside, it might appear that this segment of the Latin American population is not integrated and is living what has been called "parallel lives" (see Wills et al. 2010). However, it is the precarious nature of their experiences in London, despite contributing in important ways to London's economy, culture, and society, that influence their various engagements with London life; while they have a certain degree of agency, they are often thwarted from participating more fully due to discrimination and exclusion. At the same time, there are many Latin Americans whose experiences are different. Therefore, as Vertovec (2010) states, existing conceptual and policy frameworks for dealing with London's super-diverse population as a whole and with a specific new migrant group such as Latin Americans require to be reworked in order to have any relevance. While his suggestion that the current British integration approach reflects "post-multiculturalism" rather than assimilation is valid up to an extent in terms of its emphasis on the need to value diversity as well as cohesion, it also raises the question of the need to address some of the basic needs of some part of these diverse groups.

Acknowledgments

I would like to thank the Trust for London and Latin American Women's Rights Service for funding the research discussed here. I am also grateful to Sarah Bradshaw for her helpful comments on an earlier version of the chapter.

Notes

1. Due to restrictions in space, the chapter focuses primarily on first-generation migrants (see McIlwaine et al. 2011 for a further discussion of the second-generation).

2. It has been suggested that women are more likely to consult migrant community organizations and receive assistance in regularizing their status, especially when they have children. In addition, men are more likely to migrate to the UK alone and on an irregular basis, leaving their families behind in Latin America. Often, men will only bring their families with them when their status has been regularized.

3. This was approximately the same as official figures for the amount remitted per capita for Latin America as a whole (see http://www.ifad .org/remittances/maps/latin.htm, accessed September 23, 2010).

References

Anthias, Floya, and Nira Yuval-Davies. 1992. *Racialized Boundaries: Race, Nation, Gender, Colour and Class and the Anti-Racist Struggle*. London: Routledge.

Bauböck, Rainer. 2008. "What Went Wrong with Liberal Multiculturalism?" *Ethnicities* 8 (2): 271–76.

Bermudez, Anastasia. 2010. "The Transnational Political Practices of Colombians in Spain and the United Kingdom: Politics 'Here' and 'There.'" *Ethnic and Racial Studies* 33(1): 75–91.

Brubaker, Rogers. 2001. "The Return of Assimilation? Changing Perspectives on Immigration and Its Sequels in France, Germany, and the United States. *Ethnic and Racial Studies* 24 (4): 531–48.

Carlisle, Frances. 2006. "Marginalisation and Ideas of Community among Latin American Migrants to the UK. *Gender and Development* 14 (2): 235–45.

Cock, Juan Camilo. 2009. "Colombian Migrants, Latin American Publics: Ethnicity and Transnational Practices amongst Colombian Migrants in London." PhD thesis, London: Geography Department, Queen Mary University of London.

Datta, Kavita, Cathy McIlwaine, Jane Wills, Yara Evans, Jo Herbert, and Jon May. 2007. The New Development Finance or Exploiting Migrant Labour? Remittance Sending among Low-Paid Migrant Workers in London. *International Development Planning Review* 29 (1): 43–67.

Decho, Paul, and Claire Diamond (compilers). 1998. *Latin Americans in London: A Select List of Prominent Latin Americans in London c. 1800–1996.* London: Institute of Latin American Studies.

De Genova, Nicholas P. 2002. "Migrant 'Illegality and Deportability in Everyday Life." *Annual Review of Anthropology* 31:419–47.

Faist, Thomas. 2004. "The Border-Crossing Expansion of Social Space: Concepts, Questions and Topics. In *Transnational Social Spaces: Agents, Networks and Institutions,* ed. Thomas Faist and Eyüp Özveren, 1–34. Aldershot, UK: Ashgate.

———. 2009. "Diversity: A New Mode of Incorporation?" *Ethnic and Racial Studies* 32 (1): 171–190.

Favell, Adrian. 2001. *Philosophies of Integration: Immigration and the Idea of Citizenship in France and Britain.* Basingstoke, UK: Palgrave.

Guarnizo, Luis E. 2008. *Londres Latina: La Presencia Colombiana en la Capital Britanica.* México DF: Universidad de Zacatecas and Miguel Angel Porrúa.

Guarnizo, Luis E., Arturo I. Sánchez, and Elisabeth M. Roach. 1999. "Mistrust, Fragmented Solidarity, and Transnational Migration: Colombians in New York City and Los Angeles." *Ethnic and Racial Studies* 22 (2): 367–96.

Joppke, Christian. 1996 "Multiculturalism and Immigration." *Theory and Society* 25 (4): 449–500.

Kivisto, Peter. 2001. "Theorizing Transnational Immigration: A Critical Review of Current Efforts." *Ethnic and Racial Studies* 24 (4): 549–77.

Kymlicka, Will. 2010. "The Rise and Fall of Multiculturalism? New Debates on Inclusion and Accommodation in Diverse Societies. *International Social Science Journal* 61 (199): 97–112.

Kymlicka, Will. 2007. *Multicultural Odysseys: Navigating the New International Politics of Diversity.* Oxford: Oxford University Press.

Linneker, Brian, and Cathy McIlwaine. 2011. *Estimating the Latin American Population of London from Official Statistics.* London: School of Geography, Queen Mary, University of London (Available from: http://www.geog.qmul .ac.uk/docs/research/latinamerican/48640.pdf) (accessed May 20, 2011).

McIlwaine, Cathy. 2007. "Living in Latin London: How Latin American Migrants Survive in the City." Working Paper, London: School of Geography, Queen Mary, University of London (Available from: http:// www.geog.qmul.ac.uk/docs/staff/4400.pdf) (accessed June 12, 2011).

———. 2009. "Legal Latins? Webs of (Ir)regularity among Latin American Migrants in London. Working Paper WP-09-0. Nottingham: ICMiC, School of Sociology & Social Policy, University of Nottingham.

———. 2011. "Postcolonial Geographies of Latin American Migration to London from a Materialist Perspective. In *Postcolonial Economies: Rethinking Material Lives*, eds. Jane Pollard, Cheryl McEwan, and Alex Hughes. 157–81. London: Zed.

McIlwaine, Cathy, Juan Camilo Cock, and Brian Linneker. 2011. *No Longer Invisible: The Latin American Community in London.* London: Trust for London. (Available from: http://www .geog.qmul.ac.uk/docs/research/latinamerican/48637.pdf) (accessed May 20, 2011).

Morawska, Ewa. 2003. "Immigrant Transnationalism and Assimilation: A Variety of Combinations and the Analytic Strategy It Suggests." In *Toward Assimilation and Citizenship: Immigrants in Liberal Nation-States*, eds. Christian Joppke and Ewa Morawska, 133–76. Basingstoke, UK: Palgrave Macmillan.

Però, Davide. 2008. "Political Engagements of Latin Americans in the UK: Issues, Strategies and the Public Debate." *Focaal* 51:73–90.

Roman-Velasquez, Patria. 1999. *The Making of Latin London: Salsa Music, Place and Identity.* Aldershot, UK: Ashgate.

Schuster, Liza, and John Solomos. 2002. "Race, Immigration and Asylum: New Labour's Agenda and Its Consequences." *Ethnicities* 4:267–300.

Snel, Eric, Godfried Engbersen, and Arjen Leerkes. 2006. "Transnational Involvement and Social Integration." *Global Networks* 6 (3): 285–308.

Vertovec, Steven. 2007. "Super-diversity and Its Implications." *Ethnic and Racial Studies* 30 (6): 1024–54.

———. 2010. "Towards Post-Multiculturalism? Changing Communities, Conditions and Contexts of Diversity. *International Social Science Journal* 61 (199): 1468–2451.

Wills, Jane, Kavita Datta, Yara Evans, Joanna Herbert, Jon May, and Cathy McIlwaine. 2010. *Global cities at Work. New Migrant Divisions of Labour.* London: Pluto.

Wright, Katie. 2010. "'It's a Limited Kind of Happiness': Barriers to Achieving Human Well-being through International Migration: The Case of Peruvian Migrants in London and Madrid." *Bulletin of Latin American Research* 29 (3): 367–83.

Chapter 7

Policy Change from Below: Recognizing Migrants' Political Agency among Latin Americans in London

Davide Però

In recent years, in public debate as well as in academic circles, migrants have increasingly been represented as undermining social cohesion as well as being dysfunctional to the civic and political process for lacking, among other things, social and political capital (Putnam 2007). Part and parcel of these representations has been an unprecedented neoassimilationist assault on multiculturalism, the approach to the management of diversity that, despite some problems (Kundnani 2001, 2007), positively distinguished Britain in Europe (Giddens 2006). This chapter will critically discuss these negative representations of migrants and diversity to assess the solidity of their foundations. This discussion will be grounded in the examination of the practices of citizenship of migrants and in particular of the policy engagements that a group of migrant workers from Latin America has been articulating in London in recent years and the impact these efforts seem to have had. Prior to that it is necessary to discuss further the representations of migrants in public discourse and to introduce what is meant by practices of citizenship, policy, and policy change.

Migrant Representations in the UK

For about a decade now the overall representation of migrants and diversity in British public discourse has become less and less favorable. Key state actors such as ministers, as well as broadcasting journalists, consultants, and advisors working within the framework of the state have progressively spoken in negative terms about migrants (Però forthcoming). For instance, David Blunkett, one of the most influential home secretaries of the New Labour era, has been very active in articulating what has been referred to as a backlash against diversity (Grillo 2005). He adamantly demanded from migrants and minorities greater conformity to "British norms and values" as the following quote illustrates: "We have norms of acceptability and those who come into our home—as that is what it is—should accept those norms" (cited in Brown 2001). The former Labour prime minister Gordon Brown constitutes another example, and it is one that in my view marks a "new turn" in the neoassimilationist script against migrants and diversity of mainstream politicians, as it makes the tone much more class and "race" specific. In fact, as he pledged to "fast track British workers into jobs" at the Trade Union Congress (quoted in the *Daily Telegraph* 2007) and "to create British jobs for British Workers" at the Labour Party Conference in 2007 (quoted in BBC News 2007) throughout his speeches, he repeatedly made a coded yet clear connection between the hardships of the national (white) working class (deserving "in-group" members) and the presence of the nonnational one (undeserving out-group members). So, instead of framing inequalities and socioeconomic grievances of the working class in vertical terms—in relation to the economic elites growing wealthier and wealthier—he persistently choose a horizontal (nationalist) framing where migrant workers are represented as directly connected to the hardship of the native workers. His approach can be seen as moving dangerously on the discursive political territory of the Far Right.[1]

This increasing class and race-specific type of backlash against migrants and multiculturalism was echoed in quality broadcasting, and can be seen in documentary series such as BBC's *White Season* (2008) and Channel 4's *Immigration: The Inconvenient Truth* (2008), which claimed to contribute to an "open" and "mature" debate about migration and diversity, which until then was allegedly inhibited by political correctness and multiculturalism. Below is an excerpt taken from Channel 4's own description of one its series' documentary:

Using Enoch Powell's explosive Rivers of Blood speech as a starting point, Rageh [Omar, the journalist] explores whether the apocalyptic visions of 40 years ago have any basis in today's reality . . . Omar navigates the rocky terrain of Britain's current immigration landscape [and] discovers a sense of resentment and anger towards recent immigrants which is not restricted to the white working class. Middle-class Richard claims his area of Wibsey is the last bastion of British civilisation in Bradford. His description of feeling marginalised as a white minority elsewhere in the city and of being made to feel unwelcome in his own country echoes both the warnings Powell made in his speech and the feelings of Matt and Dave, a working-class father and son in Lichfield who tell Omar it is only a matter of time before there is violence and "Rivers of Blood" become reality (Channel 4 Dispatches April 21, 2008).

Multiculturalism has also been attacked by the then director of the authoritative Commission for Racial Equality, Trevor Phillips, who stated that "multiculturalism's legacy is 'have a nice day' racism" (Phillips 2004) and that it should be "killed off" (Baldwin 2004).

In sum, we could say that migrants have in the last ten years or so been made the object of increasingly exclusionary representations in the public discourse articulated by state actors. In addition, as migrants have also not been given space in public debates about themselves (let alone about more general matters), they have effectively been denied what Nick Stevenson (2003) has called "cultural citizenship." In this context, it is hardly surprising that in 2010 the British public emerged as having the most hostile attitudes toward migrants in an important intercontinental survey involving eight of the most economically advanced democracies (Transatlantic Trends 2010).

In the academic field, the approach to and representation of migrants have not been much more positive. To start with, the relationship between migrants and politics is normally taken to refer to the study of policies and institutional practices to do with migrants' control, management, disciplining, counting, and so forth. Recurrently taking for granted the "national order of things" (Malkki 1995), these studies have been treating migrants as objects rather than subjects of politics, thus legitimizing and mainstreaming further approaches centered uncritically around the national perspectives and that of its political institutions, an approach that Wimmer and Glick Schiller (2003) have called "methodological nationalism."[2] Then and more importantly in this context, migrants and immigration have been portrayed as actually dysfunctional to the democratic process. Indeed in studies such as Gimpel (1999), Camarota (2001), and Putnam (2007), they have been identified as "one of the primary reasons for declining civic engagement and the persistence of racial and ethnic gaps in participation" (Ramakrishnan and Bloemraad 2008, 1). In Putnam's own words: "Immigration and ethnic diversity challenge social solidarity and inhibit social capital" (2007, 138; see also Wills et al. 2010).

Practices of Citizenship

Very schematically, dominant approaches to citizenship have treated this subject as something concerning the nation-state and its legitimate members, and largely examined it with scarce grounding in people's actual lived experiences. In such an approach, citizenship refers to a set of rights and responsibilities that the state gives in a top-down manner to its formal members who passively receive them and who, by virtue of this common citizenship, become supposedly equal vis-à-vis the state. The notion of practices of citizenship departs from this approach, and refers to what individuals do as active subjects to claim, acquire, or negotiate citizens' rights in a de jure and/or de facto way (Kofman et al. 2000; Werbner and Yuval-Davies 1999; Reed-Danahay and Brettell 2008; Però 2008a). This focus on the practices of citizenship is necessary because citizenship is not as egalitarian as it is claimed in dominant approaches, but instead is exclusionary. As pointed out by Holston (2008), citizenship refers to a system that serves to sustain inequality. In fact, it is by and large accepted that not all those who are formal citizens have equal access to rights as it is accepted that out-members of the political community (for example, migrants, asylum seekers, etc.) should be excluded from it.

As I have pointed out elsewhere (Però 2008b; Però and Solomos 2010), migrants constitute an important context in which to apply the practices of citizenship approach just outlined because of their typically marginalized and disadvantaged position within society and within the policy process. For example, migrants are normally deprived of the ultimate political right—the vote—and often even of the right of being in the host society by a gamut of exclusionary and exploitative policy measures. They are located in an uneven playing field, and as we have seen, also been made the object of negative representations in public discourse and even in academic accounts.

In this context, it is important that we—as analysts—consider migrants' concrete individual and collective actions and practices of citizenship to find out what these are actually like and about, what impact they seem to have, and how they compare with the hegemonic representations discussed above. As suggested above, I am concerned with a particular set of migrants' practices of citizenship, namely, their policy engagement and the impact of such engagements.

Policy and Policy Change

Cris Shore and Sue Wright (1997, 3) persuasively argued for the inclusion of policy in the domain of anthropological inquiry. They pointed out how the concept of policy has become one of the crucial pillars of the architecture of contemporary society as well as a nodal point of intersection and articulation of ideologies, practices, power, contestation, and accommodation. Crucial for this new arena of anthropological research, and for social studies more generally, is the question, "how do policies 'work' as instruments of governance and why do they sometimes fail to function as intended?" They outlined the importance of looking at policies as processes and the messy way in which they are articulated in practice, which often contradicts the common assumptions of policy-makers and governments that see policies as somehow rational, coherent, and linear. They also outlined the inextricably political nature of policies, stressing the importance for anthropologists and social scientists more generally to dig beneath "authoritative" representations of policies as neutral and rational tools of government to reveal the power dimension of policies as well as their implications for the targeted population and social reproduction. In addition they called for a (re)conceptualization of anthropological enquiry as a committed rather than distanced set of practices (Shore and Wright 1997). Methodologically, they highlighted the importance of "studying through" the policy process, looking at both ends of the process, thus including the practices of both makers and recipients of policies. Since 1997, the anthropology of policy with its approach to policy as the "practice of power" (Levison and Sutton 2001) has been growing steadily in terms of contribution and has gained increasing recognition.

However, this growth has taken place more in terms of studying the powerful actors at the top of the policy chain and less in terms of the powerless, especially with regard to the policy change they produce (Però 2011). In that essay a key question I asked was what is policy and how do we define policy change. As Shore and Wright have argued, policies are contested practices that both reflect and create the social and cultural world they are embedded in. They are the key tools through which governments and other powerful bodies organize the spaces and the people they seek to govern. However, as the case study presented below shows, policies are not merely the performative acts of powerful collective actors but also the result of the creative practices of a number of other actors, including the governed themselves. Building on this definition of policy, I very schematically suggested that we can distinguish between two ideal typical forms of policy change. The first refers to the top-down transformations produced by powerful governmental actors. The second refers to the bottom-up activities of the governed (Però 2011).[3] In this chapter, I will focus on the policy responses of the governed to examine how policy comes to be transformed, challenged, resisted, and neutralized, as well as applied or enforced from below, through the creative engagements of disadvantaged recipients and other actors who work with these disadvantaged groups to advocate their interests (for example, trade unions, NGOs, social movements, civil society, and community organizations). In Però (2011), I also pointed out how the agency of the governed is relevant not only to complement the anthropological and other social studies of policy-makers but to rebalance the prevailing attitude in mainstream policy studies that typically treats people as "objects," "targets," or passive "recipients" of policy (Schneider and Ingram 1993). Such prevailing policy studies shed little light on the experience or agency of the governed. They do not seem to ask, for instance, what disadvantaged and marginalized groups do to ameliorate their conditions, or how they respond to unfavorable or unapplied policies and with what implications.

The critical issues to consider in this context concern the ways those who are targeted by policies and their advocates engage with and respond to such policies and with what impact (Però 2011). Appreciating the bottom-up initiatives of the governed requires a more comprehensive idea of policy change from below than that of the formal policy transformations currently in use. For example, in assessing the importance of studying the effects of social movements (Meyer 2003), policy impact, while recognized as crucial, is narrowly conceived as being limited to formal policy change. Accordingly, the more comprehensive idea of policy change I have suggested includes not only bottom-up induced formal transformations to policy produced by explicit and larger-scale collective mobilizations, but also the "smaller" policy changes produced by the everyday practices that people deploy to cope with, neutralize, and resist policy as well as those practices that seek to promote the application or enforcement of already existing "positive" policy when this is disregarded or unapplied.[4] Indeed, the main point made in the case study below is the idea that policy change from below should include the examination of the demands that the governed articulate (e.g. through mobilizations, campaigning, etc.) to apply existing "favourable" policies and legislations when these are not implemented or disregarded by powerful actors.[5]

In Però (2011), while arguing for a comprehensive idea of policy change from below, I also stressed that this idea should be critically and carefully applied. In particular, efforts to appreciate the policy responses of the governed, expressed in the form of undeclared and unorganized resistance, should be made neither at the expense of addressing larger-scale and more overt and organized practices nor at the cost of examining how these practices come about, scale up, or become overt challenges. This critical application seems necessary to avoid some of the pitfalls that have affected resistance studies lately. As Fletcher (2001) reminded us, so-called resistance studies emerged in the attempt to explain how those who see their lives as oppressed rise up in defiance of the causes of such oppression. However, this original project got lost along the way, stretching the concept of resistance into a catch-all category to cover virtually any practice deemed oppositional. In other words, resistance studies have moved away from a concern with explaining forms of opposition to descriptions of coping strategies and symbolic expressions of undeclared dissent, leading some authors to call for the end of resistance studies altogether. This chapter builds on Fletcher's critique by exploring examples of how subaltern groups such as migrant workers "scale up" their dissent and openly challenge the hegemonic policy terms set by powerful institutions and organizations, and by looking at the policy impact of such subaltern practices (see also Però 2011).[6] In focusing on policy change from below, I develop a sort of "meso-level" approach to political engagements, one that is situated somewhere between the study of coping strategies and undeclared resistance on the one hand, and the examination of larger-scale organized mobilizations on the other, as well as one that encompasses the dynamics of smaller-scale collective engagements and the impact this can have on policy.

The Case of Latin American Workers' Mobilization in London

Context

In the early 1990s, the UK, like Italy and Spain, experienced a large wave of immigration.[7] Unlike Italy and Spain, which were receiving international migrants in high numbers for the first time—for Britain this population inflow represented a second wave, the first one being that of the "colonial workers" of the postwar years (Castles and Miller 2009) who have now turned into long-standing ethnic minorities. However, it was only halfway through the first decade of the twenty-first century that the UK came to recognize that it is no longer a postmigration country (Martiniello 2005) but rather one of new immigrations as well, and indeed a country of "super-diversity" (Vertovec 2007), one where new migrants (this time from countries without colonial links to the UK) were arriving in an already multiethnic society.[8]

Latin Americans are perhaps one of the most typical groups of this second migration wave (McIlwaine this volume Section 2). They have arrived in Britain through a broad range of immigration channels and hold a variety of different statuses—for example, students, unauthorized/irregular migrants, asylum-seekers, and refugees (see Guarnizo 2008 on Colombians). The majority of Latin Americans appear to have migrated primarily for economic reasons although, as is often the case among Colombians, migration can be the result of a combination of economic and political reasons. Apart from a sizeable group of refugees, there are many people who left Colombia due to the general climate of violence, fear, and instability that, along with poverty, characterizes vast geographical areas of the country.[9] Their estimate numbers vary considerably, but there seems to be a consensus on them numbering several hundred thousands of people, with Brazilians, Colombians, and Ecuadorians being the largest groups (in this order). Latinos reside overwhelmingly in London, particularly in the areas of Lambeth, Southwark, Islington, and Camden. They are heavily employed in the cleaning sector, where they work for subcontracted companies to clean commercial and public buildings often under very exploitative conditions (see also McIlwaine 2005; McIlwaine this volume Section 2).[10] They have also developed a wide range of "ethnic" commercial and cultural activities. These "self-directed" activities include restaurants, bars, cafes, discos, food shops, *locutorios* (shops from which to phone home at discounted rates), money transfer agencies, doctors and dentists, barbers and hairdressers, launderettes and tailors, video rentals and music shops. Sometimes some of these activities are hosted in large multicultural/cosmopolitan shopping centers and markets, and sometimes they are part of smaller "all-Latino" shopping malls (see Cock this volume).

Not being from Commonwealth countries, Latinos recognize that their linguistic competence in English on their arrival is on average rather poor and tends to improve only slowly over the years. Their voice in public discourse in the UK is largely absent—as is that of the other new migrant groups. In spite of such marginalization, Latinos have a growing "ethnic" or "community" media in Spanish that includes several radio programs and news magazines widely and freely distributed covering developments in Latin American countries as well as in the UK. By addressing the entire Spanish-speaking Latin American collective in the UK, the Latino media are simultaneously facilitating the Latino population in the UK to imagine themselves as a "community" (Anderson 1983; Chavez 1991). Again, unlike migrants from Commonwealth countries or the European Union,

Latinos are not entitled to vote in any type of British elections. This, however, makes it all the more compelling to adopt a notion of politics that transcends the electoral focus of much political science to include a broader range of collective political initiatives.

It is important to note that the wide range of social, cultural, and economic initiatives outlined above has been promoting physical and virtual encounters and networks not only among Latino migrants from the same nationalities but also among Latinos of different nationalities. They are forging a growing sense of a common Latino identity that in recent years has increasingly been deployed politically in initiatives articulated by people of different Latin American nationalities and branded as "Latino/Latin."

The Latin American Workers Association (or LAWA)[11] has been one of the main expressions of Latin American sociopolitical engagement in the UK (Però 2007a, 2008b) (see figure 7.1). LAWA was set up in the second half of 2004 by three Colombians and one Chilean trade unionist as part of the British Transport and General Workers Union (T&G-Unite).[12] Forming LAWA was seen as a necessary step to protect and support more effectively the large number of Latin American workers experiencing superexploitation and abuses of various types at the workplace. Until the creation of LAWA, employment had been a crucial aspect of life which was left uncovered by the existing Latino organizations. In the words of one of its founders:

> The LAWA is the product of a necessity, which has emerged progressively after many Latinos had solved their immigration, housing and benefits problems . . . Besides addressing some of the exploitative aspects experienced by Latino workers in Britain, LAWA struggles for helping the Latino workers coming out of the invisibility with dignity not by "asking" (*pedir*) but by "demanding" (*exigir*). Together with other workers organizations—the Portuguese, the Turkish, the African—we share the same class need [*necesidad de clase*].[13]

The kind of problems that Latin Americans experience and the nature of LAWA's activity are illustrated by Ines, a volunteer at LAWA:

> Sexual harassment, psychological maltreatment . . . abuses concerning working time, verbal abuses and discrimination of all sorts. Essentially all that happens because one doesn't know the [British] laws . . . and people [employers and managers] take advantage of that and abuse the power they've got . . . I myself had a case and after solving that, I stayed on working with them [LAWA] as a volunteer. I was abused verbally and psychologically by my managers . . . It happened in a clothes shop for which I worked.

Figure 7.1 Members of the Latin American Workers Association at a migrant rally (photo by Cathy McIlwaine)

Although support in the field of employment was, in principle, available to Latino workers through the existing British trade unions, such support was not, in practice, accessible to them, for reasons of communication/language, trust, lack of relationships or links between the T&G-Unite and the Latin collective, and the lack of adequate efforts on the part of the union to reach out to migrant workers.

An important concern for those behind the setting up of LAWA was the preservation of its autonomy. LAWA founders had always been determined to form a political, rather than a civic or community charitable, organization. They wanted to avoid relying on public funding, as these organizations often do, because this would entail economic dependence on the state (an institution that they did not see as promoting the interests of working people and in particular of migrant workers) and political restrictions (for receiving public funding and a charitable status). In the end, the four founders' conviction about the need for LAWA proved correct and the organization "boomed" straight away (and with it Latino affiliations to the T&G) to the extent that after a few months of activity LAWA already struggled to keep up with the demand for assistance (see also Hearn and Bergos 2010).

LAWA's Organizing Strategy

The field of political initiative in which LAWA operates can be described as "sociopolitical." LAWA is neither very interested in playing party politics nor in lobbying national and local politicians and officials (as do other Latin American organizations such as the Latin Front—see Però 2007a and 2008a—or later by the Ibero-American Alliance and the Latin American Recognition Campaign). They privilege political initiative in the socioeconomic sphere around issues of workers' rights, and more generally material justice issues (see also Hearn and Bergos 2010). In addition to the protection of Latin American workers in the UK, they are connected to the initiatives of social forums and of the global justice movement. For example, in 2004, they participated to the European Social Forum in London and in March 2011 they were central to the Latin American Coalition against Cuts (COLACOR) and its involvement in the large-scale demonstration organized by the British trade union movement against the assault on the welfare state launched by the Cameron-Clegg/Conservative–Liberal Democrat government. They have also been developing international/transnational links with trade unions in Latin America.

In terms of "identity politics," LAWA articulates a particular blend of class and ethnicity. It aims to promote greater ethno-cultural recognition of Latin Americans within the marked class framework of the trade union movement. Overall, LAWA considers it important to be fully part of a large and organized British trade union, but its leaders feel there are ethno-cultural specificities that require a customized treatment, hence their organization as Latinos within the "T&G-Unite."[14] However, as Fernando, volunteer at LAWA said, "the objective and the essence of the struggle, as well as what unites us with other immigrant groups, is a question of class." The attitudes that LAWA members have toward unauthorized migrant workers further help us to understand LAWA's political vision. As Irene, another volunteer at LAWA, put it: "Work is a right that all human beings have. Whether they are illegal or not makes no difference to us . . . and this is why we also fight for illegal immigrants." Since 2004, Latin Americans have also become increasingly active through the mainstream T&G-Unite (rather than through LAWA). For many Latin Americans this direct involvement with the T&G-Unite developed largely as a result of the recent large-scale efforts—like the Justice for Cleaners campaign—to organize migrant workers in the cleaning sector. In terms of politics, this second and direct engagement of Latin American migrants with the T&G-Unite represents a rather classic form of class politics, one in which the focus on the socioeconomic dimension of the migrants needs at the workplace is central and the ethno-cultural one, while present (for example, in resorting to migrant organizers for carrying out the campaign), is complementary. This politics is also one that targets all workers independently of their ethno-cultural background, who in the cleaning sector happen to be essentially migrant (with a significant quota of Latin Americans). Recently, the T&G-Unite has also strengthened its promigrant stand by starting to campaign for a regularization of unauthorized immigrants as part of the London Citizens' Strangers into Citizens campaign (see Wills et al. 2010) (which LAWA criticized for not being sufficiently inclusionary) as it recognizes that their irregular immigrant status makes them vulnerable to superexploitation and abuses and condemns them to a position of permanent exclusion, marginality, vulnerability, and fear. As for LAWA, the prevailing attitude within the T&G-Unite toward unauthorized migrants tends to be on the whole inclusionary in that they are seen as workers regardless of the legal status attached to them by the state.

Achievements and Assessment of LAWA Political Organizing

LAWA and the T&G-Unite have unionized a remarkable number of Latin American workers (which in 2006 numbered about one thousand). This process has happened in a relatively short period of time and by overcoming a number of fears and prejudices including the fear of deportation (recurrent among unauthorized migrants) and the view (recurrent among Colombians) that trade unions are guerrilla supporters. The second achievement is the operationalization of the Latino workers labor protection that both LAWA and T&G-Unite have performed. Third, they have also gained a greater visibility and popularity in the eyes of the Latin American collective and among employers who are becoming aware that there is an increasing chance they will face the trade unions if they abuse immigrant workers. Fourth, all this activity has strengthened the overall integration of Latin American immigrants into British society, particularly in the civic and political fabric, and boosted confidence in their capabilities, and effectiveness.

More generally, the case study of the Latino migrants in London has revealed that the trade union is a growing form of Latino engagement (see also Hearn and Bergos 2010) that is not only important in itself but also one that is crucial to recognize if we want to avoid the "ethnicist'" (Brah 1996) or "culturalist" (Vertovec 1996, 2011) reductionism typical of much of the literature on migrants and minorities that tends to conceive and represent them only as ethno-cultural subjects, overlooking their other political identities, relationships, and engagements.

The case of Latin American workers in London has also illustrated that the form that policy assumes in practice is the result of the activity not only of powerful institutional actors but also of powerless ones who—by organizing within a trade union as in this case—were better able to demand the application of the existing legislation that protects workers from employers' abuse. It has also revealed how the policy engagement of subaltern actors need not being seen as an activity restricted to resistance or opposition to oppressive policies, but also as one that can include the promotion of policy enforcement when policy fails to be implemented.

The possibility for migrants to influence policy in this case was enhanced greatly when they scaled up their policy engagement and found allies and advocates among the native citizenry and its progressive civil society organizations. The case of the Latinos shows that migrants' needs are not just ethno-cultural, as the prevailing ideas of neoliberal multiculturalism seem to maintain, but are also material. It also shows how, from an analytical perspective, starting off assuming that migrants would automatically organize around ethnicity and/or nationality need not be necessarily the case. In addition, the case study shows how the best way to achieve working rights is probably neither by following the multicultural organizing model entailing the formation of ethnic community organizations with a political/charitable status, nor by accepting its equally neoliberal neoassimilationist alternative, but by organizing in a more democratically contentious way at the intersection of class and ethnicity, combining material and ethnic issues (as well as others) in the framework of class-based organizations.

Finally, the case of LAWA has shown that its politics centered on the advocacy of workers' rights, unionization campaigns, and advice around labor issues is very relevant to migrants who find themselves in exploitative and precarious working conditions, as the cleaners and carers laboring in the shadow of the global city often do (see Sassen 2001; Wills et al. 2010).

Conclusions

Returning to the initial question of the hegemonic representation of migrants as passive and dysfunctional to the social cohesion and the democratic process, the case of the Latin American workers' practices of citizenship seems to suggest a different picture. This is one that requires much greater caution in attributing intrinsic civic and political dysfunctionality to migrants, as these migrants have been actively involved in developing transethnic networks, connections, and alliances (what Putnam would call "the good bridging social capital") as part of their civic and political participation to the democratic process of the receiving society (see Però 2007a, 2007b, 2008a, 2011). Migrants like those connected to LAWA and UNITE, have actively been part of the local (British) civic, political, and policy process. Indeed, they have been contributing to the cause of the socioeconomically disadvantaged groups (for example, cleaners, the working class, etc.) and helped in democratizing British society by, alongside other initiatives, demanding the application of existing but disregarded progressive labor policies, and in this way they have contributed to generate more rather than less social cohesion.

Of course, a more positive reassessment of migrants' position in relation to social cohesion becomes possible only if and when one is willing to recognize the classed and ethnocentric nature of the current national neoliberal reasoning that underpins hegemonic public and academic accounts. When migrants are said not to participate in the political "game," we need to spell out better what game we are actually talking about and under whose rules migrants are expected to be "playing." In consideration of the class, legal, ethno-cultural, and racial obstacles they face, migrants do not seem to be playing in a level playing field (see also Ramakrishnan and Bloemraad 2008).

Thus, migrants such as those involved in LAWA are clearly not marginal and dysfunctional but integrated and contributing positively to the democratization of a society that is profoundly divided across class lines. Indeed, the initiatives of these migrants should be considered as remarkable given that they are taking place against a context that exploits them not only economically but also politically. In fact, public and institutional cultural practices are using migrants as a sort of "discursive glue" in the attempt to keep together different national class groups whose wealth and perspectives are polarizing more and more (Però forthcoming). In other words, political and institutional elites are attempting to reinvigorate the national unity of a socioeconomically uneven society by conveniently blaming migrant workers for the hardships of the national working classes.

In this hostile context, migrants' participation in the civic and democratic process is likely to continue but it is bound to take the form of a struggle for greater recognition, rights, and respect, a form of participation that the current political and economic elites who are thriving on migrants' presence may not like. As one Moroccan migrant protests leader once said to me in Bologna during the 1990s, "Rights are something that one takes and not a gift that somebody else makes to you" (Però 2007b, 86). Many Latin American migrants in London over a decade later have increasingly shown, through their practices and policy engagements at the intersection of class and ethnicity, to be sharing a similar active approach to citizenship.

Notes

1. Not surprisingly, the British National Party (BNP; a far-Right group) has quoted Brown's "British job for British workers" repeatedly in its political propaganda.

2. When migrants have been considered political actors, this has essentially meant focusing on the political opportunities structures provided by the national institutional environment to explain their agency in a rather mono-causal and—a little paradoxically for studying agency—structuralist way (Però 2007a, 2008a, 2008b; Però and Solomos 2010).

3. Clearly, this is a simplification as there are social actors and organizations acting on policy that find themselves somewhere in between the makers and the recipients.

4. James Scott's (1985, 1990) work on resistance and "weapons of the weak" is particularly helpful in identifying a wide range of resistance practices. Scott defines resistance as "any act(s) by member(s) of a subordinate class that is or are intended either to mitigate or deny claims (for example, rents, taxes, prestige) made on that class by superordinate classes (for example, landlords, large farmers, the state) or to advance its own claims (for example, work, land, charity, respect) vis-à-vis those superordinate classes" (1985, 290). Scott also highlights the importance of focusing on intentions, rather than consequences, in trying to understand resistance, since many acts of resistance may not succeed in achieving the intended results (1985, 290).

5. This idea of policy change from below represents an even broader concept than Levison and Sutton's appropriation (2001, 3), as it also encompasses those policy engagements of marginalized actors that "simply" resist policy without necessarily laying claims to create policy or to become formally involved the process of governance.

6. Fletcher (2001) notes the importance of focusing on how subalterns come to articulate practices of resistance particularly through alternative counterhegemonic elaborations (see also Però 2008a).

7. This case study is mostly based on ethnographic fieldwork that I conducted between 2005 and 2007, and informed by my ongoing

research. This fieldwork involved over 40 semistructured interviews, informal conversations, and participant observation focusing on the practices of citizenship of Latin American migrants in London. Research informants included Latin American migrants and representatives of civic and political organisations.

8. For a comprehensive discussion of the 'new migrants' problematic with special reference to London, see Wills et al. (2010).

9. This "political" violence is paralleled by a "common" violence that is particularly present in deprived urban areas.

10. For an analysis of Latin Americans' involvement in the contract cleaning sector, see Lagnado (2004).

11. The Latin American Workers Association (LAWA) subsequently adopted the acronym of LAWAs. However, since much of the discussion contained in this chapter refers to its practices during the "LAWA" period, I use its older acronym.

12. The year 2004 was not the first time that a Latin American Workers Association was set up in the UK. A precursor was set up and functioned in the 1980s.

13. For a more detailed account of LAWA, see Però (2008b).

14. This was the case until 2009, when LAWA left Unite and joined Industrial Workers of the World (IWW) even though a number of LAWA members still retain Unite membership.

References

Anderson, Benedict. 1983: *Imagined Communities*. London: Verso

Baldwin, Tom. 2004. "I Want an Integrated Society with a Difference. *The Times*, April 3. http://www.timesonline.co.uk/tol/news/uk/article1055207 (accessed March 17, 2011).

BBC News. 2007. "Gordon Brown's First Speech to the Labour Conference as Party Leader," Sept. 24, http://www.independent.co.uk/news/uk/politics/if-we-want-social-cohesion-we-need-a-sense-of-identity-619627.html (accessed March 19, 2011).

Brah, Avtar. 1996. *Cartographies of Diasporas. Contesting Identities*. London: Routledge.

Brown, Colin. 2001. "If We Want Social Cohesion We Need a Sense of Identity." *The Independent on Sunday*, December 9, http://www.independent.co.uk/news/uk/politics/if-we-want-social-cohesion-we-need-a-sense-of-identity-619627.html (accessed March 19, 2011).

Camarota, Steven. 2001. *The Slowing Process of Immigrants*. Washington, D.C.: Centre for Immigration Studies.

Castles, Stephen, and Mark J. Miller. 2009. *The Age of Migration*, 4th ed. Basingstoke, UK: Palgrave.

Chavez, Leo. 1991. "Outside the Imagined Community: Undocumented Settlers and the Experience of Incorporation." *American Ethnologist* 18:257–78.

Daily Telegraph. 2007. Gordon Brown's speech to the TUC in full, http://www
.telegraph.co.uk/news/uknews/1562685/Gordon-Browns-speech
-to-the-TUC-in-full.html (accessed on March 10, 2011).

Fletcher, Robert. 2001. "What Are We Fighting For? Rethinking Resistance
in a Pewenche Community in Chile. *Journal of Peasant Studies* 28 (3):
37–66.

Giddens, Anthony. 2006. "Misunderstanding Multiculturalism." *The
Guardian*, October 14. http://www.guardian.co.uk/commentisfree/2006
/oct/14/tonygiddens (accessed on April 11, 2011).

Gimpel, James. 1999. *Migration, Immigration and the Politics of Places*.
Washington, D.C: Centre for Immigration Studies.

Grillo, Ralph. 2005. *Backlash against Diversity? Identity and Cultural
Politics in European Cities*. COMPAS Working Paper No. 14. Oxford:
Centre on Migration Policy and Society.

Guarnizo, Luis E. 2008. *Londres Latina: La Presencia Colombiana en la
Capital Britanica*. México DF: Universidad de Zacatecas and Miguel
Angel Porrúa.

Hearn, Julie, and Monica Bergos. 2010. *Learning from the Cleaners? Trade
Union Activism among Low Paid Latin American Migrant Workers at the
University of London*. ICMiC Working Paper no. 7. Nottingham, UK:
Identity, Citizenship and Migration Centre, School of Sociology and
Social Policy, University of Nottingham.

Holston, James. 2008. *Insurgent Citizenship*, Princeton, NJ: Princeton
University Press.

Kofman, Eleonore, Annie Phizacklea, Parvati Raghuram, and Rosemary
Sales. 2000. *Gender and International Migration in Europe*. London:
Routledge.

Kundnani, Arun. 2001. "In a Foreign Land: The New Popular Racism."
Race and Class 43 (2): 41–60.

———.2007. *The End of Tolerance*, London: Pluto Press.

Lagnado, Jacob. 2004. *The London Service Sector and Migrant Labour in
the 1990s: Colombians in Contract Cleaning*. Unpublished MSc. dissertation. Milton Keynes, UK: Open University.

Levinson Bradley, and Margaret Sutton. 2001. Introduction: Policy as/in
Practice. A Sociocultural Approach to the Study of Educational Policy. in
Policy as Practice, ed. Margaret Sutton and Bradley Levinson, 1–22. Santa
Barbara, CA: Greenwood Press.

Malkki, Lisa. 1995. "Refugees and Exile: From 'Refugee Studies' to
the National Order of Things." *Annual Review of Anthropology* no.
24:495–523.

Martiniello, Marco. 2005. "The Political Participation, Mobilization
and Representation of Immigrants and Their Offspring in Europe."
In *Migration and Citizenship: Legal Status, Rights and Political
Participation*, ed. Rainer Bauböck, 52–64. Amsterdam: IMISCOE.

McIlwaine, Cathy. 2005. *Coping Practices among Colombian Migrants
in London*. London: School of Geography, Queen Mary University of

London (Available from: http://www.geog.qmul.ac.uk/docs/staff/4402 .pdf) (accessed May 2, 2011).

Meyer, David. 2003. "How Social Movements Matter." *Contexts* 2 (4): 30–35.

Però, Davide. 2005. "Left-Wing Politics, Civil Society and Immigration in Italy. The Case of Bologna." *Ethnic and Racial Studies* 28:832–58.

———. 2007a. *"Anthropological Perspectives on Migrants' Political Engagements.* COMPAS Working Paper no. 50. Oxford: Centre on Migration Policy and Society, University of Oxford.

———. 2007b. *Inclusionary Rhetoric/Exclusionary Practices. Left-Wing Politics and Migrants in Italy.* Oxford and New York: Berghahn Books.

———. 2008a. "Migrants' Mobilization and Anthropology. Reflections from the Experience of Latin Americans in the United Kingdom." In *Citizenship, Political Engagement, and Belonging. Immigrants in Europe and the United States,* ed. Deborah Reed-Danahay and Caroline Brettell, 103–23. Piscataway, NJ: Rutgers University Press.

———. 2008b. "Political Engagements of Latin Americans in the UK: Issues, Strategies and the Public Debate. *Focaal* 51:73–90.

———. 2011. "Migrants' Practices of Citizenship and Policy Change." In *Policy Worlds. Anthropology and the Analysis of Contemporary Power,* ed. Cris Shore, SusanWright and Davide Però, 244–263. New York and Oxford: Berghahn Books.

———. (forthcoming). "Migrants, Cohesion and the Cultural Politics of the State: Critical Perspectives on the Management of Diversity." Unpublished manuscript.

Però, Davide, and John Solomos. 2010. "Migrant Politics and Mobilisation: Exclusion, Engagements, Incorporation." *Ethnic and Racial Studies* 33 (1): 1–18.

Phillips, Trevor. 2004. "Multiculturalism's Legacy Is 'Have a Nice Day' Racism." *The Guardian,* May 28. http://www.guardian.co.uk /society/2004/may/28/ equality.raceintheuk (accessed on March 17, 2011).

Putnam, Robert D. 2007. "E Pluribus Unum: Diversity and Community in the Twenty-First Century. The 2006 Johan Skytte Prize Lecture." *Scandinavian Political Studies* 30 (2): 137-174.

Ramakrishnan, Karthick, and Irene Bloemraad. 2008. Civic and Political Inequalities. In *Civic Hopes and Political Realities. Immigrants, Community Organisations, and Political Engagement,* ed. Karthick Ramakrishnan and Irene Bloemraad, 1–42. New York: Russell Sage Foundation.

Reed-Danahay, Deborah, and Caroline Brettell. 2008. "Introduction." In *Citizenship, Political Engagement, and Belonging. Immigrants in Europe and the United States,* ed. Deborah Reed-Danahay and Caroline Brettell, 1–17. Piscataway, NJ: Rutgers University Press.

Sassen, Saskia. 2001. *The Global City,* 2 nd ed. Princeton, NJ: Princeton University Press.

Schneider Anne, and Helen Ingram. 1993. "Social Construction of Target Populations: Implications for Politics and Policy. *American Political Science Review* 87 (2): 334–47.

Scott, James 1985. *Weapons of the Weak: Everyday Forms of Peasant Resistance.* London: Yale University Press.

———. 1990. *Domination and the Arts of Resistance. Hidden Transcripts.* London: Yale University Press.

Shore, Cris, and Susan Wright. 1997. "Policy a New Field of Anthropology." In *Anthropology of Policy. Critical Perspectives on Governance and Power*, ed. Cris Shore and Susan Wright, 3–30. London: Routledge.

Stevenson, Nick. 2003. *Cultural Citizenship. Cosmopolitan Questions.* Milton Keynes, UK: Open University Press.

Transatlantic Trends. 2011. *Immigration 2010 Key Findings.* Washington: German Marshall Fund of the United States.

Vertovec, Steven. 1996. "Multiculturalism, Culturalism and Public Incorporation. *Ethnic and Racial Studies* 19:49–69.

———. 2007. "Super-Diversity and Its Implications." *Ethnic and Racial Studies* 30 (6): 1024–54.

———. 2011. "The Cultural Politics of Nation and Migration." Annual *Review of Anthropology*, 40: DOI: 10.1146/annurev-anthro-081309-145837.

Werbner, Pnina, and Nira Yuval-Davis. 1999. "Introduction: Women and the New Discourse of Citizenship." In *Women Citizenship and Difference*, ed. Pnina Werbner and Nira Yuval-Davis, 1–38. London: Zed.

Wills, Jane, Kavita Datta, Yara Evans, Joanna Herbert, Jon May, and Cathy McIlwaine. 2010. *Global Cities at Work. New Migrant Divisions of Labour.* London: Pluto.

Wimmer, Andreas, and Nina Glick Schiller. 2003. "Methodological Nationalism, the Social Sciences, and the Study of Migration: An Essay in Historical Epistemology." *International Migration Review* 37 (3): 576–610.

Chapter 8

Conceptualizing Human Well-Being from a Gender and Life Course Perspective: The Case of Peruvian Migrants in London

Katie Wright

This chapter examines the construction of human well-being among migrants from a gender and life course perspective. A human well-being perspective deepens understandings of how gendered roles and identities are constructed by focusing analysis on what is needed to live well and how this varies throughout the life course. Conceptual debates in this area have tended to center on how gender influences migration, and how migration shapes gender relations as well as health-related quality of life (including gender differences in health-seeking behaviors). Such approaches have paid less attention to examining explicitly how the construction of human well-being itself is gendered, how it varies across the life course, and how it is transmitted intergenerationally in the context of migration. The research presented here uses a human well-being approach to explore how these processes intersect in the context of international migration using the case of Peruvian migrants in London.

Human Well-Being, Gender, and Migration

The broader literature exploring human well-being outcomes has highlighted how the construction of what is needed to "live well" is gendered, varies over time, across space, and over the life course (Bevan 2004; White 2008). For example, gender underpins how men and women's health status and health-seeking behaviors differ, which, in turn, impact on wider health and human well-being outcomes

(Cloutier-Fisher and Kobayashi 2009). Similarly, the construction of human well-being varies according to age and across the life course. For example, what babies need to "live well" will be different from the needs of widows. There is also evidence that life satisfaction outcomes vary by age. Interestingly, surveys of North American adults (Campbell, Converse, and Rodgers 1976) record how negative scores on human well-being for those aged below 55 subsequently become positive scores (Offer 2008 cited in White 2008). In the case of Latin America, a slight reduction in life satisfaction levels is apparent during the first years of Latin Americans' adult lives followed by an increase in their latter years with life satisfaction and age having a "U" shaped relation (Graham and Behrman 2009).

Alongside gender and age, stage in the life course also impacts on human well-being outcomes as what is needed to "live well" will vary, for example according to whether individuals have dependent children. For instance, the birth of a child may leave less time and energy for paid work, and at the same time create the need for more resources (Offer 2006, 318). How far such needs can be met will influence levels of life satisfaction and human well-being outcomes.

The extent to which life satisfaction varies by gender remains contested. First, indications show that women respond to life satisfaction questions differently from men (Graham and Behrman 2009, 7). According to a study of quality of life in Latin America, following a universal trend, despite lower educational opportunities and widespread gender-based discrimination (Schuldt 2004), Latin American women tend to give higher scores in terms of life satisfaction than men: "Although men usually have more favorable financial circumstances, it is women who feel more satisfied overall" (Lora, Chaparro, and Rodriguez 2009, 100). By contrast, in a recent study of happiness determinants on households in Peru, being a woman was found to be negatively related to happiness (Copestake et al. 2008).

This literature on the gendered construction of human well-being has emerged independently from that on gender and migration. Within migration studies, recognition of the increased feminization of migration (including such categories as young single women, female family breadwinners, and low-skilled women from urban backgrounds migrating autonomously to flee divorce, gender-based or other forms of violence and poverty [Sørensen 2005]) has led to an increased focus on the gendered nature of migration processes. This literature first examines how gender shapes patterns and processes of migration and the extent to which the decision to migrate is facilitated or constrained by gendered norms and institutions in the home country (Hondagneu-Sotelo 1994). Another dimension explored is the gendered nature of labor markets of receiving countries into which migrants are inserted (Escrivá 2003). A third dimension is the impact of this migration on gender roles, ideologies, and divisions of labor (McIlwaine 2010) and the extent to which traditional understandings of motherhood and fatherhood are maintained or transformed though migration processes (Hondagneu-Sotelo and Avila 1997; Parreñas 2005; Pribilsky 2004; see also Herrera this volume).

These bodies of literature reveal three main gaps. First, despite an increasing recognition of the diverse experiences of male and female migrants (Datta et al. 2009, 2010; Mahler and Pessar 2006; McIlwaine 2010), research on the gendered nature of migration has tended to neglect how gender identities vary across the life course or how gendered experiences of migration are constructed intergenerationally. In addition, work on gender and the life course has tended to be heavily biased toward health dimensions, and its impact on other domains of human well-being remains little understood. Third, the focus within the literature on human well-being has been on how gender affects life satisfaction and quality of life measures rather than how it shapes understandings of human well-being. Such areas of neglect can be addressed by tracing gendered experiences of migration across different stages of the life course in order to examine differences in the construction and achievement of human well-being. Analysis of what is needed to live well varies over the life span. This can deepen understanding of the ways in which gender roles and identities are constructed and the extent to which these are reinforced or transformed intergenerationally. Exploring how gender and the life course intersect in the context of international migration enhances understanding of the specific gender and life course issues that low-income migrants in particular are likely to face. Similarly, analyzing how these processes intersect in the context of international migration can potentially improve understanding of how the construction of human well-being varies across different kinds of population groups.

Therefore, it is argued that there is a need to use a more holistic conceptual framework that goes beyond health outcomes to focus attention on the dynamic interplay between material, perceptual, and relational domains of human well-being in the context of a gendered approach to international migration. Building on a particular human well-being approach presented by White (2008), this chapter examines women and men's own self-assessment of the factors influencing their human well-being via the interaction of three different dimensions— material, perceptual, and relational. According to this framework, the material dimension encapsulates income, wealth, and assets; employment and livelihood activities; education and skills; physical health and (dis)ability; access to services and amenities; and environmental quality. The perceptual dimension includes aspects such as understandings of the sacred and the moral order; self-concept and personality; hopes, fears, and aspirations; sense of meaning/meaninglessness; and levels of (dis)satisfaction, trust, and confidence.

The relational encapsulates relations of love and care; networks of support and obligation; relations with the state (law, politics, welfare); social, political, and cultural identities and inequalities; violence, conflict, and (in)security; and scope for personal and collective action and influence (White 2008).[1] In addition, it is argued that this approach has the advantage of explicitly assessing differences in how well-being is constructed across these domains. Third, by tracing respondents at different life stages, it responds to the call by Rosser (1991, cited in Katz and Monk 1993, 17) to consider all phases of the life course. Finally, this study grounds this theoretical approach in empirical understanding by examining the case of Peruvian migrants in London.

Peruvian Migration to London

The following sections explore the construction of human well-being across the life course and how it is gendered through the examination of Peruvian migrants in London. This group has been chosen because it has received less attention in the UK context than other Latin American groups. While the 2001 Census revealed that London's population included 46,325 Latin Americans, these appear to be significant underestimates (McIlwaine 2007). According to a Foreign and Commonwealth Office strategy paper on Latin America (FCO 2007, 5) there are between 700,000 and 1,000,000 Latin Americans visiting or living in the UK. This includes 70–90,000 Ecuadorians and 10–15,000 Peruvians (McIlwaine 2007).

This study forms part of a larger research project in which 99 interviews were conducted with the migrants between 2005 and 2007, with 49 conducted in London and 50 in Madrid (Wright 2010). Peruvian migrants in London were contacted via gatekeepers from the Latin American community with entry points through informal sporting events. The interviews comprised closed questions on objective states of human well-being and more open questions related to what respondents felt they needed to "live well" in London and Lima using subjective perceptions of life satisfaction via multidimensional assessment of their daily lives. A further ten interviews were conducted in Lima with direct relations and close friends of those interviewed in Europe.[2]

The London sample included 49 Peruvian migrants, with 37 of the respondents aged between 15 and 45. It incorporated 32 men and 17 women. Respondents were well educated (20 had university education, 16 had technical institute level education, and 11 had secondary-school level). In total, 37 respondents were from Lima. Respondents had left Peru mainly for economic reasons—two were unemployed, nine left due to economic uncertainty, and six moved for greater economic opportunity. However, the reasons were rarely singular—other motivations included joining a family member in London. Migrants were employed in low-paid occupations, such as cleaning. The vast majority in the sample were low-income with 16 earning less than £7,999 per year, 13 earning between £8,000 and £14,999 per year, and 10 earning between £15,000 and £22,999 per year.

The research presented here first examines men and women's constructions of human well-being. It then develops the life course analysis, which focuses specifically on women. In order to understand the gendered construction of human well-being, respondents were first asked to identify what they felt they needed to "live well" in the contexts of Lima and London, which was classified by age group. For the life course analysis that focuses on women, responses were classified due to availability of data using two main categories: single women and women with dependent children. Building on the work of Monk and Katz (1993, 20) and Hopkins and Pain (2007), it is argued that it is important to identify the specific "cohorts" to which respondents belong as behaviors associated with a specific life stage may affect the conditions through which a group has lived collectively (such as different patterns of labor force participation). Similarly, examination of women's roles requires identifying them not only as "wives and workers" but also intergenerationally, for example, as daughters (Monk and Katz 1993, 20). Where possible, the generation they belonged to (for example, mothers or daughters) was also identified since cohort, generation, and stage in the life cycle appeared to be important for understanding variance in human well-being outcomes.

"Living Well' in Lima and London

Given that human well-being "travels" and is constructed across spatial boundaries, this research first identified what low-income Peruvian migrant men and women identify as important for "living well" in the context of Lima. Respondents were then asked to identify what they considered important for living well in the context of London. This section first examines the needs identified by women and then explores those highlighted by men.

Women in their 20s and 30s highlighted how living well in Lima was predicated upon having a family to ensure economic support but also required particular attitudes and learned behaviors such as personal initiative as well as relational needs including personal contacts as suggested by Cynthia,[3] aged 26, from Lima, working as an administrative assistant in London: "You need money; family—parents for good economic support. You need a lot of personal initiative and good contacts." These women also associated human well-being with being able to afford material comforts as suggested by Maya, aged 22, a student in London: "You need a good job, to be well economically, have your family close by, a good education and comforts—a telephone, television, radio and computer." This corroborates findings by Lora, Chaparro, and Rodriguez (2009, 107), who suggest that life satisfaction in the Latin American context currently depends on access to a telephone and other material assets.

Others in this age group highlighted a combination of needs essential for living well, including conforming to particular gendered and sexualized norms relating to physical appearance as suggested by Susy, aged 34 and from Cusco, working in a grassroots organization: "[To live well you need] to have qualifications in science or technology, to have good contacts, to live in Lima (because all the power is centered in the capital), qualifications from abroad, to speak English and have a Western outlook . . . to be sexy, pretty and to have a good appearance." The term "good appearance" is ambiguous and also encompasses racialized norms about appearance, which intersect with gendered and age-related expectations that are socially determined (Wade 1997). By implication, to have an appearance that is "sexy," to be young and to be lighter-skinned will all enhance one's ability to "live well" in a society where gender, age, and ethnic discrimination are widespread. Material needs were identified by this age group as the hardest to fulfill as suggested by Magda, aged 32, from Lima, married with two children under five: "You need material things. The rest you already have." The material demands implied by having more than one child were also highlighted by other cohorts of women such as Flor, aged 48, from Lima, working as a cleaner in London, who suggested: "You need to have your own terrain, to be able to feed your children and clothe yourselves." Women stressed the importance of going beyond subsistence needs to achieve human well-being in the material domain. This was the case for Rossy, aged 47, from Lima, currently married with two children and also working as a cleaner in London, who associated living well with having "job opportunities for one's children." In terms of relational needs, women with children highlighted the importance of security and protection from street violence, as Rossy noted: "You need security for citizens." This corroborates findings of Cárdenas, Mejía, and Di Maro (2009, 155) that personal security (related to being free from victimization by mugging or absence of gangs) is a strong predictor of satisfaction with one's standard of living.

By contrast, for men in their 20s, living well in Lima was related directly to the material sphere, including being able to run a business and to build new floors in one's house. Economic opportunities and access to remittances were considered important to achieve this. However, equally important was being part of a "united" family to ensure economic support as suggested by Abel, aged 23, from Cañete, and a student at a London-based university: "[To live well you need] a good job and not to be out of work, though the family will always help you so it is not always so important." In terms of perceptual needs, the ability to live harmoniously within a large or extended family unit was also identified as essential, as suggested by Abel's cousin, Federico, aged 28, working as a shop assistant in a supermarket: "You need to know how to live across the generations."

Men in their 30s felt less able to "coast" in a large family unit for economic protection than men in their 20s and considered being employed as essential for living well, such as in the case of Pepe, aged 30, from Lima, working in a restaurant in London: "You need a favorable economic situation and a good job." Without employment, men in their 30s felt vulnerable to falling into crime, such as the case of Martín, aged 37, from Lima, working as a vending machine supervisor in London: "[You need] capital—those who have it live well; those that do not . . . drink . . . you fall into it, bad ways, drugs, prostitution, unemployment. I have two unemployed brothers in San Martin de Porres where I am from. Both are drug addicts." These respondents also suggested that men in their 30s who had failed to enhance self-esteem though acting as breadwinners for their families often engaged in criminal activity in order to feel "more manly." Finally, although men in their 30s could not "coast" in the economic unit of the family as much as men in their 20s expected to, family union was still considered important in providing informal social protection and insurance in case of shocks requiring the need to return to the family unit, as highlighted in the case of Martín: "The important thing is to have work, not to be unemployed . . . and to maintain yourself unified to the family. Being divided is of no use because that way you cannot return." For men in their 40s, having a business and economic security to maintain children and a home was perceived as important such as in the case of Felipe, aged 44, from Trujillo, working as a cleaning supervisor in London, who suggested: "You need a good job to maintain your family . . . a family is important." Whereas women in this age group highlighted relational needs such as protection from violence, men highlighted the importance of having good contacts and access to social networks, which could be ensured by having studied in the "right" places as suggested by Juan, aged 46, from Lima, working as an independent tour operator in London: ["You need] contacts, political influence—everything you do depends on relationships, who your friends are and this depends on who you studied with."

In this section I have explored how men and women constitute "living well" in the context of Lima. Although in their 20s both men and women highlighted the family as an economic unit that is essential for "living well," for men in their 30s "coasting" in a large family unit was no longer considered possible, and living well was predicated on obtaining paid employment and keeping good relations with the family unit to ensure economic support as an informal social protection mechanism. Where men were unable to acquire paid employment, finding other ways to feel "manly" were sought, which may include crime and delinquency. For women in their 30s, living well was also dependent on fulfilling gendered expectations but in different ways, such as via a youthful, white, and sexualized appearance. By their 40s, for women living well is based upon being able to fulfill children's needs as well as protection from street violence. For men, it required being able to maintain children, and these material needs were fulfilled via the relational dimension to ensure personal contacts obtained through extended social networks.

Focusing specifically on what respondents identified as important for living well in the London context in terms of needs, women who had migrated in their 40s complained of feeling trapped in cleaning work and highlighted the importance of material needs such as education and qualifications recognized in the UK as a route to skilled employment and better human well-being outcomes, such as in the case of Flor: "[You need] to have a high level of education which allows access to good jobs. You cannot live without education here [London] or you end up cleaning. Over there [Lima] you can sell potatoes." This was also the case for Aurora, aged 46, divorced with three children (two of whom were in their mid-20s), from Lima, working as a cleaner: "[You need] to work, have a house and learn the language well." A good income was also identified as important, as indicated by Sara, aged 46, with four children, from Lima, working as a housekeeper in a private dwelling: "You need a well paid job." Part of the explanation for this emphasis on material well-being for women in this age group relates to their social history and migration trajectory. Women in their 40s were less likely to have had the opportunity to obtain formal qualifications in the UK and little opportunity for learning English given the need to take whatever work they could find on arrival to maintain their children. This highlights the importance of understanding the conditions through which particular cohorts have lived collectively that influence, for example, employment experiences of a particular group (Monk and Katz 1993, 20), as well as wider structural conditions that influence what women are able to be and do in the host country.

Women in their 20s and 30s highlighted that in contrast to Lima, having contacts in London is not enough to secure employment—human capital (including knowledge of English) was also required, as suggested by Cynthia: "[To live well] you need to know the language or it's a struggle. Though you may have initiative and contacts, without the language you cannot." Interestingly, they also signaled the importance of perceptual needs for achieving human well-being including awareness of social conventions and the need to reconstruct one's values and sense of family, as suggested by Susy: "[You need] to know the English system, to understand the social codes such as how to get a job and maintain it . . . to reconstruct your sense of family and social values." Thus, "having family around you" either through members being physically present or via transnational linkages was identified as important.

There was some overlap with these findings in the material domain for men in their 20s and 30s. For example, having legal documentation, good English, and qualifications acquired in the UK were identified as important for living well. Interestingly, in the perceptual domain men highlighted the importance of protecting their pride and self-esteem. For example, Alex, aged 29, from Lima, working as a kitchen porter suggested: "You need self-esteem, courage, never to lower your head to anyone, to know how to manage solitude." This was also the case for Marco, aged 33, from Surco in Lima, living as a busker in London: "[You need not feel] that they are giving you things via charity, to have dignity, be self-sufficient, not to depend on anyone." Deskilling and finding oneself without the personal contacts to get ahead in London in the same way that one might have enjoyed in Lima can be an infantilizing experience with the added challenge of a hostile environment for migrants who are subject to racism and other kinds of inequalities. In such a context high levels of self-esteem are required in order to foster resilience and "live well."

Having explored what women and men identify as important for living well in the contexts of Lima and London according to age group, the following section investigates how human well-being is constructed in London across the life course and how it is transmitted intergenerationally. This analysis focuses only on women and on two specific domains—material and perceptual well-being.[4]

Life Course Analysis and Intergenerational Transmission of Human Well-Being

In the material domain, women were affected in different ways across the life course. Most women in their 40s and 50s had children, and many women in this cohort complained that they had formerly lacked the ability to train in the UK given the need to maintain children. This had meant that they had never been able to access higher-paid employment, such as in the case of Esther, aged 57, a housekeeper with one teenage daughter: "Finding a better job is difficult. I was never able to get the skills because I had to maintain my daughter." Daughters also highlighted the particular vulnerabilities of their mothers (in their late 40s) in the material domain related to living in high-rise council blocks in London. For example, Miriam, referring to her mother, suggested: "Sometimes the tower blocks are very high and there are no lifts and my mother gets repeatedly ill because of this."

In terms of intergenerational transmission of human well-being in the material domain, it became apparent that daughters who had migrated to join their mothers in London had also been frustrated in their abilities to live well by having their opportunities for obtaining qualifications in the UK curtailed, due to the need to support their mothers financially. This was the case of Cynthia, aged 26, working as an administrative assistant in London, whose mother worked as a cleaner: "I would like to study, live my teens, be able to study, not have to work straight after; I would have liked to have studied more; not have to have helped my mum. Most first children have to help the parent. I'd like to study psychology." Daughters in the same cohort but at a different life cycle stage complained of being caught in the poverty trap, such as Miriam, aged 20, a single mother with one child under five: "As I have the baby I cannot work. If I do they take away my benefits." Although daughters could speak better English than their mothers, they still felt uncomfortable using it, as Cynthia continues: "I would like to have studied more but the language is difficult, I learnt it by force. I don't feel secure in the language."

In the perceptual domain, the emotional and psychosocial impacts of this migration affected women in positive and negative ways at different stages of the life course. Negative impacts included vulnerability to loneliness and depression. Interestingly, in the wider literature on gender, life satisfaction, and social isolation, risk factors include age, gender, marital status, and place. In turn, having a strong social network is related to greater resilience and better health outcomes (Cloutier-Fisher and Kobayashi 2009). Migrant women at particular stages in the life span are less likely to benefit from strong social networks as other population groups given the lack of social contact implied by the need to work longer hours to send remittances, as illustrated in the case of Esther, aged 47, divorced with one teenage child: "We [Peruvian friends] do not see each other very regularly—one tends to work a lot, there is no time to socialize." This was the case for younger cohorts of women in their 30s who had found it hard to make friends in the UK while at the same time were losing touch with family in Peru, such as in the case of Susy, aged 34, from Cusco: "I went through some very dark periods, family members who died over there [Peru]. Furthermore, I have lost contact with my family and friends which is invaluable." Loss of social networks in Peru and negative impacts in the perceptual domain also affected women at a different life stage, such as Flor, aged 48, with four children (two of whom were residing in Peru), who suggested: "I was unable to bless my mother when she died . . . I cannot leave this country [UK]. Neither can my children come here and if I leave I risk everything . . . I have this country as a prison. I am grateful but it is a limited kind of happiness."

The human well-being literature suggests that individuals suffering serious physical illness or disability adapt (via social comparison with others with these disabilities), and so return to their initial happiness levels. By contrast, individuals suffering depression are much less likely to experience this kind of adaptation (Dolan 2006 cited in Graham and Lora 2009, 189). This study builds on this finding by suggesting that there is a need to understand in more detail how migrant women's emotional and psychosocial needs vary across the life course and by generation. Women without dependent children in their 20s and 30s often still felt uncomfortable speaking in a foreign language even where they speak it well, giving rise to feelings of insecurity and lack of confidence. They may also be hindered in their ability to take opportunities to develop their human capital and skills development due to the need to work to support their mothers financially, which may frustrate their ability to achieve their personal goals and compound low self-esteem. For women at a different stage in the life cycle who migrated with children, difficulties associated with speaking English and the need to work to support dependents on arrival are likely to have meant they are even more constrained in their ability to develop their skills. For the same reasons they are also restricted to low-skilled employment, offering few opportunities for self-realization in the workplace and limiting time for creation of social networks that bolster resilience.

Notwithstanding these negative psychosocial impacts, there were also positive impacts of this migration in the perceptual domain. The migration literature examining the extent to which women are empowered through migration processes presents contradictory evidence (Mahler and Pessar 2001). This study showed that despite the material difficulties experienced by women in their 40s and 50s, with children, such as lack of opportunity to study, migration was also considered a route to independence and empowerment. The way that this was experienced varied across the life cycle. Unlike their mothers, some daughters, such as Alba, aged 19, benefitted from opportunities to study in the UK (while concurrently holding down cleaning jobs passed down via her mother). For this generation of women, migration was perceived as a route to self-realization: "I can fulfill my potential more as a person. When you study here [London] it serves to get you to where you want to be." Other cohorts of women without children also saw migration as a means to bolster their human capital, such as in the case of Maya, aged 22: "We have a better education— you can study Latin American Studies, Spanish, at North London Metropolitan University." For women in their thirties without children, other positive perceptual impacts included no longer being dependent on their own mother's or male partner's incomes, such as in the case with Susy, aged 34, from Cusco: "I no longer depend on my mother's income, I am independent." Women in the same cohort but at a different life course stage signaled that they were enjoying new respect for women and children found in the host country and were aware of financial benefits available in London for single mothers, such as Magda, aged 32, a housewife with two children under five: "[In London] there is a lot of respect for children, for women, there is a lot of support for women, for example, single mothers." Notwithstanding the material difficulties that had curtailed their own mothers' opportunities to develop human capital and knowledge of English, daughters in their 20s, such as Miriam, were aware of the positive perceptual impacts of migrating to London for their mothers, which included leaving behind male-dominated or abusive relationships: "In Peru my mother was not able to work as it is more *machista* [male-dominated], here [London] she can work. In Peru you have to depend on men for things that are needed. Here she is more independent." Her mother Aurora, whose abusive husband had died in Peru leaving her a widow in London, suggested: "I have what I could not have before. I maintain my children. I develop as a woman. I hold the highest position in the home, I give orders at home, I do not depend on anyone, I am more independent and I go out when I want."

What these narratives suggest is that notwithstanding the negative psychosocial impacts, migration can also have empowering effects and how this is experienced varies according to gender, stage in the life cycle, and generation. Findings from this study suggest that mothers leaving *machista* relationships in Peru (in spite of the arduous and exploitative nature of the work they are forced to undertake in the host country) perceive migration as a route to financial independence and self-realization (see also McIlwaine 2010; also Herrera, Moser this volume). For daughters migration is also perceived as an opportunity for cultivating independence and self-reliance in the perceptual domain. For daughters this requires opportunities to study or train as well and the negotiation of cleaning jobs passed down by their mothers in such a way to ensure that they do not become trapped in low-skilled employment themselves.

Conclusions

These findings suggest that both understandings of what is needed to live well in particular contexts as well as ways in which human well-being is constructed varies according to gender and stage in the life course. The discussion here deepens theoretical and empirical insights into the processes through which this occurs in the context of international migration. This is achieved by situating research on gender, the life course, and migrant well-being within a more holistic analytical frame that captures how these processes intersect across material, perceptual, and relational dimensions. Interestingly, this reveals that constructions of human well-being are transmitted and renegotiated intergenerationally in ways that can reinforce or transform gender relationships. This matters because rather than providing a single snapshot of migrants' experiences at a particular life stage, it offers a richer and more nuanced understanding of how needs vary by gender and across the life course and across different generations of women, providing information of potential use to policy makers and other stakeholders interested in enhancing migrant well-being. It also moves discussion beyond examining gendered experiences of migration to a broader consideration of how the construction of human well-being is itself gendered. Adoption of a human well-being approach thus offers additional insights into the gendered aspects of intergenerational transmission of migrant well-being. In addition, it also offers two empirical insights. First, it highlights the need to target training programs at migrant women in their 20s and 30s to help break the cycle of generations of migrant women being trapped in unskilled employment. Second, it highlights the need to consider ways of strengthening the resilience and psychological well-being of low-income migrants. This study suggests that migrants' needs in this area vary by gender, at different stages of the life course and by generation and that programs need to be targeted accordingly. This might be achieved for example by extending knowledge and information of the range of services available in order to support women at different stages of the life course in achieving their goals and enhancing their quality of life across material, perceptual, and relational domains.

Acknowledgments

I would like to thank Katie Willis and Cathy McIlwaine for their very helpful comments on an earlier draft of this chapter.

Notes

1. Whereas White (2008) uses the term "subjective" as the second dimension of human well-being, I have chosen to use the term "perceptual" to avoid potential confusion associated with the particular branch of literature within human well-being approaches known as "subjective well-being approaches."
2. These are analyzed in a separate article (Wright 2011b).
3. Pseudonyms are used throughout this chapter in order to preserve anonymity.
4. Further discussion of the relational domain as well as men's experiences across the life course are explored in a book by Wright (2011a) currently under preparation for Palgrave Macmillan.

References

Bevan, Pip. 2004. "Exploring the Structured Dynamics of Chronic Poverty: A Sociological Approach. Bath: University of Bath, Wellbeing in Developing Countries ESRC Research Group Working Paper Series.

Campbell, Angus, Phillip. E. Converse, and Willard. L. Rodgers. 1976. *The Quality of American Life: Perceptions, Evaluations and Satisfactions.* New York: Russell Sage Foundation.

Cárdenas, Mauricio, Carolina Mejía, and Vicenzo Di Maro. 2009. "Vulnerabilities and Subjective Wellbeing. In *Paradox and Perception: Measuring Quality of Life in Latin America,* ed. Carol Graham and Eduardo Lora, 118–57. Washington, D.C.: Brookings Institution Press.

Cloutier-Fisher, Denise, and Karen M. Kobayashi. 2009. "Examining Social Isolation by Gender and Geography: Conceptual and Operational Challenges Using Population Health Data in Canada." *Gender, Place and Culture* 16 (2): 181–99.

Copestake, James, Monica Guillen-Royo, Wan-Jung Chou, Tim Hinks, and Jackeline Velazco. 2008. "Economic Welfare, Poverty and Subjective Wellbeing." In *Wellbeing and Development in Peru: Local and Universal Views Confronted,* ed. James Copestake, 103–20. New York: Palgrave Macmillan.

Datta, Kavita, Cathy McIlwaine, Yara Evans, Joanna Herbert, Jon May, and Jane Wills. 2010. "A Migrant Ethic of Care? Negotiating Care and Caring among Migrant Workers in London's Low-Pay Economy." *Feminist Review* 94:93–116.

Datta, Kavita, Cathy McIlwaine, Joanna Herbert, Yara Evans, Jon May, and Jane Wills. 2009. "Men on the Move: Narratives of Migration and Work among Low-Paid Migrant Men in London." *Social and Cultural Geography* 10 (8): 853–73.

Escrivá, Ángeles. 2003. Mujeres Peruanas en España: conquistando el espacio laboral extradoméstico, *Revista Internacional de Sociología* 36:59–83.

Foreign and Commonwealth Office (FCO). 2007. Latin America to 2020: A UK Public Strategy Paper. London: FCO.

Graham, Carol, and Jere. R Behrman. 2009. "How Latin Americans Assess Their Quality of life: Insights and Puzzles from Novel Metrics of Well-Being." In *Paradox and Perception: Measuring Quality of Life in Latin America,* ed. Carol Graham and Eduardo Lora, 1–21. Washington, D.C.: Brookings Institution Press.

Graham, Carol, and Eduardo Lora. ed. 2009. *Paradox and Perception: measuring Quality of Life in Latin America.* Washington, D.C.: Brookings Institution Press.

Hondagneu-Sotelo, Pierrete. 1994. *Gendered Transitions: Mexican Experiences of Immigration.* Berkeley: University of California Press.

Hondagneu-Sotelo, Pierrette, and Ernestine Avila. 1997 "'I'm Here, But I'm There': The Meanings of Latina Transnational Motherhood." *Gender and Society* 11:548–71.

Hopkins, Peter, and Rachel Pain. 2007. "Geographies of Age: Thinking Relationally." *Area* 39 (3): 287–94.

Katz, Cindi, and Janice Monk. 1993. "Making Connections: Space, Place and the Life Course." In *Full Circles: Geographies of Women over the Life Course*, ed. Cindi Katz and Janice Monk, 264–77. London: Routledge.

Lora, Eduardo, Juan Camilo Chaparro, and María V. Rodriguez. 2009. "Satisfaction Beyond Income." In *Paradox and Perception: Measuring Quality of Life in Latin America*, ed. Carol Graham and Eduardo Lora, 96–117. Washington, D.C.: Brookings Institution Press.

Mahler, Sarah J., and Patricia R. Pessar. 2001. "Gendered Geographies of Power: Analyzing Gender across Transnational Spaces. *Identities* 7 (4): 441–59.

———. 2006. "Gender Matters: Ethnographers Bring Gender from the Periphery toward the Core of Migration Studies." *International Migration Review* 40 (1): 27–63.

McIlwaine, Cathy. 2007. "Living in Latin London: Surviving in the City". London: Leverhulme and Queen Mary, University of London.

———. 2010. "Migrant Machismos: Exploring Gender Ideologies and Practices among Latin American Migrants in London from a Multi-Scalar Perspective." *Gender, Place and Culture* 17 (3): 281–300.

Monk, Janice, and Cindi Katz. 1993. "Where in the World are Women? In *Full Circles: Geographies of Women over the Life Course*, ed. Cindi Katz and Janice Monk, 27–54. London: Routledge.

Offer, Avner. 2006. *The Challenge of Affluence: Self-Control and Well-Being in the United States and Britain since 1950.* Oxford and New York: Oxford University Press.

Parreñas, Rhacel. 2005. "Long Distance Intimacy: Class, Gender and Intergenerational Relations between Mothers and Children in Filipino Transnational Families." *Global Networks* 5(4): 317–36.

Pribilsky, Jason. 2004. "'Aprendemos a convivir': Conjugal Relations, Co-Parenting, and Family Life among Ecuadorian Transnational Migrants in New York City and the Ecuadorian Andes." *Global Networks* 4 (3): 313–34.

Schuldt, Jürgen. 2004. *Bonanza Macroeconomuca y Malestar Microeconomico: apuntes para el estudio del caso Peruano, 1988–2004.* Lima: Universidad del Pacifico.

Sørensen, Nina N. 2005. "Globalización, género y migración transnacional." In *Migración y Desarrollo*, ed. Ángeles Escrivá and Natalia Ribas, 87–109. Córdoba: Publicaciones del Consejo Superior de Investigaciones Científicas.

Wade, Peter. 1997. *Race and Ethnicity in Latin America*. London: Pluto Press.

White, Sarah C. 2008. But What is Wellbeing? A Framework for Analysis in Social and Development Policy and Practice. Bath: University of Bath, Wellbeing in Developing Countries ESRC Research Group Working Paper Series.

Wright, Katie. 2010. "'It's a Limited Kind of Happiness': Barriers to Achieving Human Wellbeing through International Migration: The Case of Peruvian Migrants in London and Madrid." *Bulletin of Latin American Research* 29 (3): 367–83.

Wright, Katie. Forthcoming, 2011a. "Constructing Migrant Wellbeing: An Exploration of Life Satisfaction amongst Peruvian Migrants in London." *Journal of Ethnic and Migration Studies.*

———. Forthcoming, 2011b. "Connecting Wellbeing in North and South: Negotiating Meanings in Transnational Migration." *Global Networks.*

Chapter 9

Gender Transformations and Gender-Based Violence among Latin American Migrants in London

Cathy McIlwaine and Frances Carlisle

The examination of gender-based violence and domestic abuse among migrant women across the world has received very limited attention to date. This is partly because the gendered nature of migration processes has only received sustained consideration in the last decade or so, together with the fact that gender-based violence has only recently been fully recognized as an important issue both academically and in policy terms. However, the limited research available on gender-based violence suggests that gendered power relations are at the root of such abuse and that migrant women are especially vulnerable. Yet, while research on gender-based and domestic violence among immigrant communities is increasing, there remains very little work in the European or British context, with most concentrated on North America and especially among Asian and to a lesser extent among Latin Americans (however, see Beckett and Macey 2001; Gill and Rehman 2004; Macey 1999).

In addressing this neglect, this chapter explores the nature of gender-based violence and domestic abuse among Latin American migrants in London. Drawing on qualitative research with 70 women and men migrants from Colombia, Ecuador, and Bolivia in London as well as casework conducted by the Latin American Women's Rights Service, this chapter argues that it is impossible to understand gender-based violence and domestic abuse among Latin American migrants without consideration of the wider context of the migration process and concomitant transformations in gender ideologies. In turn, it argues that migration offers opportunities and constraints for female and male migrants and suggests that migrants' specific circumstances in relation to immigration and employment status are critical in negotiating their experiences and responses to gender-based violence. More specifically, the discussion highlights that in general terms, women were more likely to emphasize the advantages associated with migration, while men consistently stressed their loss of status. This has resulted in some transformations in gender ideologies and power relations with some especially ambiguous outcomes for gender-based violence. In relation to the latter, this chapter highlights the problems relating to immigration legislation, and especially the situation where irregular women migrants who are survivors of abuse have "no recourse to public funds," exacerbating their vulnerability.

Conceptualizing Gender-Based Violence among Immigrant Communities

Dealing first with the meanings of gender-based violence and acknowledging that violence itself is a highly contested concept (McIlwaine 2008), most definitions draw on the 1993 United Nations Declaration of Violence against Women Article 1 that states that "any act of gender-based violence that results in, or is likely to result in, physical, sexual or psychological harm or suffering to women, including threats of such acts, coercion or arbitrary deprivations of liberty, whether occurring in public or in private life." Article 2 continues that it may occur in the "family, community, perpetrated or condoned by the State, wherever it occur" and may refer to assault, sexual abuse, rape, female genital mutilation and other "traditional" practices, as well as sexual harassment, trafficking in women, and forced prostitution (Heise, Pitanguy, and Germain 1994, 3). This was further reinforced in the Beijing Platform for Action in 1995 that identified how "acts or threats of violence, whether occurring within the home or in the community, or perpetrated by the State, instill fear and insecurity in women's lives and are obstacles to the achievement of equality and peace" (Pickup, Williams, and Sweetman 2001, 2). These definitions reflect how gender-based violence is multidimensional and occurs in both the private sphere of the home and the public sphere. Although the focus here will be on abuse within the home between conjugal partners, it is important to refer to and recognize wider dimensions of gender-based violence (McIlwaine 2008).

Just as definitions and interpretations of gender-based violence are contested, so are the causes that are multiple and complex. At the core, however, gender-based violence is closely associated with the construction of gender identities, which, in turn, are linked with constructions of masculinities and femininities (Barker 2005). Under this broad rubric, there are two main ways of viewing violence against women. The first is the "biological approach" that accepts male violence as "natural" and rooted in biological differences; this view makes it difficult to try and change male behavior. A dimension of this is the psychological perspective that argues that men who abuse women have "impaired masculinity" often thought to be the result of socialization processes involving witnessing violence. The second main approach strongly influenced by feminist scholarship attributes the primary causes to patriarchal relations and the exercise of male power against women (and to a lesser extent against children) (McIlwaine 2008). In turn, these forces may be altered or shaped by a range of external factors such as poverty, [un]employment, or migration. Therefore, violence is the expression of power of one gender over the other, which is aggravated or ameliorated by various individual and structural risk factors at different levels (WHO 2005). Because of the recognition that is possible to address and reduce gender-based violence, the second approach has gained most currency in the social sciences and forms the foundation for understanding such conflict in the current context in relation to Latin American migrants.

Turning to the gendered nature of international migration, it is now acknowledged that mobility disrupts and changes gender identities. Gender is also recognized as being deeply embedded in the migration process in relation to who moves, why, and the forms of settlement in the destination country (Hondagenu-Sotelo 2001). Gender ideologies are also understood to be fluid and mutable. Yet, there is little agreement as to the exact nature of the transformation of gender identities and ideologies. While early research tended to emphasize the empowering effects of migration for women, this has since been revised to suggest that the outcomes are contradictory (Zentgraf 2002). These outcomes depend on a range of intersecting factors such as the type of labor force participation undertaken by migrant women, the nature of family and household structures, and the routes of entry and residence in a country, particularly whether migrants are documented or undocumented (Anthias and Lazaridis 2000; Parreñas 2001). Also critically important is the nature of gender ideologies in the home country before departure (Menjívar 1999).

Therefore, while migration can provide opportunities for women in terms of being able to assert financial independence through their labor force participation in destination countries, this does not necessarily bring equality or transformations in other spheres (Pessar and Mahler 2003). In recent years, there have been increasing calls for caution when assuming that migrants move from "backward" patriarchal societies to "enlightened" or modern ones (Gutmann 2004). Indeed, the costs of migration have been increasingly emphasized. Of particular relevance here is that migration can lead to feelings of disempowerment among migrant men who struggle to deal with deteriorating social and occupational status as well as exclusion and racism (Datta et al. 2009). In these circumstances, it has been suggested that some men try to reassert themselves through gender-based violence as the only way they can feel powerful again (Hondagneu-Sotelo and Messner 1999; Kim 2006). It has therefore been suggested that migrant women are especially vulnerable to gender-based violence (Menjívar and Salcido 2002; Raj and Silverman 2002). In addition, processes of exclusion and the depiction of migrant women as "exotic others" can serve to exacerbate their vulnerability further (Das Dasgupta 2005).

A useful framework that summarizes the gendered outcomes of international migration within which experiences of gender-based violence play a role has been developed by Patricia Pessar (2005) based largely on her research with Latin Americans in the United States (see also McIlwaine 2010 on Latin Americans in the UK). She identifies three potential sets of outcomes. First, migration can lead to a positive renegotiation of premigration gender ideologies and practices that prevailed in home countries; second, movement can reinforce any changes that had previously set root in home countries prior to departure; third, asymmetrical gender beliefs and norms from the premigration stage can be intensified. These outcomes are not mutually exclusive with considerable overlaps among them which are further crosscut by social position such as race, class, and nationality, among others. Yet, the framework provides a helpful way of categorizing the complex gendered experiences of migrants that are outlined below in relation to Latin American migrants in London. As noted above, only by understanding these experiences, is it possible to understand the nature of gender-based violence among this group (Carlisle 2006).

As for the research on which this paper is based, in-depth interviews were conducted with 70 Latin American migrants in London as well as three focus group discussions (including 17 migrants), and series of key informant interviews with people working with the Latin American community between November 2006 and July 2007. Three main Latin American nationalities were interviewed: Colombians, Ecuadorians, and Bolivians. Colombians were chosen as the most established and largest (besides Brazilians), Ecuadorians as the second largest, and Bolivians as the most recent arrivals. The sample for the in-depth interviews was based on nonpurposive sampling techniques; 20 were conducted through a migrant community organization with a further 50 carried out through a range of people identified through a range of snowballing techniques and different networks.

This research is complemented by casework undertaken by the Latin American Women's Rights Service (LAWRS), which works with Latin American women living in London. LAWRS campaigns with Latin American women to empower them to pursue social, personal, and fundamental change to their lives and livelihoods, through providing information, and tools to take action. Their programs include financial literacy; prevention and support to overcome gender-based violence; employability; social inclusion and civic participation; and advocacy for greater recognition of Latin American women in local planning. Their work around violence against women includes preventative campaigns and information; advocacy, securing legal remedies, safety planning, and long-term resettlement; and psychotherapy to overcome all forms of domestic and sexual abuse, trafficking, and elder abuse.

Gender Practices and Ideologies among Latin American Migrants in London

Examination of gender ideologies among Latin American migrants in London revealed a complex picture of some profound changes in how women and men lived their lives in both positive and negative ways. While migration to London provided many women with significant opportunities vis-à-vis their previous lives, many men had to deal with considerable losses as hegemonic masculinities were continually challenged. As women and men struggled to assert and reassert themselves and deal with their new gender roles, more negative ramifications of gender transformations emerged, among which was gender-based violence and especially domestic violence.

Understanding gender ideologies among any migrant group requires some consideration of the patterns prevailing in home countries. At a very general level, gender ideologies in Latin America are dominated by the complex of machismo. Although hegemonic discourses on masculinity remain important throughout the region, it is increasingly acknowledged that machismo is flexible and malleable, just like gender ideologies more generally. This is especially true when it comes to how gender identities transform when women and men migrate as evidenced in extensive research on Latin American migrants to the United States (Hondagneu-Sotelo 2001; Pribilsky 2004).

Yet, while gender ideologies are certainly changing in Latin America, there was a general tendency among the migrants interviewed to portray gender relations as traditional, restrictive, and dominated by machismo. Here, machismo refers broadly to the ways in which men dominate women ideologically and practically in relation to "exaggerated masculinity." This entails protection and asserting control over women, sometimes violently, as well as performing virility and various "masculinized" activities such as drinking heavily and gambling (Chant with Craske 2003, 14). Adriana,[1] aged 44, from Quito in Ecuador, noted: "In my country men are always *machista* . . . there men want to dominate women or keep them in line, there are violent and aggressive men there." Although most men had a more positive interpretation of machismo back home, they agreed that gender relations were very different, reflecting strict gender divisions of labor, as Dario, 26, from Santa Cruz, Bolivia, pointed out: "Bolivia is very *machista*. There, women depend completely on men, they expect him to go out to work, to give them money, while they stay at home looking after the children."

Yet, despite these rather monolithic views and although hegemonic discourses on masculinity remain important throughout the region, machismo is also flexible and malleable (Pineda 2001). Among the respondents, there was some indication that gender identities were changing in home countries especially among more educated and middle-class migrants. For example, educated Colombian women in particular were the most likely to report positive changes. Sandra, 27, who was from Medellín, noted that she and her boyfriend had a completely equal relationship in London but that this was also the case in Colombia where she had worked as a graduate social worker on a government nutrition project. Indeed, the vast majority of women had been working or in full-time education before they migrated, with only two calling themselves housewives. On the one hand, this highlights how people uphold hegemonic gender roles in theory while in practice may carry out very different ones (McIlwaine 2010). On the other, it reflects Pessar's (2005) second set of outcomes in relation to the recognition that changes in gender regimes had occurred in home countries before people migrated.

This complex picture of traditional gender regimes was also reflected in migrants' views of how relationships between women and men changed when they migrated to London. Very generally, and reflecting Pessar's (2005) suggestion that gender ideologies are renegotiated when people migrate, women tended to speak positively about changes, while men found transformations very difficult to accept. Most women stated that their lives were more independent of men and that they had more opportunities than in their home countries.

Women's entry into the labor market is fundamental in understanding changes in gender ideologies, reflecting a central tenet of feminist thought, although the changes do not occur in clear-cut ways. Most significant was that women and men worked side-by-side in similar jobs, mainly in cleaning and catering, earning broadly comparable wages. The majority of migrants stated that it was easier for women to get jobs than men because they were "naturally" suited to cleaning work, but also because they could get higher paid jobs cleaning in houses—that was much more difficult for men. The fact that women tended to earn broadly similar wages to men with the same terms and conditions was significant for women who were accustomed to routinely earning less than men in their home countries. Women reported feeling valued as a result, as well as having financial power that had eluded them back home. For example, Helena, 38, from Bolivia, who had worked as a hairdresser in La Paz before she migrated, spoke of her various jobs cleaning in houses and offices in London:

> When I came here, I realized that I was worth a lot. He [her husband] always looked down on me, that I wasn't worth anything, but I've realized that I can work and that I can look after children on my own.

While there are certain advantages for women in London, it is essential not to romanticize the working experiences of women (or men). Cleaning and catering work is characterized by low status and low pay and is rife with exploitative working practices (see McIlwaine this volume Section 2). Most jobs are part-time, involving working unsociable hours early in the morning or late at night, creating safety issues for women in particular (two women reported being assaulted in the early hours of the morning on their way to work). Although most people were paid the National Minimum Wage (£5.35 per hour at the time of study), this was much less than the Living Wage for London (£7.20 at the time). Exploitative working practices were common especially among those without papers, including people not being paid for their work or being given large workloads (see McIlwaine, Cock, and Linneker 2011).

While men were also subject to these poor working conditions and exploitative practices, their experiences were exacerbated by having to work in feminized workplaces doing what many considered to be "women's work." Edgar, 41, from Pereira, Colombia, stated:

In my life, I had never done cleaning, but to arrive and to have to dust, to wipe, to brush-up, it affects your self-esteem, you feel really, really bad, bad because you come with the idea of improving your life.

These challenges for men strongly contributed to a reinforcement of preexisting gender inequalities as outlined by Pessar (2005) as well as the creation of new asymmetries created by the migrant experience. This was further reinforced by a perception that migrant women received preferential treatment from the British state. Not only did many think that women were more likely to get their asylum claim approved, but access to benefits, housing, and social services were seen to allow women to live independent lives or at least garner advantages over their male counterparts (see also Escrivá 2000). Indeed, experiences from LAWRS show that women speak of having greater protection and more rights in the UK as a sign of greater equality and respect for women. However, for many migrant women who were irregular, their relationship with the state actively undermined their well-being (see below).

At the level of the household itself, there was also evidence that some changes in domestic divisions of labor were taking place, albeit linked with the need to deal with the practicalities of living in London with two people working all the time. Most migrants agreed that men had to start doing housework, especially childcare, which was often viewed as the least threatening to hegemonic masculine norms (Boehm 2008). Sebastian, 40, from Palmira, Colombia, mentioned changes at home: "Now I cook, I make some really good dishes, I look after the children, sometimes I wash the dirty clothes, I mow the lawn . . . and I like doing these things." The contradictory nature of the outcomes of women's and men's well-being as a result of migrating abroad served to fuel resentment and ambivalences, some of which had a direct bearing on the emergence of gender-based violence.

Gender-Based Violence in the Home among Latin American Migrants

Although gender-based violence has been associated with the migrant experience, it is not necessarily a direct result of the migrant process per se. Instead, it has been shown to be the result of a convergence of a range of forces that cause men to abuse women within systems underpinned by patriarchal relations (Gamburd 2000, 2006; Menjívar and Salcido 2002). In the current case, one in four women reported having been subject to physical abuse at the hands of their husbands or partners, with two noting that their partners had also abused their children. Around half of the women spoke of verbal abuse by their partners.

While rates of violence against women are difficult to obtain or compare to national UK rates, LAWRS receives six to seven cases per week. Incidences span all nationalities, although it is interesting to note that some nationalities are clearly more likely to be involved in so-called sex- or marriage-tourism, trafficking, or having been groomed by Latin Americans settled in London, returning home, and promising a different or better life in the UK, only for this not to be the case after women arrived. Bolivians and Brazilians, in particular, seem to be more vulnerable to abuse (this correlates to a greater likelihood of being irregular—see McIlwaine, Cock, and Linneker 2011); but in some cases they also present severe cases of physical abuse, which may relate to attitudes in countries prior to migration. It is also very important to highlight that significant numbers of cases of gender-based violence involve perpetrators from the UK or other countries in Europe, and that violence is not confined to within the Latin American community.

There was no agreement among those interviewed that the incidence of domestic violence was more or less common in London. Three women stated explicitly that they had left their homelands in order to escape abusive partners, and most who discussed their experiences of abuse said that they had also experienced it back home. However, all women agreed that domestic violence was more hidden and more accepted in Latin America. This was partly because the state rarely intervened in cases of domestic violence (see also Alcalde 2006; Arriagada 1998). Manuela, 43, from La Paz, Bolivia, stated: "Here, if a woman gets a black eye, it's published in the press; there, you could kill a woman and nobody would do anything." Women and men recognized that the UK provided legal protection for women who had suffered gender-based violence. For example, Isabel, 32, discussed how in Colombia most women don't report domestic violence, instead suffering in silence. She noted:

> With my problem [of domestic abuse] in Colombia, I would have denounced my case and that would have been that. Here, in contrast, there was protection. Only the Home Office knew my address, he [her husband] had to continue to support my son by law. Here there are laws that protect women who have suffered domestic violence.

Most migrant women recognized that support was available from the state, the police, and specific nongovernmental organizations, although this does not guarantee that women actually seek help (see also below).

In a high proportion of cases presented at LAWRS (who see women in different stages, and often abuse arises as an issue in the "preventative stage"), women do not recognize abusive behavior, particularly emotional abuse, as violence: "He is rude and insults me, but doesn't hit me" being a comment frequently heard by a caseworker. Knowing what rights women have is one of the many barriers to women seeking help. A combination of ignorance of the law and the justice system, lack of trust in the police, and deep-rooted acceptance of violence as something women must endure make reporting abuse far removed from reality.

This recognition of much protection for those who were experiencing domestic abuse was also reported by men, although this often fuelled further resentment. One man, Eduardo, 44, from Quito, Ecuador, complained: "Women have it easy here because the government helps them. When a man abuses a woman, the state protects her . . . In contrast, men are at the last to be helped."

Furthermore, while some women certainly felt much more protected and safe because of the role of the state, this was only fully possible among those with settled immigration status and rights. It is essential to recognize that although the law criminalizes abuse against all women, many women felt completely unable to go to the police or any other state authority because of their undocumented status and in some cases because of their lack of language skills (Bui and Morash 1999; Menjivar and Salcido 2002). They were willing to put up with the abuse in order to avoid being deported back home (Erez 2000). Alba, 45, from Santa Cruz, Bolivia, was irregular and had lived for a year in a hotel room with her husband and two small children. Not only was Alba afraid to leave her hotel room for fear of being caught by the police and deported, but her husband regularly raped her.

Responses from police are typically hit-and-miss, resulting in a postcode lottery for some migrant women. The more positive cases show police departments in areas with significant Latin American populations to be proactively encouraging women to work with them (Southwark police); and others to publicly announce that immigration status will not be a concern for women disclosing violence (although in reality this should be the stance universally).

Alba's case also illustrated another situation that emerged as common among Latin American women, which was the manipulation and immigration status in order to assert power and control on the part of men (Bui and Morash 1999). It is widely acknowledged that UK immigration policy views women migrants as dependants of men rather than individuals in their own right (Yuval-Davis, Anthias, and Kofman 2005). As dependents, women are much less able to report or escape domestic violence. For example, Alba's husband was a British citizen, yet he had advised his wife and children to come to the UK on tourist visas and allowed them to expire. Alba felt that her husband did this on purpose in order to be able to control her. In another case, Helena from Bolivia (see above) was dependent on her husband's student visa (along with her two children) despite the fact that she was officially his financial sponsor. Although her husband did not actually study but worked full-time as a janitor in a hotel, she had to prove to the Home Office that she had the funds in order to support him. They had a very difficult relationship that involved both verbal and physical abuse, yet, she couldn't leave him because of her dependent status. She was willing to stay with him and endure the abuse for her children's sake.

From the perspective of LAWRS, this was also an important issue that it saw through its casework—immigration as an excuse for abuse was a key vantage point for many men, irrespective of their partner's actual status (threats to have women deported, hiding their passports, not renewing their papers, or reporting them to the authorities are incredibly common and instill fear in women to not report the violence). Equally, the threat of having their children removed (especially where the abuser has a "more" settled migration status) is enough for women to retreat from reporting violence, or to call and ask for more information on her rights.

Once women are informed, however, this knowledge can be extremely powerful, and in many instances (particularly where women are irregular), it is used to prevent abuse, threaten a violent partner with legal action, or for women to take direct action and pursue justice.

As to the causes of domestic abuse, women were in agreement that violence was rooted in the nature of patriarchal relations, coupled with a combination of external circumstances, such as women and men's labor force participation in the same occupational sectors with similar conditions, and the pressures of exclusion and discrimination that are part of being a migrant in the UK (Das Dasgupta 2005; Menjívar and Salcido 2002). In particular, the disempowerment of men and the empowerment of women through their paid employment and perceived preferential access to state benefits caused some men to assert themselves in violent ways. The practicalities of men and women working at different times and living in overcrowded housing lead some men to react violently. Rosa, 42, from Santa Cruz, Bolivia, experienced severe daily violence at the hands of her husband for three years after they migrated to London. Although her husband had always been violent, the conditions they found themselves in London made the violence worse. Rosa noted that the abuse was ultimately about power and that her husband felt disempowered in London, thus exacerbating the violence:

> The power of money and because men in Bolivia are accustomed to hit women with no comeback. They come here, they fear the police and realize it's not a game. But they also lose power. It made him even worse . . . Women begin to earn some money which they are not used to, they start to become more independent, to do what they want and then partnerships begin to disintegrate.

While not talking about their experiences directly, men discussed how these types of situations left them embittered. As Pedro, a Peruvian man in one of the focus groups, noted:

> For those who come with their wives, here women don't know how to value men and in their work they take value from men. A point arrives when they don't value men at all and instead of helping them, they criticize.

Women have different perspectives, however. Eva is a user at LAWRS. She left violence in Colombia, to come to London. Only after arriving in London, with all the changes in circumstance and status that it brings, her husband began to control her—he would stop her from going out, from learning English, or from making friends. When she had a child, he couldn't stand their baby's cries, so he would scream at her and beat her up until he got tired. She had been so controlled and beaten she could barely walk. She repeatedly visited LAWRS, but the fear of harming her husband, or of what he would do to her, made it a long process before she finally broke the cycle.

The process of seeking help from health or other support services was fundamentally affected by immigration status (see also Salcido and Adelman 2004). Not only were irregular migrants very wary of associating with anyone they did not know extremely well, but those who did have regular immigration status or residency were often reluctant to have any dealings with irregular migrants for fear of being inadvertently stigmatized. Furthermore, the complexities of migration status concern the recourses women have, but also the ability of the authorities to adequately respond to the plight of irregular survivors of violence. Until very recently, women on spouse visas had no recourse to public funds, even when faced with domestic violence, meaning they had no right to a space in a refuge, emergency shelter, housing, or benefits—the state effectively criminalizing violence on the one hand, while on the other punishing victims by disallowing them any real protection. Recent government changes (following campaigns by migrant women's and women's organizations) now allow for spouses to claim public funds in cases of violence—although this must be proven. However this still leaves irregular women, older family dependents, and students with no access to state support other than to claim justice or have the perpetrator arrested. This is complicated by the fact that many women still do not want to harm their partner.

From the perspective of LAWRS, the value of women's lives weighs in much less than the financial cost of protection where the state is concerned. Authorities bend over backwards to avoid providing shelter (witnessed ever more as anti-immigration feelings are stirred, and then government cutbacks hit) for those irregular women they have a duty to protect. These are women with children who should be protected as a duty of care for the children in order to conserve their own funds. Indeed, some social service departments now house immigration officers for just such cases. In these instances, migrant women's organizations are vital to providing support for women who have nowhere else to turn to. Their contacts, networks, and resources (for safe housing, benevolent or emergency funds) and intricate knowledge of the impact of migration status on domestic violence and the law are crucial for safeguarding women who most other agencies turn away, be it out of lack of knowledge or duty. The following case is a case in point.

Violeta came to the UK on a tourist visa, to join her mother, stepfather (a UK resident), and the couple's child. She was abused and raped by her stepfather repeatedly, eventually becoming pregnant. When she sought help from social services, their response was that they could do nothing, as she had no recourse to public funds. She was given the same response by a women's refuge organization who were unable to fund her a place. It was several years before she managed to get help. Eventually, an immigration solicitor referred her to LAWRS, which, within three days, secured her counseling, a specialist solicitor, who obtained an occupation order to remove the stepfather from the house, and a court ruling for her abuser to pay maintenance and rent for the children.

Although some women reported positive experiences with the authorities in terms of response to gender-based violence, they were all regular migrants. Most irregular migrants either did not report it or, if they did call the police during an attack, failed to follow through with charges. In the case of Rosa, the police offered to prosecute her husband and to facilitate his deportation to Bolivia, yet, she refused because she didn't want her children to be left without a father. Therefore, while increased independence can provide women with more opportunities to assert themselves, this did not always translate into seeking help in situations of abuse or following through with this help, although all but one of the women who experienced abuse left their partners (Erez 2000).

More specifically, from LAWRS's perspective, women seek support from the organization at various stages of their experiences of abuse, ranging from seeking information, with which to arm themselves for decisions they will make later and to (in many instances successfully) prevent further abuse from occurring. The lack of apparent action in some cases translates into action further down the line for some women, while for others the knowledge that they can disprove their partners' threats, or effectively threaten them with redress, seems to be enough for the short-term. Many women also seek support from organizations when they have tried all other remedies and found no support, or ironically, are referred from the authorities themselves—in these instances such organizations can be crucial to providing the escape needed (Raj and Silverman 2002; Walton-Roberts 2008).

Conclusions

This chapter has attempted to shed some light on the gendered power relations that can result in gender-based violence among a much-neglected population group. Drawing on qualitative empirical research with female and male migrants as well as casework examples from LAWRS, the discussion has highlighted how understanding gender-based violence among this group, especially domestic abuse, requires an in-depth understanding of how gendered power relations are reconfigured with the migration process and subsequent settlement. Recalling Pessar's typology of outcomes, it has shown that women experience both gains and losses through their migration. Some dimensions of gender ideologies have undergone fundamental restructuring in positive ways especially in relation to changing domestic divisions of labor. Yet some gender inequalities have been reinforced or recreated as a result of migration mainly linked with migrant men coming to terms with threats to hegemonic masculinities, which leads some men to resort to violence as their only route to assert power and control.

This also suggests that addressing gender-based violence and domestic abuse requires much greater recognition and understanding of the lives of migrants. In line with existing research on domestic violence among immigrant groups elsewhere, it is not necessarily the case that the incidence of abuse is higher, but that the migrant experience can create a range of exclusions that can make it more difficult to deal with domestic abuse in relation in particular to immigration status. As Menjívar and Salcido (2002, 900) note: "Women's experiences of domestic violence [are] intimately linked to broader structural forces—political, economic, social—for these create multiple layers of oppression and hierarchies within which immigrant women's lives are enacted." It appears that the key to reducing domestic abuse among Latin American migrants in the future is to tap into some of the positive changes and foster them in order to ameliorate the negative dimensions that can result in gender-based violence, while simultaneously encouraging the government to protect women living in the UK regardless of their immigration status.

Acknowledgments

We would like to thank the Leverhulme Trust who funded the research project on which this chapter is based. We are also grateful to Flor Alba Robayo and Carolina Velasquez for their research assistance.

Note

1. All names are pseudonyms.

References

Alcalde, M. Cristina. 2006. "Migration and Class as Constraints in Battered Women's Attempts to Escape Violence in Lima Peru." *Latin American Perspectives* 33 (6): 147–64.

Anthias, Floya, and Gabriela Lazaridis. 2000. "Introduction: Women on the Move in Southern Europe." In *Gender and Migration in Southern Europe: Women on the Move*, ed. Floya Anthias and Gabriela Lazaridis, 1–14. Oxford: Berg.

Arriagada, Irma. 1998. "Latin American Families: Convergences and Divergences in Models and Policies." *CEPAL Review* 65:85–102.

Barker, Gary T. 2005. *Dying to be Men: Youth and Masculinity and Social Exclusion*. London: Routledge.

Beckett, Claire, and Marie Macey. 2001. "Race, Gender and Sexuality: The Oppression of Multiculturalism. *Women's Studies International Forum* 24 (3–4): 309–19.

Boehm, Deborah. A. 2008. "'Now I Am a Man and a Woman!' Gendered Moves and Migrations in a Transnational Mexican Community. *Latin American Perspectives* 35 (1): 16–30.

Bui, Hoan N. and Merry Morash. 1999. "Domestic Violence in the Vietnamese Immigrant Community: An Exploratory Study. *Violence Against Women* 5 (7): 769–95.

Carlisle, Frances. 2006. "Marginalisation and Ideas of Community among Latin American Migrants to the UK." *Gender and Development* 14 (2): 235–45.

Chant, Sylvia, with Nikki Craske. 2003. *Gender in Latin America*. London: Latin America Bureau.

Das Dasgupta, Shamita, 2005. "Women's Realities: Defining Violence against Women by Immigration, Race and Class. In *Domestic Violence at the Margins: Readings on Race, Class, Gender, and Culture*, ed. Natalie J. Sokoloff, Christina Pratt, and Beth E. Richie, . Rutgers, 56–70. New Brunswick, NJ: University Press.

Datta, Kavita, Cathy McIlwaine, Yara Evans, Jo Herbert, Jon May, and Jane Wills. 2009. "Men on the Move: Narratives of Migration and Work among Low Paid Migrant Men in London." *Social and Cultural Geography* 10 (8): 853–73.

Erez, Edna. 2000. Immigration, Culture Conflict and Domestic Violence: Woman Battering. *Crime Prevention and Community Safety: An International Journal* 2:27–36.

Escrivá, Angeles. 2000. "The Position and Status of Migrant Women in Spain." In *Gender and Migration in Southern Europe: Women on the Move*, eds. Floya Anthias and Gabriela Lazaridis, 199–226. Berg: Oxford.

Gamburd, Michele R. 2000. *The Kitchen Spoon's Handle: Transnationalism and Sri Lanka's Migrant Housemaids*. Ithaca, NY: Cornell University Press.

Gill, Aisha, and Gulshun Rehman. 2004. "Empowerment through Activism: Responding to Domestic Violence in the South Asian Community in London." *Gender and Development* 12 (1): 75–82.

Gutmann, Mathew C. 2004. "Dystopian Travels in Gringolandia: Engendering Ethnicity among Mexican Migrants to the United States." *Ethnicities* 4 (4): 477–500.

Heise, Lori, Jaqueline Pitanguy, and Adrienne Germain 1994. *Violence against Women: The Hidden Health Burden*. Washington, D.C.: World Bank,

Hondageu-Sotelo, Pierette. 2001. *Doméstica: Immigrant Workers Cleaning and Caring in the Shadow of Affluence*. Berkeley: University of California Press.

Hondagneu-Sotelo, Pierette, and Michael A. Messner. 1999. "Gender Displays and Men's Power: The 'New Man' and the 'Mexican Immigrant Man.' In *American Families: A Multicultural Reader*, eds. Stephanie Coontz, Maya Parson, and Gabrielle Raley, 342–58. London: Routledge.

Kim, Nadia Y. 2006. "Patriarchy Is So Third World: Korean Immigrant Women and 'Migrating' White Western Masculinity." *Social Problems* 53 (4): 519–36.

Macey, Marie. 1999. "Religion, Male Violence and the Control of Women: Pakistani Muslim Men in Bradford." *Gender and Development* 7 (1): 48–55.

Mahler, Sarah J. and Patricia R. Pessar. 2006. "Gender Matters: Ethnographers Bring Gender from the Periphery toward the Core of Migration Studies." *International Migration Review* 40 (1): 27–63.

McIlwaine, Cathy. 2008. "Gender- and Age-Based Violence." In *The Companion to Development Studies*, eds. Vandana Desai and Robert Potter, 445–49. London: Arnold.

———. 2010. "Migrant Machismos: Exploring Gender Ideologies and Practices among Latin American Migrants in London from a Multi-Scalar Perspective." *Gender, Place and Culture* 17 (3): 281–300.

McIlwaine, Cathy, Juan Camilo Cock, and Brian Linneker. 2011. *No Longer Invisible: The Latin American Community in London*. London: Trust for London. (Available at: http://www.geog.qmul.ac.uk/docs/research/latinamerican/48637.pdf) (accessed May 20, 2011).

Menjívar, Cecilia. 1999. "The Intersection of Work and Gender: Central American Immigrant Women and Employment in California." *American Behavioral Scientist* 42 (4): 601–27.

Menjívar, Cecilia, and Salcido, Olivia. 2002. "Immigrant Women and Domestic Violence: Common Experiences in Different Countries. *Gender and Society* 16 (6): 898–920.

Parreñas, R. 2001. *Servants of Globalization: Women, Migration, and Domestic Work*. Stanford, CA: Stanford University Press.

Pessar, Patricia. 2005. "Women, Gender, and International Migration across and beyond the Americas: Inequalities and Limited Empowerment." *Expert Group Meeting on International Migration and Development in Latin America and the Caribbean* (available from: http://www.un.org/esa/population/publications/IttMigLAC/P08_PPessar.pdf accessed February 1, 2009).

Pessar, Patricia R., and Sarah Mahler. 2003. "Transnational Migration: Bringing Gender In. *International Migration Review* 3:812–46.

Pickup, Francine, with Suzanne Williams and Caroline Sweetman. 2001. *Ending Violence against Women: A Challenge for Development and Humanitarianism*. Oxfam: Oxford.

Pineda, Javier. 2001. "Partners in Women-Headed Households: Emerging Masculinities? In *Men at Work: Labour, Masculinities, Development*, ed. Cecile Jackson, 72–92. London: Routledge.

Pribilsky, Jason. 2004. "'Aprendemos a Convivir': Conjugal Relations, Co-Parenting and Family Life among Ecuadorian Transnational Migrants in New York City and the Ecuadorian Andes. *Global Networks* 4 (3): 313–34.

Raj, Anita, and Jay Silverman. 2002. "Violence against Immigrant Women: The Roles of Culture, Context, and Legal Immigrant Status on Intimate Partner Violence. *Violence Against Women* 8 (3): 367–98.

Salcido, Olivia, and Madelaine Adelman. 2004. "'He Has Me Tied with the Blessed and Damned Papers": Undocumented-Immigrant Battered Women in Phoenix, Arizona." *Human Organization* 63 (2): 162–172.

Walton-Roberts, Margaret. 2008. Weak ties, immigrant women and neoliberal states: Moving beyond the public/private binary." *Geoforum* 39 (1): 499-510.

WHO 2005. *Multi-Country Study on Women's Health and Domestic Violence against Women*. Geneva: World Health Organization.

Yuval-Davis, Nira, Floya Anthias, and Eleonore Kofman. 2005. "Secure Borders and Safe Haven and the Gendered Politics of Belonging: Beyond Social Cohesion. *Ethnic and Racial Studies* 28 (3): 513–35.

Zentgraf, Kristine M. 2002. Immigration and Women's Empowerment: Salvadorans in Los Angeles. *Gender and Society* 16 (5): 625–46.

Chapter 10

Latin American Commercial Spaces and the Formation of Ethnic Publics in London: The Case of the Elephant and Castle

Juan Camilo Cock

The year 2010 was a presidential election year in Colombia and it was a tight presidential race. The Colombian diaspora in London had not been very active in elections in the past, but on this occasion a group of migrants got together to campaign heavily for one of the candidates. It was a group made up mostly of students and professionals who met through Facebook and decided to organize a campaign for the Green Party's candidate. They quickly realized that if they wanted to have any impact they would have to find ways of reaching the Colombian population in London, to which they had limited access. The key question they asked themselves was: where could they find Colombians in London? They concluded that the way to achieve this was to actively campaign in the places where Colombians gathered, and two key places to do this were the Elephant and Castle and Seven Sisters, two of the most important commercial spaces used by Colombian migrants in the city. Even though their candidate lost the presidential race in the end, he was the winner in London. The leaders of the campaign agreed that reaching out to people in the Colombian areas and meeting face to face with "the community" had been a key success factor in their campaign.

A year earlier, the Colombian foreign affairs minister had visited London and as part of his visit attended a meeting with the Colombian community organized in a hall in Chelsea. At the meeting, two traders stood up and asked the minister to support their campaign to save the Seven Sisters market. This market in north London is occupied mostly by Latin American traders and has been dubbed by them the "Pueblito Paisa" in reference to an area of Colombia from where many of the traders originate. The market was (and still is at the time of writing) under threat of being demolished to make way for a housing development and there is an ongoing campaign among the traders and the local community to save it. The Latin American shops in the Elephant and Castle, an area of south London, were similarly under threat (and still are) due to a redevelopment plan. The campaigners noted that not only did the markets provide employment to many Colombian traders but that they were community hubs and a "part of Colombia in London." The minister said that he was aware of the campaign, pledged his support, and commented that people like them showed the enterprise and leadership of Colombians abroad. However, a few minutes later another of the participants at the meeting made the remark to the minister that Colombians were not only found in Elephant and Castle and Seven Sisters and that there were lots of them in other areas of the city. Sounding aggrieved, she argued that Colombians in London should not be reduced to what happens in those two areas.

These two vignettes highlight some of the ambivalent relations between place and an ethnic community for Colombian, and more generally Latin American, migrants in London. On the one hand, clearly there are spaces in London that have become important social arenas for a large number of the Colombian migrant population and have achieved a visibility among Colombians and the wider population. On the other hand, many people feel excluded from these spaces and resent the relationship between community and spaces that is constructed through them.

In this chapter, I examine the role that places within the city play in creating a sense of community and identity among Latin Americans migrant in London. The chapter is based on ethnographic research through participant observation in these spaces and on 62 interviews with Colombian migrants between 2006 and 2008.

Ethnicity and Place in Migrant-Receiving Cities

At the heart of the relationship between places, identity, and community is the idea of ethnicity as a social phenomenon in which groups of people are differentiated according to a shared origin or culture (Eriksen 1993). The concrete manifestations of ethnicity vary significantly and can refer to various aspects of social life. In this sense, ethnicity can refer to at least three related but distinct phenomena (Anthias 1992; Jenkins 1997). First, it can refer to a form of categorization based on shared origin or culture. Thus, the state and individuals within a society use "ethnic" categories to identify other individuals according to ethnic criteria. A second use refers to a form of self-identification based on ethnic criteria. Thus individuals may identify themselves as members of an ethnic group regardless of how others perceive them. The third element refers to the concretion of social groups based on ethnic criteria. This refers to putting to actual use the perceived belonging to an ethnic group by forming social networks or other social structures based on these criteria. This is what is commonly referred to as the ethnic group or the ethnic community, an actual social formation based on ethnicity.

For migrants, the emergence of a sense of ethnicity is often a part of their process of incorporation into the new society over time. The salience and reach of a sense of ethnicity may be temporary in some cases, while for other groups it extends over time for a number of generations in various domains of economic and social life. It is also a phenomenon that happens alongside other processes such as integration (or assimilation) and transnationalism with different segments of a social group moving in different directions simultaneously, or with a group moving in one direction in one domain of social life and in another direction in other domains (Morawska 2003; Alba and Nee 2003).

The sense of ethnicity is often tied to a relationship with places. Most often this connection manifests itself in the connection between "a people" and "a territory" (Gupta and Ferguson 1997). However, in the context of cities it is also present in the association between ethnic groups and parts of a city. One form of this association is that of ethnic enclaves or ghettos—areas of a city where one cultural and social group dominates. However, this is not the only form of association between place and ethnicity in the contemporary city, and the notion of ethnic neighborhoods itself has come under close scrutiny. In many cities, "ethnic neighborhoods" are not as homogenous as many people believe, and they contain a diverse set of relations within and across ethnic groups (Baumann 1996).

In a city like London there are no clear physical lines dividing one ethnic area from another. For ethnic groups, however, certain areas and specific locations within them do play important symbolic and social roles in their sense of ethnicity. Therefore, ethnic space within the city "needs to be conceptualized not as territory or circumscribed locality but as networked and socially produced" (Werbner 2001, 673).

The specific spaces where ethnic discourses and identities emerge have different forms and can include community organizations, temples and other faith spaces, public spaces, and commercial spaces. These spaces are key to the formation of a sense of ethnicity because they are publicly and collectively accessible, and they generate representations of those that are part of them.

An emerging sense of ethnicity is the product of a dialectic process of collective representations and the positionality of individuals in relation to those representations. Different individuals relate to different conceptions of the ethnic group in varied ways. It is a political process in which differing views are confronted, resisted, and negotiated. It is also a communicational process. Different versions of who is part of the group and what characterizes the group vie for acceptance within the group by its members and outside the group by mainstream actors. Ethnicity in this sense can be thought of as a manifestation of a public.

When thinking about ethnic groups in cities the notion of publics can be useful. Craig Calhoun has defined publics as "self-organizing fields of discourse in which participation is not based primarily on personal connections and is always in principle open to strangers. A public sphere comprises an indefinite number of more or less overlapping publics, some ephemeral, some enduring, and some shaped by struggle against the dominant organization of others" (2002, 162). He then states that publics can facilitate the formation of social relations: "engagement in public life establishes social solidarity partly through enhancing the significance of particular categorical identities and partly through facilitating the creation of direct social relations" (ibid.). The utility of the idea of an ethnic public lies in the fact that it is not an essentialist concept. People do not belong to a public naturally nor do they dictate the behavior of those who are a part of it. Rather, discourses are open to participation and, in the case of ethnicity these discourses rely on the idea of a common origin or belonging.

Ethnic spaces are important for the formation of an ethnic public in two ways. First, they create a space for people with a shared origin to come together, interact socially, and publicly discuss and debates ideas, including those about themselves as a group. Second, they become part of the representation of the ethnic group itself. Through the aesthetics of the spaces, the activities that happen in them, their naming practices, and the people they attract, these spaces become an important part of the discourse of the ethnic group (see Cock 2009).

In the remainder of the chapter I focus on how one type of space, commercial spaces, has become an important arena for the emergence of discourses of ethnicity for migrants coming from Latin America living in London and how different people relate to them.

Commercial Spaces as Social Spaces

Research on commercial activities among migrants has tended to focus on ethnic entrepreneurship and its effects in the economic integration of migrant populations rather than on social and cultural relations that arise from them. Despite this, many of the benefits of ethnic enclaves lie less with economics than with enabling networks that cut across class distinctions and provide a meeting point for dispersed migrants where valuable information is exchanged and opportunities shared (Zhou 2004).

Therefore, the spaces created by ethnic entrepreneurs, especially by businesses aimed at having a clientele made up of coethnics, are not just arenas of economic activity but also social and representational spaces. Businesses that cater to coethnics are spaces of consumption, an issue that is also often neglected in the ethnic entrepreneurship literature but that has received a growing amount of attention in the past few decades in several disciplines, not least geography (see Miller 1994; Crewe 2000; Jackson and Thrift 1995; Kneale and Dwyer 2004 for reviews).

One interesting strand of consumption studies has focused on the spaces where consumption happens (Goss 1993; Miller et al. 1998) and has looked not just at the transactions happening within them but at the social interactions in these spaces (Miller et al. 1998). Commercial spaces often become representational spaces that are identified with particular groups. This generates particular reactions both from wider society and from members of the ethnic group (Dávila 2004; Garbin 2008; Lin 1998).

In examining shopping spaces and identity, Miller et al. (1998) found that for several ethnic groups in London the spaces where shopping occurred had a strong relationship with their ethnic identity: "For many people terms such as Cypriots, Asian and Jewish were of importance not simply as background classifications evoked by relevant questions, but were categories which many people expected would and should stand for particular styles of interaction with the two shopping centers under study" (Miller et al. 1998, 159).

They also found that this relationship was one that was related to the process of settlement, with groups developing a stronger sense of ethnicity tied to space as they settled in the new location: "For such groups, as long as their orientation remains focused upon a site abroad, local sites have little implication for identity. Rather their identity is mainly affected by their sense of difference from the local population. It is only when they become immigrant as against merely diasporic groups that this situation changes" (Miller et al. 1998, 164).

More recently, Rabikowska and Burrell (2009) considered the use of food shops by Polish migrants in the UK and found that these as well as Polish food in mainstream shops were important identity markers. However, they found that there was little social interaction in the shops themselves, and that the association between food and identity was carried out mostly in the private space of home.

The connection between consumption and identity happens at different levels. While Polish migrants emphasize their individual identity, for other groups, such as those studied by Miller and his colleagues, the collective identity and social function of the shopping spaces is emphasized. In the case of Latin Americans in London, I argue that both these tendencies are evident. On the one hand, commercial spaces play a wider role than the transactions that occur within them, becoming associated with the identities of many and providing an arena for social and cultural interaction. On the other hand, many migrants do not develop this sort of relationship, and in some cases they actively distance themselves from it.

Latin American Commercial Spaces in London

In the decade since the year 2000, two places in London have become most commonly identified as "Colombian/Latin American" areas of the city: the Elephant and Castle south of the river Thames and Seven Sisters in the North (see figures 10.1 and 10.2). They are recognized as such by many Colombian and other Latin American migrants but also increasingly by local authorities, politicians, the wider local population, and the media. However, these areas are not ethnic neighborhoods. Latin Americans in fact live spread across the city and, although there are concentrations in the neighborhoods around these two places, Latin Americans do not make up anywhere near the majority of the population there. These are, rather, very multicultural areas of London, with a variety of different ethnic groups sharing the same space. What marks them as "Latin American" is the agglomeration of commercial spaces owned by and aimed at Latin American migrants as well as the recurrent use of local public and community spaces for gatherings and faith meetings. The Elephant and Castle and Seven Sisters undoubtedly concentrate a wide variety of specialized services and events in a way that is not found in other areas of the city.

Figure 10.1 La Bodeguita, Elephant and Castle Shopping Centre, London (photo by Juan Camilo Cock)

In this chapter the focus will be on the Elephant and Castle. This is an area located more or less equidistant from the political center of Westminster, the commercial center of the West End, and the financial center of the City of London. Its main feature is its position as a confluence of major transport routes from across south London leading towards the northern side of the river. It is therefore one of the busiest transport hubs in the city, funneling and distributing thousands of commuters every day. Historically, it has been a working class area but also an entertainment hub with music halls, theatres, and cinemas. Following widespread destruction by bombs during World War II, new roads were laid out, the housing stock replaced with high-rise housing estates, and London's first urban shopping center built in 1965.

However, the area has not aged well and has been cited as an example of the failure of postwar architecture, with low-quality housing, busy roads with terrible pedestrian crossings and unloved buildings. The shopping center has been voted the city's ugliest structure by the readers of London's most popular listings magazine (McAusian 2006).

Like most of inner-city London, the Elephant and Castle is today a multicultural area, its white working-class character having been transformed over the last 50 years. It is located in the London borough of Southwark, where there are also significant West African and, in more recent years, Eastern European populations. In official statistics the numbers and proportions of Latin Americans living in the area are low, although toward the higher end for London as a whole. In a recent survey it was found that Southwark and the neighboring borough of Lambeth were the areas of London where Latin Americans were most likely to be living (McIlwaine, Cock, and Linneker et al. 2011). However, overall, as noted above, the Latin American population in London is residentially dispersed, suggesting that the cluster of Latin American commercial spaces around Elephant and Castle is not due to population concentration.

The shopping center that dominates the area is mostly occupied by standard British high-street outlets such as Tesco, Iceland, and Boots, and several discount stores. However, the southern side of the upper floor of the shopping center housed the first Colombian/Latin American shops and restaurants in the area that appeared in the early 1990s, occupying previously empty units and stalls in the corridors of the mall. Around 2005, there was a Colombian restaurant, a cafeteria, and several stalls on the southern side of the shopping mall. In this area, people from different Latin American countries gathered in the afternoons and weekends.

Figure 10.2 Seven Sisters Market, London (photo by Juan Camilo Cock)

It is around the shopping mall where there is a more varied offer of outlets serving the Latin American community. Several of these followed a particular model by which an entrepreneur would take a lease or acquire a commercial property and would then make an arrangement with other entrepreneurs who would set up smaller businesses in that space. These, despite being modest in size, have become known among migrants as "shoppings," short for shopping centers. Even though they are not exclusive to Elephant and Castle, in this area there are at least six of these "shoppings," making it the area of London with the highest offer of services and goods aimed at Latin Americans.

The Latin American "Shopping"

Typically, the Latin American "shopping" in London offers several services and goods in the same space, frequently having a combination of shops/stalls including the sale of food staples, cafeterias, money transfer services, parcel sending services, hairdressers, clothes sales, jewelers, legal advice services, and DVD and music shops. The "shoppings" often have at least one area with space for sitting down and gathering and this is often a shared communal space. In some of them this is used by patrons to meet and chat but is also used for special events such as meetings and celebrations. The "shoppings" often offer services and goods to people from a variety of national origins throughout Latin America but in practice are frequently dominated by services and clients from a particular country.

Recent research has confirmed the high incidence of use of ethnic commerce among Latin American migrants. In a survey with 453 Latin American migrants, 85 percent said that they used Latin American shopping areas, and among Colombians the rate was 87 percent (McIlwaine et al. 2011). Most commonly this involved visiting restaurants, buying cooking ingredients, and sending money. Similarly, 70 percent of Latin Americans who remitted money did so from Latin American service points such as those found in the "shoppings." It is therefore clear that Colombian migrants have widespread contact with Latin American commercial spaces in one way or another.

Use of and Relations with Latin American Commercial Spaces

The ample use of Latin American commercial spaces does not mean that all those using them do so in the same way. In fact the use of and relationship to these spaces varies significantly between different migrants. For some migrants, Colombian and Latin American commercial spaces form an important part of their weekly or monthly routines even if this is exclusively to buy goods and services and without much engagement with other consumers or activities.

Carolina was such a person. Carolina had been living in London with her husband and their daughter since 2001. They had successfully claimed asylum and in 2007 had become British citizens. Carolina maintained close contact with her mother in Colombia in that she called her every week by telephone and sent her £500 pounds every month. To send the money she travelled from Lewisham in South East London to a transfer agent in one of the "shoppings" in Elephant and Castle because it was the most convenient Colombian place for her to send money from.

As well as sending money to her family, Carolina also went there to buy cooking ingredients and to send presents to Colombia or to buy music and videos. She told me how "sometimes we go out just to go to the shops. We often go to the shopping to buy Latin products. You can find everything there: music, videos, everything." However, despite frequently going to the Latin American "shopping" to send money and buy food and other products, Carolina also said she did not like the place and usually would not stay there for long: "I do not like the atmosphere, you see a lot of people I do not like. I only go to buy my things and then leave. I am not the sort of person who sits down to listen to music. I do the errands I go for and then I leave immediately."

For Carolina, Colombian commercial spaces were a key feature of the practices that kept her in constant contact with Colombia. This was especially the case because she had not travelled back home in the years since she had arrived in London; being an asylum seeker, Carolina could not leave the UK while her case was under consideration. Once she was granted asylum, even though she could leave the UK with a travel document, she could not travel to Colombia. Only recently had she become a British citizen and was looking forward to visiting her family back home. The contact Carolina kept with her family and the reproduction of her ties to them through financial support and gifts were facilitated by the services she used in the Latin American "shoppings." They also enabled her to keep updated with Colombian music and videos, and to cook food from her home country.

For people like Carolina, commercial spaces facilitated the transnational practices that kept them in contact with their families.

Commercial spaces, however, did not play an important role within their social lives in London, nor did they show any sense of identification with them. In their case, commercial spaces functioned only as a conduit for their transnational activities that had a private and familial character.

Carolina's social life was carried out in more private spaces like the homes of acquaintances where she got together with friends: "We get together to celebrate birthdays. I mean, that is what we do because we never go out to nightclubs or things like that, but our get-togethers are usually to celebrate a birthday or Christmas if our friends are in England, or we go out to the beach in the summer with a group of friends."

Social and Cultural Connections in Latin American Commercial Spaces

Other migrants used Latin American commercial spaces for their services and products but also as spaces where they could socialize and be involved in an ethnic public arena within London. This was common among a group of people I interviewed. One of them was Adriana, who had lived in London since 1993, where she had a large family, including parents, uncles, aunts, and cousins. With most of her family living in London, Adriana had few obligations in her home country and only occasionally sent some money to her mother-in-law. Despite not needing to send money or packages to Colombia, and having travelled there on several occasions, Adriana liked to frequent Colombian restaurants, shops, and nightclubs.

She said,

"I love to go to Colombian shops because I can go and eat a *buñuelo* or eat a *pandebono* [bakery products], and I feel just as if I was in Colombia. I have a lot of nostalgia for Colombia. I love Colombia and, if I could, I would live there. I love London too but my roots are Colombian and I feel strong ties to my country . . . Let's say, I go out almost every weekend, to restaurants, discos, Latin events. I don't know, you feel as if you were there in Colombia. I like our people, our traditions, our things."

For her, Latin American spaces in London were more than a way of keeping social and economic ties with people in her place of origin; they were a way of maintaining emotional and cultural ties to Colombia. She had a well-established life in London, successfully managing properties, and it would be difficult for her to start her life anew in Colombia and these commercial spaces were the next best alternative to living there. It was where she could recreate in London all those things she missed and she would use these spaces avidly, having lunch in Colombian restaurants at least once or twice every week. Adriana also followed Colombian news and popular TV programs from her house where she had Colombian TV channels. In addition, she enjoyed socializing with other Colombians in restaurants and Latin American events. For Adriana, the Latin American shops around Elephant and Castle offered, besides the circulation of physical goods and money, a place where she could reproduce and identify with cultural practices associated with Colombia.

Intensive users of commercial spaces frequent them for reasons that go beyond engaging in the use and consumption of services and products that link the UK to Colombia—they are a meeting place, a space to socialize and share information. In many "shoppings," for example, special events were organized on weekends. These ranged from parties with a regional theme to live performances of London-based Colombian or other Latin American artists, to live Colombian acts touring the UK. Special events were also organized on dates that Colombians usually mark during the year. Those who went to the regular and special events were usually the same people every weekend. They were regular customers who bought products and used services but also liked to spend some of their free time at the "shopping," interacting with the traders and with other customers.

One particular "shopping" in the Elephant and Castle frequented by Colombian migrants was located under the arches of the railway line that crosses the area. Inside the arch there was a cafeteria and grocer shop together with a DVD and CD rental place, a money transfer agent, a parcel service, a small clothes shop, and a "community adviser." In the center there were tables and chairs and in the far end a small stage. The wife of the manager explained that she viewed their "shopping" as a way of building a community. She believed that the space they set up had a role beyond selling products and services. It was a space where people could get together and discuss politics and share information and where migrants could meet other people with whom they had things in common. Christmas, for example, was a time to develop and cement the bonds between the people who frequented this shopping. The manager, along with the other traders, organized a Christmas party and a New Year's Eve celebration where the traders and some of their frequent customers took Christmas food for the celebrations. Nobody had to pay for the food or for entry to the party; everybody was contributing a different dish to the large buffet of Christmas foods. Latin American Christmas music was also played and people danced into the early hours of the morning. At the party there was a sense of nostalgia in the air.

For many Colombians, Christmas is the most important time of the year to reunite with family and friends, and many migrants make an effort to visit Colombia during this period (see figure 10.3). For many of those who did not, the celebrations in these spaces was the next best alternative. The close relationships between this group of traders and clients meant that the "shopping" was for many like a second family. This is, in effect, one of the ways that the "shopping" advertises itself, as a second home for people who are far from their families. One of their ads in the Spanish-language Latin American newspapers used to say: "If you feel lonely, come to 'shopping' X where you will feel at home."

Although in December there are a lot of events in these commercial spaces, activities are not limited to the Christmas period. In the summer of 2007, the manager, together with the owners of several

Figure 10.3   Christmas celebrations at Elephant and Castle (photo by Juan Camilo Cock)

Figure 10.4 A Latin American football tournament (photo by Juan Camilo Cock)

other "shoppings" and Latin American businesses, organized a football championship in a south London park in the vicinity of Elephant and Castle. The teams were made up of entrepreneurs and customers and they played every Sunday for most of the summer, with crowds of up to a hundred people coming to watch. When the tournament was finished, the winners received a trophy, and there was a celebration back in one of the "shoppings" (see figure 10.4).

Not all the social activities held in these spaces were leisure activities. A group of traders and some customers at the "shopping" also organized a self-help finance group called a *cadena* (chain), which is a very simple form of rotating credit. These cadenas are well known but not too common among this group who lack access to mainstream financial services. There are numerous stories of people running away with the money and not fulfilling their obligations, and people often feel weary of joining one. However, knowing one another through the "shopping" was enough to generate the trust among these customers and traders to participate in this type of arrangement, which in other contexts could have been hampered by mistrust. More recently, following a series of devastating floods in Colombia during 2010, people from one of the affected towns organized a music and talent show at the "shopping," to raise funds for the flood relief. The event was organized with more than a hundred attendees, and all the proceeds sent back to the town.

Another role of commercial spaces was helping in the diffusion of information among Colombian and Latin American migrants. Sometimes this was done informally; in parties and during the day people who were looking for work shared information about job opportunities in that people who knew that a company was hiring people would inform others. In other cases, the diffusion of information was made through other means. Event promoters advertised their events with fliers and posters in Latin American shops and "shoppings," and they used some of the shops as outlets to sell tickets for events.

Latin American restaurants, shops, and "shoppings" were also the main form of distribution of the three main Spanish-language Latin American free newspapers at the time in London. Most migrants picked up the newspapers in these commercial spaces when doing errands. Some even reported going to a shop or restaurant just to pick up a copy of the paper whenever they were passing by. The newspapers therefore relied on commercial spaces to reach their audiences. At the same time, the businesses within the commercial spaces used the papers to advertise their products and services with both creating a Latin American reading public and clientele base.

Figure 10.5   A procession on its way to the Carnaval del Pueblo (photo by Juan Camilo Cock)

Similarly, meetings and rallies are frequently held in some of the commercial spaces around the Elephant and Castle. In this particular "shopping," one activist organized meetings between the "Latin American community" and public service providers such as the police and transport for London. It has also been used as the starting point for the parade of the largest Latin American themed festival in London, the Carnaval del Pueblo (see figure 10.5).

In some cases, the public meetings were convened by activists leading campaigns for the ethnic recognition of Latin American migrants. These campaigns have taken different approaches to the question of the appropriate category, with one camp looking for the category "Iberian-American" and another camp the category "Latin American." For many of their activities and meetings, it was the commercial spaces in the area that provided the arena for debate.

In summary, for some migrants Colombian commercial spaces play an important social and cultural role. For many it is there where they remember and reproduce aspects of their countries of origin and keep up-to-date with new developments in popular culture. They are also spaces where they establish strong interpersonal links of friendship. But they also play a wider role as community hubs in terms of providing support through activities such as cadenas or as spaces where Latin Americans can interact with public service providers. The owners and managers of these spaces make an effort to turn these spaces into places where a sense of community is formed, and they perceive themselves as playing a role as community builders. Through these multiple leisure, commercial, and communal activities, they have become a social hub for Colombian and other Latin American migrants.

In the current UK context of diminishing public investment in community centers and the questioning of funding for single ethnicity groups, migrants have to create their own spaces for communal activities with limited public support. In this context, for relatively recent communities such as the Latin American, commercial spaces provide an arena where alongside commercial transactions there are other social and cultural activities organized on an ethnic basis.

"Colombia Isn't That": Ambivalence toward Ethnic Spaces

As in Carolina's case, not everyone shares the outright enthusiasm for Latin American commercial spaces exhibited by some. While for some migrants they have become important social spaces and many identified with them, a common attitude was one of ambivalence. They are valued for the products they sell and the services they offer, but at the same time many feel fear or apprehension. In other cases, people reject the image they project, contrasting this "bad" image of Colombia with other "good" images that they have from home or from other spaces in London itself.

Some associate these spaces with poverty and marginality, often the conditions that migrants were trying to leave behind when leaving their country of origin. Carlos was one of them. When I met him, he was 26 years old, having arrived in London in 1999 at the age of 19. He lived undocumented for some time, working as a cleaner and washing up dishes at a restaurant but eventually managed to legalize his status when he married his Danish girlfriend, whom he later divorced. Carlos studied and learned English and then managed to land a job in the marketing department of an international magazine. He used to frequent Colombian commercial spaces in his first years in London and when I met him he still did, especially because his Colombian girlfriend liked to go there, but he had a negative perception of them:

> "I think [Colombian places in London] are hell-holes. I will tell you this in a simple way, I think they are the recollection of the worst

qualities of Colombia. I think it is the worst image that Colombia can have abroad . . . It's terrible because Colombia isn't that. Colombia is not those stalls that look like a shanty town, as if they were just scraping a living. Colombia is more than that. I think it is a very intimidating place. It is a place where from the moment you arrive you are being observed, in a good or bad way. It is a place where you know that good things cannot be occurring very often. It is dark things more probably, ugly business and hidden things. I do not think it is a nice place, it is a place where you have to be careful."

Another interviewee, Carolina, mentioned earlier, shared this view of Colombian spaces in London:

"I don't like them. Sometimes I tell my husband that in England there is a lot of money and you have more chances to have a better life, these places should not be so poor. I mean, you can't even compare it with our country because over there they keep the shops in a nice state."

There is a class dimension to these views of marginality because some migrants associate these spaces with working-class migrants who come from lower income and educational backgrounds in Colombia. Migrants hailing from the upper-middle classes and some of those with professional education can sometimes look at these spaces with scorn. For them they represent what in Colombia is frequently referred to as popular culture. Popular in this context means the cultural practices and artistic forms of the mass of low-income working-class people.

Rosario, who worked as a cleaner in London, but in Colombia was a graduate and was involved in development work, expressed this view: "[Elephant and Castle] is where you find a lot of popular [meaning poor or working class] people, the most popular from our countries . . . I do not see people from the middle or upper classes in those places." Another interviewee, Alicia, who had a similar background having been a professional in Colombia yet worked cleaning homes in London, shared this view:

"Elephant and Castle is a terrible place. It is a place of gossip, you cannot find progressive people there. It is a good place to make contacts for a lot of people who need to find work or someone or some sort of help. I never go to Elephant, which is an area of a lot of Latin Americans. I do not have an anxiety or interest to go and see Latin American people, of talking to them. I don't do it. I do not feel right doing it."

For these people, the activities, aesthetic, and narratives of Colombian commercial spaces in Elephant and Castle did not provide an ethnic discourse that was appealing, and they often constructed a sense of identity in opposition to those areas. It was this same sentiment that was expressed by the woman in the meeting with the minister who was concerned with the idea that the Elephant and Castle and Seven Sisters were the representation of the Colombian community in London. In their cases, other narratives of being Colombian in London are constructed through their individual stories, rather than through a collective community.

Conclusion

Even though surveys suggest that a majority of Colombians and Latin Americans living in London use or have used the commercial spaces set up to cater to them as an ethnic group, the relationships that different people create with these spaces are conflicting. The spaces that entrepreneurs have created in London to serve the Colombian and Latin American population have become an important source of goods and services but give rise to different patterns of use and appropriation. Their role as commercial areas coexists alongside their role as spaces where a Colombian/Latin American community takes form in London through sporting activities, celebrations, the sharing of employment opportunities, and support groups such as the cadenas. A sense of a group arises from the social interaction in these ethnic spaces.

But this conflicts with the identities of other Colombians in the city and is challenged by them in their personal accounts and in public meetings. Clearly, these spaces have become an important element of the representation of the Colombian and Latin American community in London, but while for some this is a cause to celebrate, for others it is a representation that is avoided and rejected. As a population they do not feel interpolated by the discourse taking form in these places, and they decide to construct their identity apart from the ethnic social structures that take form in these spaces and the collective representations they generate.

Acknowledgments

I would like to thank Queen Mary, University of London for the doctoral studentship that funded this research and the Central Research Fund of the University of London that funded part of the fieldwork.

References

Alba, Richard D., and Victor Nee. 2003. *Remaking the American Mainstream: Assimilation and Contemporary Immigration.* Cambridge, MA: Harvard University Press.

Anthias, Floya. 1992. *Ethnicity, Class, Gender, and Migration: Greek-Cypriots in Britain.* Aldershot, UK: Avebury.

Baumann, Gerd. 1996. *Contesting Culture: Discourses of Identity in Multi-Ethnic London, Cambridge Studies in Social and Cultural Anthropology.* Cambridge: Cambridge University Press.

Calhoun, Craig. 2002. "Imagining Solidarity: Cosmopolitanism, Constitutional Patriotism, and the Public Sphere." *Public Culture* 14 (1): 147–71.

Cock, Juan Camilo. 2009. "Colombian Migrants, Latin American Publics: Ethnicity and Transnational Practices amongst Colombian Migrants in London." PhD thesis, London: Geography Department, Queen Mary University of London.

Crewe, Louise. 2000. "Geographies of Retailing and Consumption." *Progress in Human Geography* 24 (2): 275–90.

Dávila, Arlene M. 2004. *Barrio Dreams: Puerto Ricans, Latinos, and the Neoliberal City.* Berkeley: University of California Press.

Eriksen, Thomas Hylland. 1993. *Ethnicity and Nationalism: Anthropological Perspectives, Anthropology, Culture, and Society.* London: Pluto Press.

Garbin, David. 2008. "A Diasporic Sense of Place: Dynamics of Spatialization and Transnational Political Fields among Bangladeshi Muslims in Britain." In *Transnational Ties: Cities, Migrations, and Identities,* ed. Michael. P. Smith and John Eade, 147–161. New Brunswick, NJ: Transaction Publishers.

Goss, Jon. 1993. "The "Magic of the Mall": An Analysis of Form, Function, and Meaning in the Contemporary Retail Built Environment." *Annals of the Association of American Geographers* 83 (1): 18–47.

Gupta, Akhil, and James Ferguson. 1997. "Culture, Power, Place: Ethnography at the End of an Era." In *Culture, Power, Place: Explorations in Critical Anthropology,* ed. Akhil Gupta and James Ferguson, 1–30, Durham, NC: Duke University Press.

Jackson, Peter, and Nigel Thrift. 1995. "Geographies of Consumption." In *Acknowledging Consumption: A Review of Studies,* ed. Daniel Miller, 203–36, London: Routledge.

Jenkins, Richard. 1997. *Rethinking Ethnicity: Arguments and Explorations.* London: SAGE.

Kneale, James, and Claire Dwyer. 2004. "Consumption." In *A Companion to Cultural Geography,* ed. James S. Duncan, Naula C. Johnson, and Richard H. Schein, 298–315, Oxford: Blackwell.

Lin, Jan. 1998. *Reconstructing Chinatown: Ethnic Enclave, Global Change.* Minneapolis: University of Minnesota Press.

McAusian, Fiona. 2006. Elephant and Castle Shopping Centre. *Time Out Magazine*, September 4, 2006.

McIlwaine, Cathy, Juan Camilo Cock, and Brian Linneker. 2011. *No Longer Invisible: The Latin American Community in London*. London: Trust for London.

Miller, Daniel. 1994. *Acknowledging Consumption: A Review of New Studies, Material Cultures*. Abingdon, UK: Routledge.

Miller, Daniel, Peter Jackson, Nigel Thrift, Beverly Holbrook, and Michael Rowlands. 1998. *Shopping, Place, and Identity*. London: Routledge.

Morawska, Ewa. 2003. Immigrant Transnationalism and Assimilation: A Variety of Combinations and the Analytic Strategy It Suggests. In *Toward Assimilation and Citizenship: Immigrants in Liberal Nation-States*, ed, Christian Joppke and Ewa Morawska, 133–76. Basingstoke, UK: Palgrave Macmillan.

Rabikowska, Marta, and Kathy Burrell. 2009. "The Material Worlds of Recent Polish Migrants: Transnationalism, Food, Shops and Home." In *Polish Migration to the UK in the "New" European Union after 2004*, ed. Kathy Burrell, 211–32. Aldershot, UK: Ashgate.

Werbner, Pnina. 2001. "Metaphors of Spatiality and Networks in the Plural City: A Critique of the Ethnic Enclave Economy Debate." *Sociology* 35 (3): 671–94.

Zhou, Min. 2004. "Revisiting Ethnic Entrepreneurship: Convergencies, Controversies, and Conceptual Advancements." *International Migration Review* 38 (3): 1040–74.

Chapter 11

Colombian Migrant Families in the North of England: Sociocultural Invisibility and Young People's Identity Strategies

Rosa Mas Giralt

Introduction

Research to date has provided important insights into the experiences of Colombian migrants in the United Kingdom (Bermúdez Torres 2003; Guarnizo 2008; McIlwaine 2005; Open Channels 1998). However, most studies have been conducted in London, where the population is larger and more organized (for example, support groups and cultural initiatives). In contrast, less is known of the experiences of Colombians who settle outside of the capital, or of their children's lives and their degree of social inclusion in the places where they live.

This chapter contributes to these areas by drawing on an exploratory project undertaken with Latin American informants and families of Colombian origin in the north of England in 2008,[1] a region where potential support networks are not as developed as in London and where shared community spaces are rare. By joining scholarship focusing on the integration experiences of second generations,[2] I consider the identity strategies of relatively isolated young people of Colombian and dual descent (Colombian-British) who live in conditions of sociocultural invisibility. I argue that, within a context characterized by a lack of opportunities to relate to fellow Colombians and reproduce their culture outside of the household and the extended family, the young participants establish friendships on the basis of shared experiences (for example, migration stories, multiple cultural backgrounds) and resort to notions of inclusive multicultural diversity in order to negotiate belonging in their localities.

The chapter starts by exploring the scholarship on the integration experiences of the children of migrants and continues by introducing the case-study with families of Colombian descent in the north of England. The next two sections present the findings of this study by exploring the sociocultural invisibility that characterizes this population in the northern regions and by considering the strategies of identification that the young participants displayed against the background of these contextual circumstances. The chapter concludes with a summary of the main contributions and related reflections.

Integration Experiences of Migrants and Their Children

Integration has been the approach favored by the UK, and many other Western immigrant-receiving countries, to conceptualize the way in which migrants and ethnic minorities incorporate into their societies (Nagel and Staeheli 2008, Phillips 2007). From a policy perspective, this term has been used to emphasize that both host society and immigrants are involved in processes of "mutual adjustment and participation" (Atfield, Brahmbhatt, and O'Toole 2007). In the UK, criticisms of the multicultural model brought about by racial tensions and the perceived terrorist threat (mainly centered on young British Muslims disaffections) have shifted state efforts toward neoassimilationist positions (Kofman 2005; Nagel and Staeheli 2008).

Traditionally, empirical research on integration and assimilation has made use of statistical indicators, such as language acquisition, labor market participation, educational attainment, or residential patterns, to measure the level of incorporation and acculturation of migrant and ethnic minority populations in their host society (Phillips 2007; Schneider and Crul 2010). However, there has been a considerable amount of debate regarding the methodological constraints of these quantitative approaches as they are often designed on the basis of available statistical data, for example, census-based figures (Findlay and Graham 1991), where processes of collection, interpretation, and representation are embedded in politicized debates around immigration, conceptualizations of ethnic minorities, and understandings of segregation (Phillips 2007; Simpson 2007). Although this approach has provided important insights into the socioeconomic differences between minority and majority groups in given societies and the different patterns of social, economic, and geographical mobility of these groups in specific localities (Nagel 2009, 402), it cannot illuminate how minority groups or immigrants themselves interpret segregation or integration (Nagel and Staeheli 2008, Phillips, Davis, and Ratcliffe 2007). In the light of this, it has been suggested that focusing on migrants' and ethnic minorities' senses of affiliation and belonging are essential if we are to comprehend processes of integration in all their complexity (Ehrkamp 2006; Nagel and Staeheli 2008, Phillips, Davis, and Ratcliffe 2007).

Researchers have turned their attention toward the social worlds of migrant and second-generation children and have documented the development of identities among these young people as strategies of integration or resistance to cope with the conditions they face in their receiving society (Colombo, Leonini, and Rebughini 2009, Griffiths 2002; Valentine, Sporton, and Nielsen 2009). For example, Rutter's (2006) research with young Southern Sudanese found that males from this group adopt both British and Sudanese cultural forms with ease in order to negotiate the social terrains of their settlement society, while young Southern Sudanese women are more constrained by traditional gender norms.

Additionally, research within the transnational paradigm has provided insights into the role of transnational attachments in the lives of the children of migrants. Despite the increasing consensus that only a minority of second-generation members engage in material cross-border activities (for example, visiting, remitting, participation in kin networks) and that their involvement tends to decline over time (Lee 2007, Rumbaut 2002), scholars have pointed out that the study of generations as a linear process does not capture properly the experience of living embedded in transnational social fields. Within these fields, the comings and goings of migrants blur the distinctions among cohorts, and the ethnification of migrant communities provides new terms of cultural reference (Fouron and Glick Schiller 2002 Gowricharn 2009; Levitt and Waters 2002; Levitt 2009).

From this basis, some research has highlighted the important role that the emotional circuits of the transnational family play in recreating or reproducing attachments that may figure saliently in the senses of belonging and identification of the second generations, even for those who have never experienced their parents' societies of origin (Le Espiritu and Tran 2002; Louie 2006, Wolf 2002). In fact, there is a growing perspective that emphasizes that incorporation and transnational attachments should be seen as simultaneous dynamics in the lives of migrants and their descendants (Levitt and Glick Schiller 2004), with several studies documenting how they negotiate coexisting ties (Morawska 2004; Nagel and Staeheli 2008).

In many instances, the transnational or collective identifications of the second generations have been found in children who live among other young people from the same geographical origin or religious background, as in the case of research mentioned above (Le Espiritu and Tran 2002; Louie 2006; Valentine, Sporton, and Nielsen 2009; Wolf 2002). Much less is known about the circumstances and the circuits of identification of second generations from sparse migrant populations and invisible minorities. The case of Colombians in the north of England provides us with the opportunity to explore how relatively isolated migrants and their children experience their lives in a geographical area without visible community groups or networks of fellow Colombians or Latin Americans. Furthermore, it allows us to consider how the young participants negotiate their senses of identification against the background of this sociocultural invisibility and in relation to the multiple frames of reference available to them (cf. Levitt and Glick Schiller 2004; Levitt 2009).

The Case-Study of Families of Colombian Descent in the North of England

The empirical material presented here is the result of an exploratory project undertaken in the north of England during 2008. Due to the scarce information available about Latin Americans residing outside of London, it was considered necessary to conduct a small-scale preliminary study that could help illuminate the circumstances that characterize this population in the north of the country and that could also cement the basis for further research. The first phase of this preliminary project comprised a benchmarking exercise of the statistical data available (both from official sources and from researchers and support organizations) and ten semistructured interviews with key informants and stakeholders from the northern regions. This was followed by a second stage that consisted of an exploratory case-study (Yin 1994), with four families of Colombian descent living in a specific metropolitan area of Yorkshire.[3]

The fieldwork with the four participant families (of middle-class background) included all the adults and young people over eight years of age within the household,[4] a total of five adults (four mothers of Colombian descent, one British stepfather) and four children (12 to 18 years of age, two male and two female, one had come to live in the United Kingdom at a young age and the other three had been born in the country, one was of Colombian origin and the other three were Colombian-British). Independently from their nationality (or nationalities as most hold dual citizenship, British and Colombian), the young participants displayed fluid self-identifications that, as they explained, depended on the context in which they were asked about their heritage and by whom (for a contrast see the findings of a recent survey among second-generation Latin Americans in London, McIlwaine Cock, and Linneker 2011). On occasions, this diversity of self-identifications was related to perceptions of being "mixed race" (cf. Ifekwunigwe 2004; Tizard and Phoenix 2002); however, in this chapter I am not focusing on the degree to which participants fore-grounded their ethnic or racial background but on the rich frames of reference they resorted to when narrating their senses of identity and belonging.

Each young participant took part in three semistructured inter-views with participatory tools, mainly diagramming, to talk about their family, attachment to places, social networks, and everyday lives. Their accounts were complemented by in-depth interviews with their parents, during which we completed a family diagram and discussed settlement experiences. Additionally, they all participated in family group semistructured interviews. Both Spanish and English were used in conducting the fieldwork activities, according to the prefer-ences of the participants; I have indicated which ones were originally spoken in English and which ones I have translated. All the names used are pseudonyms to protect the identities of the informants.

The Colombian Population in the North of England: Encountering Sociocultural Invisibility

The Census 2001 (Office for National Statistics 2003, 38) situated the overall size of the South American[5] population in England and Wales as 73,785 people, of whom over 12,000 were of Colombian origin (Organisation for Economic Co-operation and Development 2005). A comparison between the data provided by the Labour Force Survey (LFS) from March to May 1998 (Office for National Statistics and Northern Ireland Statistics and Research Agency 2004) and the data collected by the LFS from January to March 2007 (Office for National Statistics and Northern Ireland Statistics and Research Agency 2007) would suggest that this population doubled during this period, although remaining a fairly small group (around 24,000 people). However, estimates from researchers and support organiza-tions suggest that the real size of the Colombian population ranges from between 50,000 and 140,000 people, most of whom are settled in London (McIlwaine 2007, 7).

Statistical data for outside of the capital is limited, but if we take into account the LFS January–March 2007 (Office for National Statistics and Northern Ireland Statistics and Research Agency 2007), it would suggest that, overall, less than 10 percent of the total Colombian population lives in the north of the country. This edition of the survey identifies small clusters of Colombians residing in the north east and north west of England.[6] In addition, the National Insurance Number Allocations to Overseas Nationals entering the UK (previously Migrant Workers Statistics) (Department of Work and Pensions 2002/2003–2006/2007) also shows small numbers of applications being made by Colombians in the large cities of the northern regions (for example, Manchester, Liverpool, Newcastle, and Leeds).[7]

The growth of this population in England and Wales has been accompanied by an increasing awareness of the presence of Latin American children in schools around the country. This awareness has translated into the fact that several local education authorities have started to use extended "Other ethnic group ethnicity codes" in their annual School Census, which include a category for pupils from Central/South America, Cuba, and Belize (Department for Education and Skills 2006, 13). The Schools' Census for Autumn 2008 indicated that only around 1 percent of Latin American students, out of a total of 4,000 (2 to 19 years of age), attend northern schools (Department for Children Schools and Families 2008). However, this is a partial figure as not all the local education authorities include this category as a possible choice to describe ethnic affiliation, and it is not possible to disaggregate the information further to ascertain more specific backgrounds.

An example of the alleged recent growth of the Latin American population in the north can be found in Liverpool, where there are reports of a considerable increase in the number of Bolivians, Colombians, Brazilians, and Peruvians coming to the city since 2004. Francisco Carrasco, cofounder of "All Things Latin" in Liverpool, a restaurant and club promoting Latin American culture, believes that his city could now be host to the second-largest Latin American population in the country after London (Liverpool.com 2007 and in conversation with the author).

If we consider the data provided by the LFS October to December 2007 (Office for National Statistics and Northern Ireland Statistics and Research Agency 2007) for the type of jobs that Colombians in the north are undertaking, the majority are employed in the higher end of the labor market in professional positions. However, the stakeholders and informants I spoke to reported that there is a more invisible recent migration, compounded by people who have arrived as students or, initially, as tourists. Within this group, some are working in very low-skilled jobs and sometimes unofficially (mainly cleaning and restaurant work) and are not accounted for by official statistics.

This diversity of new residents also includes asylum seekers and refugees who have been dispersed to towns and cities in the north by the National Asylum Seekers Support Service. However, these cases are few in number (one to ten in all instances) in line with the low numbers of Colombians who claim asylum at the present time (Home Office 2008). They tend to be highly invisible as their presence goes unnoticed among other larger populations of asylum seekers.

The low numbers and the sociodemographic diversity of Colombians and other Latin Americans living in this region of the country translate into a pronounced social invisibility, which in material terms manifests itself in a virtual absence of support groups and shared spaces that can act as sites of cultural reproduction and socialization. There are only a few initiatives, such as a community magazine for the Spanish-speaking community, a few organized gatherings (for example, conversation circles), specific cultural groups (for example, Chilean Community in South Yorkshire, university student associations), and some professional enterprises promoting Latin American culture, music, and dance (for example, "All Things Latin" in Liverpool).

There is a complexity of factors that play a role in the persistent invisibility of this population. Due to the lower number of immigrants in this region, Colombians report having social networks that transcend their country of origin and include other Latin Americans. However, their sociodemographic diversity also leads to a lack of cohesion as migrants tend to relate to people of similar backgrounds or with similar life situations. For example, those in Anglo-Colombian relationships, often talk about having different social networks, feeling more blended into British society, with occasional Latin American friends in parallel lifecourse stages (for example, with young children). Some Colombians express an additional wish to pass as British because of what they perceive as a significant level of prejudice in their host society due to the stereotyping of their country as drug ridden and violent. In fact, some of the informants recounted being discriminated against when trying to obtain jobs, and they attributed this prejudice specifically to their Colombian nationality, as they considered such discrimination as more prevalent than that suffered by Latin Americans in general (McIlwaine 2007).

There have also been external support initiatives that seemed to reinforce this invisibility through the assimilation of Latin Americans into their local societies. For example, another one of the informants, a Colombian Evangelist pastor, explained that he had been sent to the north by a faith group based in London to help newly arrived families incorporate into existing English-speaking church congregations so they could achieve equality in their new places of residence.

In summary, the sociocultural invisibility that characterizes the Colombian population (and Latin Americans more generally) in the north of England plays a crucial role in the practical possibilities that these migrants and their children have to relate to fellow compatriots or reproduce their cultural heritage. One of the participant families, which included Susana (47, Colombian mother) and Duncan (12, son, of Colombian-Scottish descent), reflected on the difficulties of maintaining their language and traditions in these circumstances.

> *Susana*. It becomes another exercise, an *added job* to the daily routines and then for me . . . maybe because we are, again a minority, if we were more people, then there would be restaurants, groups, we wouldn't have the problem of abandoning our food or our music, but being . . . *Duncan*. No, the music not! *Susana*. No, we don't lose the music, no, we listen to music (laughs). But yes, this is, it is not very practical to be a minority, minority. [My translation]

In order to understand further how this everyday invisibility is experienced by the young participants, the next section focuses on the frames of reference that underline their strategies of identification and affiliation.

The Strategies of Identification of the Young Participants of Colombian Descent

Against the background of a lack of possibilities to meet and socialize with young people of similar descent, all the participants told me about different kinds of attachments that helped them negotiate their own senses of affiliation and identity in relation to their families, their local lived experiences, and their own social networks.

Attachments in Relation to Their Family Heritage

The two issues that became most salient during the fieldwork were the participants' potential engagement with their extended family networks and the degree of intensity of their own relationships with these relatives. These two themes were normally discussed in relation to the transnational links that their families maintained with their extended kin living in Colombia, or third countries, and in relation to the degree of involvement that the young people had in these practices (Levitt and Waters 2002). The participants talked about the importance of having the opportunities (visits) and the means (language) to engage with these extended family relations as independent individuals.

With the use of family diagramming, the perception that the young people had of their family and relatives contrasted significantly with those of their parents. Examples of this contrast were provided by the diagrams of Martina (mother, Spanish-Colombian background) (see figure 11.1), and Mia (18-year-old daughter, Chilean-Spanish-Colombian background) (see figure 11.2).

Martina has maintained strong emotional bonds with her extended family in Spain and Colombia and has tried to pass on these connections to her daughter through constant communication and family visits. Mia's parents divorced a few years ago and she has always lived with her mother but has seen her Chilean father regularly. Although Martina and Mia used the diagram in similar ways, making use of the space on the paper to express the proximity they felt to the people they were talking about, there is a strong contrast between the

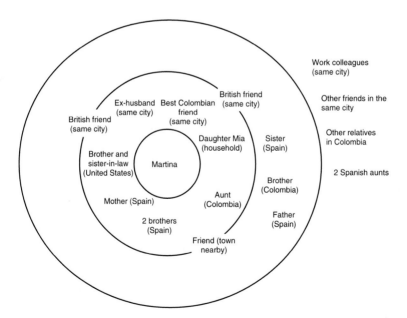

Figure 11.1 Martina's family diagram (anonymized reproduction, translated from Spanish)

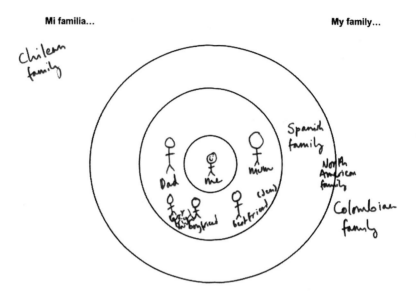

Figure 11.2 Mia's family diagram (reproduction of the original)

two. In general, Martina talked about every single individual that she thought was part of the diagram, personalizing her relationship to every one of them and only reverting to talking about groups as she moved further away from the people whom she considered were more important in her life. Mia, however, emphasized the people closer to her and then talked about her extended family in relation to the possibilities that she had had to meet them herself. She referred to them as groups, without individualizing the attachments that she experienced. For example, she placed her Chilean family completely apart from the rest of her extended family as she felt she had never had the chance to establish real relationships with them. As she explained:

> Like when my Dad tells me about Chile I really like it but it just sounds like story to me because I don't really understand. Yeah, I do feel a connection with my Colombian family because I remember how much I loved visiting and all the people, I know all the people involved, so yeah I would say that I do feel a connection. [Original English]

As I talked to the different participants, it became clear that their sense of attachment to their extended family often depended on the possibilities that they themselves had had to recreate and nurture the family relationships they had inherited from their parents, otherwise, this family inheritance was purely perceived as an ancestral story. In general, although "people, values, goods and claims from somewhere else" (Levitt and Jaworsky 2007, 134) were present in their lives, these young participants felt that they only became significant if they had had the chance to engage with them personally and as independent members of the family.

However, family bonds were only one of the frames of reference that the participants referred to. In the context of the lack of possibilities to meet fellow Colombians or Latin Americans in the places where they live, friendships and social networks were established in relation to senses of shared life experiences and notions of diversity.

Attachments to Other Young People with Similar Life Experiences

Another way in which the participants talked about their feelings of belonging was on the basis of their attachments to other young people who had similar personal stories to their own or similar diverse cultural backgrounds (independently of the geographical origin of their parents). They explained how it was easier for them to form friendships or relate to other young people who had shared understandings of life in Britain. For example, during the group interview with his family, Salvador (14-year-old Colombian) talked about his closest friends who, he emphasized, had diverse cultural origins.

> *Step-father.* But your friends are more from other countries than English.
> *Salvador.* Yes, yes . . . from Pakistan and India and . . . Bangladesh . . .
> *Mother.* How is the culture? What is the difference between cultures when making friendships?
> *Salvador.* Well I don't know how to explain it . . . the ones that were born in England don't know how to have fun . . . the ones that were born in other countries know, have stories to tell and all that, then we can talk, but no, not with the others. [My translation]

Salvador felt he belonged to this group of friends with whom he shared experiences of mobility and settlement; however, these commonalities functioned independently from their senses of national affiliation or cultural identity (Mas Giralt and Bailey 2010).

In a similar way, 12-year-old Duncan also spoke of the type of friendships that he likes to establish. Duncan has a dual background, with his mother from Colombia and his father from Scotland. His parents divorced many years ago, and he has not had any contact with his father for a long time. Like Salvador, Duncan spoke of wanting to interact with people who had similar backgrounds to his own, that is, parents with different geographical origins (not necessarily Colombian or Latin American). He felt that their characters, ways of being, and approaches to establishing friendships were similar to his own.

> I think that people who are, who have some relation with another European or Latin country, but who have another, like me being Colombian, well, yes, I have a friend whose mother is from Hungary, this, these are the people I want to interact with. [My translation]

In fact, these friendships based on shared experiences and notions of diversity were at the basis of how the participants understood their inclusion into the multiethnic locales in which they live (Mas Giralt and Bailey 2010).

Negotiating Invisibility through Lived Diversity

All the participants highlighted the scarcity of opportunities that they had had to interact with children of a common descent while growing up. In addition, they had experienced the generalized lack of awareness regarding the presence of Colombians or Latin Americans among other people in the places where they reside. Mia (18-years–old, Chilean-Spanish-Colombian), whom we met in the first section, explained her own experience in terms of the size of the population and its invisibility.

> The only thing I can really think to add is just the obvious, that it is, it is quite a minority . . . like aside from, from the introductions that have been sort of probably made by my parents, my parents' friends, I've met one person from South America, who wasn't related so . . . it's, I think, I still think it's quite unusual. [Original English]

However, they negotiated this social invisibility by using an inclusive notion of cultural diversity, which provided them with a sphere of belonging in the multiethnic places where they reside (Mas Giralt and Bailey 2010). They did so by highlighting their cultural background and making it selectively and strategically visible (see Bailey et al. 2002, 136, for "strategic visibility"); in this way, the participants actively subverted the structural conditions that characterize their everyday experiences in the locales where they live.

For example, Duncan (12-year-old Colombian-Scottish) explained how, when in England, he always stressed the diversity of his background.

> I would say [that I am] Scottish and Colombian but not English. When I'm in England I don't feel that I'm English . . . I don't know but when I was saying about people who are English and something European, that's something similar. [My translation]

He also explained that, while living in Spain for a year, he described himself purely as British, if asked. However, back in the UK, he felt it was important to highlight his dual heritage: "I don't know, I like other people to know . . . not in a boasting way but I like them to know that I speak another language, that I have different customs and that" (my translation).

A similar approach was adopted by Jo (16, Anglo-Colombian), who was born in the UK and has not had many possibilities to establish relationships with her extended Colombian family, which is dispersed across many different countries. She usually defined herself as British but also by adding information about her maternal heritage.

> Well I say oh, my mum is from South America and they're always like "waa!" a South American mum but normally not many people know about it, they just think that is quite interesting and then they move on [laughs]." [Original English]

For the participants, their diverse backgrounds provided them with membership of the multicultural places they inhabit (Mas Giralt and Bailey 2010). This notion of multiculturalism must be understood in terms of what scholars have described as "multiculturalism as lived experience" (Malik 2002, n. p.) as they all reside in multiethnic metropolitan areas and, as we have seen, have friends with a variety of cultural origins. The experience of lived multiculturalism among these participants allows them to reimagine "Britishness" in inclusive terms, terms that accommodate their own and their friends' diverse cultural heritages, as Mia summarized it: "What is British?, there is so many types of British" (original English).

Conclusion

The small-scale cross-sectional study presented in this chapter has aimed at starting to explore the situation of Colombian migrants and their children in the north of England. The sociocultural invisibility that characterizes this population in the northern regions is rooted in the small number of Colombians and other Latin Americans who settle in this part of the country (although it is difficult to establish its real size and the rate at which it is growing) and their sociodemographic diversity. In turn, the scarcity of shared spaces and networks of fellow Colombians, or Latin Americans in general, translates into a lack of opportunity to reproduce their cultural heritage outside of the household and extended family.

Against this background, the young participants of Colombian and dual descent reported different types of attachments that allowed them to negotiate their senses of identity and belonging. The influence of familial transnational attachments as potential frames of reference depended on the intensity of the family relationships and on the possibilities that the young people had had to recreate and live these relationships as independent individuals and family members in their own right. In addition, commonalities based on their personal stories of mobility and settlement or on diversity of cultural background were at the basis of feelings of belonging to their friendship groups. In this sense, they displayed what Bryceson and Vuorela have described as "a more elastic relationship to their places of origin, ethnicity or national belonging" (2002, 9). By resorting to an inclusive notion of diversity and strategically highlighting their cultural background (Bailey et al. 2002), the young participants negotiated membership of the multicultural lived worlds they inhabit (Mas Giralt and Bailey 2010). Despite the crisis of the multicultural model in the policy debates of the United Kingdom (Morrell 2008), these participants provided an example of its persistence at the level of everyday lived experiences (Colombo 2010, Wise and Velayutham 2009).

The study presented here was continued through a second stage of research that focused on Latin American adults and children living in northern English regions. This second stage responded to the need to explore further the social networks that transcend national origins and that the participants had highlighted as being important for the way they organized their lives. There is, however, a need for more research to build our understanding of the experiences of young people of Colombian and Latin American descent who may be growing up in very different sociocultural environments, as in the example of London were the populations are much larger and more visible (McIlwaine, Cock, and Linneker 2011).

Acknowledgments

I would like to acknowledge the support of the Economic and Social Research Council in the United Kingdom for funding the research that informs this paper. I am very grateful to all the adults and young people who took part in the research and to Adrian J. Bailey for his constructive comments on the earlier paper on which this chapter is based.

Notes

1. For the purposes of this project, the north includes the regions of Yorkshire and the Humber, north west and north east of England.
2. Understood here as both children who were born in the homeland and immigrated at an early age and those born in the host land to immigrant parents. I recognize that this category is constructed and the boundaries between generations are often blurred (Levitt and Waters 2002).
3. In order to protect the anonymity of the participant families, it is not possible to identify specifically the localities in which they live.
4. The lack of existing information about Colombians or Latin Americans in this region and the scarcity of cultural or support organizations make them a *hard-to-reach group*. Recruitment of participants was conducted with the invaluable help of a few stakeholders who provided contacts with other informants, who, in turn, connected the researcher with potential participant families (snowballing technique).
5. In the Census of 2001, the category of South America includes the following countries: Argentina, Bolivia, Brazil, Chile, Colombia, Ecuador, Falkland Islands, French Guiana, Guyana, Paraguay, Peru, Suriname, Uruguay, and Venezuela (Office for National Statistics 2003).
6. It must be emphasized that due to the methodology employed in collecting the Labour Force Survey, which is based on 60,000 responding households every quarter and is consequently applied weighting measures, its accuracy decreases when dealing with very small populations. Therefore, this data must be approached with extra caution.
7. This data must also be approached with caution as we cannot assume that all these Colombian workers stay in the localities where they have obtained their number.

References

Atfield, Gaby, Kavita Brahmbhatt, and Therese O'Toole. 2007. *Refugees' Experiences of Integration*. Birmingham: Refugee Council, University of Birmingham.

Bailey, Adrian J., Richard A. Wright, Alison Mountz, and Ines M. Miyares. 2002. "(Re)producing Salvadoran Transnational Geographies." *Annals of the Association of American Geographers* 92:125–144.

Bermúdez Torres, Anastasia. 2003. *Refugee Populations in the UK: Colombians.* ICAR Navigation Guide. Available from: http://www.icar .webbler.co.uk/?lid=2021 (accessed October 15, 2007).

Bryceson, Deborah, and Ulla Vuorela, eds. 2002. *The Transnational Family: New European Frontiers and Global Networks.* Oxford and New York: Berg.

Colombo, Enzo. 2010. Crossing Differences: "How Young Children of Immigrants Keep Everyday Multiculturalism Alive." *Journal of Intercultural Studies* 31:455–70.

Colombo, Enzo, Luisa Leonini, and Paola Rebughini. 2009. "Different but Not Stranger: Everyday Collective Identifications among Adolescent Children of Immigrants in Italy." *Journal of Ethnic and Migration Studies* 35:37–59.

Department for Children Schools and Families. 2008. *National Pupil Database: Autumn 2008.* DCSF. [Data File].

Department for Education and Skills. 2006. *Ethnicity and Education: The Evidence on Minority Ethnic Pupils Aged 5–16.* Department for Education and Skills. Available from: http://www.teachernet.gov.uk/publications (accessed March 7, 2007).

Department of Work and Pensions. 2003/2003–2006/2007. *National Insurance Number registrations in respect of non-UK nationals in 2002/03–2006/2007 by Local Authority and Country of Origin.* Department of Work and Pensions. National Insurance Recording System (NIRS). [Excel datasets].

Ehrkamp, Patricia. 2006. "'We Turks Are No Germans': Assimilation Discourses and the Dialectical Construction of Identities in Germany." *Environment and Planning A* 38:1673–92.

Findlay, Allan M., and Elspeth Graham. 1991. "The Challenge Facing Population Geography." *Progress in Human Geography* 15:149–62.

Fouron, Georges E., and Nina Glick Schiller. 2002. "The Generation of Identity: Redefining the Second Generation within a Transnational Social Field." In *The Changing Face of Home: The Transnational Lives of the Second Generation,* ed. Peggy Levitt and Mary C. Waters, 168–208. New York: Russell Sage Foundation.

Gowricharn, Ruben. 2009. "Changing Forms of Transnationalism." *Ethnic and Racial Studies* 32:1619–38.

Griffiths, David. 2002. *Somali and Kurdish Refugees in London: New Identities in the Diaspora.* Aldershot, UK: Ashgate Books.

Guarnizo, Luis E. 2008. *Londres Latina: La Presencia Colombiana en la Capital Britanica.* México DF: Universidad de Zacatecas and Miguel Angel Porrúa.

Home Office. 2008. *Asylum Statistics United Kingdom 2007.* Home Office Statistical Bulletin,11 (08). Available from http://www.homeoffice.gov .uk/rds (accessed September 9, 2008).

Ifekwunigwe, Jayne O., ed. 2004. *"Mixed Race" Studies*. London and New York: Routledge.

Kofman, Eleonore. 2005. "Citizenship, Migration and the Reassertion of National Identity." *Citizenship Studies* 9:453–67.

Le Espiritu, Yen, and Thom Tran. 2002. "'Viet Nam, Nuoc Toi' (Vietnam, my country): Vietnamese Americans and Transnationalism." In *The Changing Face of Home: The Transnational Lives of the Second Generation*, ed. Peggy Levitt and Mary C. Waters, 367–98. New York: Russell Sage Foundation.

Lee, Helen. 2007. "Transforming Transnationalism: Second Generation Togans Overseas." *Asian and Pacific Migration Journal* 16:157–78.

Levitt, Peggy. 2009. "Roots and Routes: Understanding the Lives of the Second Generation Transnationally." *Journal of Ethnic and Migration Studies* 35:1225–42.

Levitt, Peggy, and Nina Glick Schiller. 2004. "Conceptualizing Simultaneity: A Transnational Social Field Perspective on Society." *International Migration Review* 38:1002–39.

Levitt, Peggy, and Nadya B. Jaworsky. 2007. "Transnational Migration Studies: Past Developments and Future Trends." *Annual Review of Sociology* 33:129–56.

Levitt, Peggy, and Mary C. Waters, eds. 2002. *The Changing Face of Home: The Transnational Lives of the Second Generation*. New York: Russell Sage Foundation.

Liverpool.com. 2007. *Liverpool's Latin Quarter: Just around the Corner [December 18, 2007]*. Available from: http://www.liverpool.com/news/liverpool-s-latin-quarter-just-around-the-corner.html (accessed June 2, 2009).

Louie, Vivian. 2006. "Growing Up Ethnic in Transnational Worlds: Identities among Second-Generation Chinese and Dominicans." *Identities-Global Studies in Culture and Power* 13:363–94.

Malik, Kenan. 2002. *Can Multiculturalism Work?* Institute Français. Attention Seeking: Multiculturalism and the Politics of Recognition. Available from: http://www.kenanmalik.com/lectures/multiculturalism_if.html (accessed 12 February 2009).

Mas Giralt, Rosa, and Adrian J. Bailey. 2010. "Transnational Familyhood and the Transnational Life Paths of South Americans in the UK." *Global Networks* 10:383–400.

McIlwaine, Cathy. 2005. *Coping Practices among Colombian Migrants in London*. London: Queen Mary. University of London. (Available from: http://www.geog.qmul.ac.uk/docs/staff/4402.pdf) (accessed May 2, 2011).

———. 2007. *Living in Latin London: How Latin American Migrants Survive in the City*. London: Queen Mary, University of London. (Available from: http://www.geog.qmul.ac.uk/docs/staff/4400.pdf) (accessed May 2, 2011).

McIlwaine, Cathy, Juan Camilo Cock, and Brian Linneker. 2011. *No Longer Invisible: The Latin American Community in London*. London: Trust for

London. (Available from: http://www.geog.qmul.ac.uk/docs/research/latinamerican/48637.pdf) (accessed May 20, 2011).

Morawska, Ewa. 2004. "Exploring Diversity in Immigrant Assimilation and Transnationalism: Poles and Russian Jews in Philadelphia." *International Migration Review* 38:1372–1412.

Morrell, Gareth. 2008. *Multiculturalism, Citizenship and Identity*. London: Information Centre about Asylum and Refugees (ICAR).

Nagel, Caroline R. 2009. "Rethinking Geographies of Assimilation." *The Professional Geographer* 61:400–7.

Nagel, Caroline R., and Lynn A Staeheli. 2008. "Integration and the Negotiation of 'Here' and 'There': The Case of British Arab Activists." *Social and Cultural Geography* 9:415–30.

Office for National Statistics. 2003. *Census 2001: National Report for England and Wales*. TSO. Office for National Statistics (ONS). Available from: www.statistics.gov.uk (accessed October 19, 2007).

Office for National Statistics and Northern Ireland Statistics and Research Agency. 2004. *Quarterly Labour Force Survey: March–May 1998*. ONS and NISRA. Economic and Social Data Service. Available from: www.esds.ac.uk/governments/lfs/ (accessed October 5, 2007).

———. 2007. *Quarterly Labour Force Survey: January–March 2007*. ONS and NISRA. Economic and Social Data Service. Available from: www.esds.ac.uk/government/lfs/ (accessed October 5, 2007).

Open Channels. 1998. *La comunidad colombiana en Londres*. Peterborough, UK: Open Channels.

Organisation for Economic Co-operation and Development. 2005. *Database on Immigrants and Expatriates: Total Population by Nationality and Country of Birth (Detailed Countries)*. OECD. Available from: http://www.oecd.org (accessed August 15, 2007).

Phillips, Deborah. 2007. "Ethnic and Racial Segregation: A Critical Perspective." *Geography Compass* 1:1138–59.

Phillips, Deborah, Cathy Davis, and Peter Ratcliffe. 2007. "British Asian narratives of Urban Space." *Transactions of the Institute of British Geographers, New Series* 32:217–34.

Rumbaut, Rubén G. 2002. "Severed or Sustained Attachments? Language, Identity, and Imagined Communities in the Post-Immigrant Generation." In *The Changing Face of Home: The Transnational Lives of the Second Generation*, ed. Peggy Levitt and Mary C. Waters, 43–95. New York: Russell Sage Foundation.

Rutter, Jill. 2006. *Refugee Children in the UK*. Maidenhead, UK: Open University Press.

Schneider, Jens, and Maurice Crul. 2010. "New Insights into Assimilation and Integration Theory: Introduction to the Special Issue." *Ethnic and Racial Studies* 33:1143–48.

Simpson, L. 2007. "Ghettos of the Mind: The Empirical Behaviour of Indices of Segregation and Diversity." *Journal of Royal Statistical Society A* 170:405–24.

Tizard, Barbara, and Ann Phoenix. 2002. *Black, White or Mixed Raced? Race and Racism in the Lives of Young People of Mixed Parentage.* Revised ed. London and New York: Routledge.

Valentine, Gill, Deborah Sporton, and Katrine B. Nielsen. 2009. "Identities and Belonging: A Study of Somali Refugee and Asylum Seekers Living in the UK and Denmark." *Environment and Planning D-Society & Space* 27:234–50.

Wise, Amanda, and Selvaraj Velayutham, eds. 2009. *Everyday Multiculturalism.* Basingstoke, UK: Palgrave Macmillan.

Wolf, Diane L. 2002. "There's No Place Like 'Home': Emotional Transnationalism and the Struggles of Second-Generation Filipinos." In *The Changing Face of Home: The Transnational Lives of the Second Generation,* ed. Peggy Levitt and Mary C. Waters, 255–94. New York: Russell Sage Foundation.

Yin, Robert K. 1994. *Case Study Research: Design and Methods.* 2nd ed. Thousand Oaks, CA: Sage.

Chapter 12

Political Transnationalism and Gender among Colombian Migrants in London

Anastasia Bermudez

Introduction

Political participation among migrant communities and diasporas has received renewed attention recently, whether from a transnational or local integration perspective. However, research considering this in the context of Latin American migration tends to focus on Latinos in the United States. In contrast, little is known about this from a European perspective, despite the growing importance of Latin American migration to the region. A gendered approach to the study of migrants' transnational politics has also only emerged more recently, with most studies emphasizing women's lesser involvement. Empirically, although Latin Americans are currently one of the fastest-growing migrant communities in the UK, little is known about them (see McIlwaine this volume Section 2). This chapter focuses on the experiences of Colombian migrants in London, who represent one of the largest national groups within the wider Latin American community in the UK, and who play a prominent role in community initiatives, organizations, and businesses. The chapter draws on recently conducted research with Colombian migrants in the UK and Spain on the gendered nature of transnational political practices. The chapter shows that Colombian women (and men) are involved in a variety of political initiatives, oriented both toward the host and home countries, and at the individual and collective levels, with types and levels of involvement varying across gender, but also depending on other factors such as type of migration and social class. Following an outline of the conceptual and methodological framework used in the research, I will provide a brief background on Colombians in London, before focusing on some of the core issues to emerge from my research.

Conceptual and Methodological Approach to the Study of Migrant Politics

Currently, the issue of migrants' political participation in host societies has received renewed attention, especially in the European context and linked to the debates on integration, citizenship, and democracy (see Reed-Danahay and Brettell 2008). At the same time, new transnational approaches to the study of international migration have encouraged a move away from the traditional focus on the incorporation and acculturation of migrants in host societies toward the recognition of the linkages that migrants maintain with their country of origin (see Levitt, DeWind, and Vertovec 2003). This theoretical approach emerged strongly in the second half of the 1990s, concentrating mainly on Latin American and Caribbean labor migration to the United States, with most research initially focused on migrants' transnational economic and social relations. However, work later expanded to cover other types of migration and different world regions and established that "transnational social fields" also encompass political and symbolic links (Itzigsohn et al. 1999). In the case of Europe, the transnational focus on migration is more recent, and the work available has focused on more established migrant/ethnic groups in those countries with a longer history of immigration. Only more recently has Latin American migration to Europe received sustained attention, prompted by the large flows directed mainly toward southern Europe in the last two decades. However, little is known about Colombians in the UK and their transnational politics.

Until quite recently, gender had also been largely absent from these fields of study. Mahler and Pessar (2006, 27) point out that most research does not consider gender "as a key constitutive element of migrations." Women and gender have also been traditionally excluded from the study of politics and again, only relatively recently has work on the political incorporation of migrant groups begun to view gender as central to analyses (Piper 2006). However, as scholarship in migration and transnationalism has expanded, it has gradually started to investigate "the degree to which participation in transnational activities and in transnational social fields in general is gendered" (Mahler 1998, 83). Gendered analyses of the transnational political involvement of Latino migrants in the United States generally conclude that "[m]en appear to be more committed to the maintenance of public and institutionalized transnational ties than are women, while women appear more committed to participating in the life of the receiving country" (Itzigsohn and Giourguli-Saucedo 2005, 896; see also Goldring 2001; Jones-Correa 1998). However, Gammage's (2004) study of transnational migration from Haiti has contested these conclusions, highlighting the economic and political contributions of migrant women to their country of origin. The current research conducted with Colombians in London also shows that both men and women become involved in transnational politics, although types and levels of participation vary according to gender, as well as other factors (see McIlwaine and Bermudez 2011).

Conceptually, the research data explored here used a wide definition of what constitutes "transnational political practices," including both formal/conventional and informal/unconventional manifestations (see Østergaard-Nielsen 2003). It also distinguished between transnationalism "from below" and "from above," but went beyond the traditional focus on one or the other to try to understand convergences and tensions present in the transnational political field (Smith and Guarnizo 1998). Finally, the research explored transnational political practices both from the individual and state levels, as well as the meso level by considering the work of migrant and wider civil society groups and organizations. Methodologically, the discussion draws on qualitative research based mainly on one-to-one semistructured interviews, participant observation, and content analysis of Web sites and other materials.[1] In total, 50 people were interviewed during 2006–2007, mostly Colombian men and women migrants, but also Colombian officials and experts and non-Colombian experts. Migrant interviewees were mostly first generation and included refugees and asylum-seekers, labor migrants, and professionals, as well as Colombians who had migrated for other reasons.

Colombian Migration Abroad and the Community in London

Colombia has a long history of internal and external migrations, forced and voluntary. However, the phenomenon of Colombian migration abroad in large numbers is very recent and as such has not been explored in great depth. Emigration rates started to climb in the 1960s and rapidly accelerated throughout the 1990s and into the twenty-first century, as violence and insecurity in Colombia increased and economic conditions deteriorated. Recent migration flows from

Colombia are also the result of global economic factors, part of current population movements from the Global South to the North (and South to South). Based on the 2005 census, current official estimates suggest that there are just under 3.4 million Colombians living abroad (Conpes 2009). Traditionally, Colombian emigration has tended to be across neighboring borders (mainly to Venezuela) and to the United States. However, from the 1990s, flows have diversified, both in terms of destinations and regarding the regional and social background of migrants (Guarnizo 2008). New destinations now include other countries in the region (Ecuador, Panama, Costa Rica), and outside (Canada, Japan, Israel, and several European countries). Europe was traditionally only a destination for the Colombian elite, political refugees, intellectuals, artists, and students. However, this started to change in the 1970s, and more rapidly from the 1980s–1990s. The UK is home to the second largest Colombian community in Europe, after Spain (by a large difference), with significant communities also present in Italy, France, Germany, and Belgium (Guarnizo 2008).

According to Guarnizo (2008), England, and London in particular, has always occupied a special place for the Colombian upper classes, political leaders, young professionals, and students. Indeed, several Colombian migrants interviewed in London, from middle- or upper-class backgrounds, said they had come to London because as children they had learned or heard a lot about Europe or Britain, and were attracted by European culture. These linkages were later widened to include all sectors of the Colombian population, especially from the 1970s, when many Colombians arrived in the UK as the British government authorized the entry of nonskilled migrants to work in services. Although the work permit system ended in 1979, an increasing number of Colombians continued to arrive as migration networks became established and stronger visa restrictions were imposed in other destinations (Open Channels 2000). The arrival of Colombian refugees in the UK also dates back to the 1970s, when other Latin Americans escaping human rights abuses settled in the country, but numbers increased significantly during the 1980s and 1990s as violence in Colombia intensified, to decline subsequently as immigration laws became stricter. In addition, there are also significant numbers of Colombian students and professionals in the UK. Estimates of the number of Colombians in the UK range from 50,000 to 150,000 (Guarnizo 2008).

Most Colombians, and Latin Americans in general, have settled in or around London, concentrating mostly in the boroughs of Lambeth, Islington, Southwark, and Camden (Open Channels 2000).[2] The majority of migrants have an urban, working- or middle-class background, coming from Bogotá and other large and medium-size cities in the Valle del Cauca, Eje Cafetero, and Antioquia. There is also a significant proportion of upper-middle-class professionals and students, who do not mix much with the wider community. Most migrants have relatively high levels of formal education, especially the women. Despite this, a large majority work in low-skilled activities, such as domestic and industrial cleaning, and in catering or retail (see also McIlwaine 2005). A significant minority are also self-employed, while a small number work in skilled professions. Suggestions are that there are more women than men, the female ratio being 53.5–58.7, which contrasts with the higher feminization of flows to other European countries, such as Spain and Italy (but is similar to the US context) (Guarnizo 2008). The majority of Colombians in London are aged between 20 and 50, with most being 30–40 years old and in the economically active age bracket. While some studies suggest that most Colombians emigrate for socioeconomic reasons, other research has highlighted the interrelationships between different types of migration and the relevance of violence and insecurity for explaining Colombian migration flows (McIlwaine 2005, 2008).

A Gendered Analysis of Transnational Politics among Colombians in London

Studies on the transnational political activities of Colombian migrants in the United States argue that, compared with other Latin Americans, they are "the least likely to take part in home country politics" (Guarnizo, Portes, and Haller 2003, 1232; see also Guarnizo and Díaz 1999). This research points out that Colombians become more involved at the individual than the collective level and in general avoid continuous political engagement. This is mainly explained by the divisions and fragmentation affecting Colombian migrant communities, which are the result of class, regional, and ethnic differences, as well as the mistrust caused by the armed conflict and the illegal drugs trade in Colombia (Guarnizo, Sánchez, and Roach 1999; also Guarnizo 2008). In addition, such work suggests that in the case of Colombian migrants' transnational political participation, gender plays a limited role, especially when compared with other Latin American migrant communities in the United States, which has been explained mainly by the mostly urban and middle-class origin of these Colombian migration flows (Guarnizo, Portes, and Haller 2003; Guarnizo 2008).

My research also showed a high density of transnational links at the individual and private levels between Colombians in London and the home country, and other migrant destinations. These involved activities such as engaging in regular communication with family and friends, sending remittances, and in some cases travelling frequently to Colombia or other destinations, as well as involving in business transactions. Sometimes these transnational linkages did not happen in the expected direction, with some respondents admitting to receiving monetary transfers from Colombia rather than sending remittances (McIlwaine 2005). Also, sustaining these links had been easier for some migrants than others, depending on migrant status, socioeconomic background, and gender. However, in this section I explore how a gendered transnational political field has been developing based not only on individual activities but also on collective efforts from above and below. Although this research also examined the political participation of these migrants in relation to the host country, and the many connections between the transnational and local political fields (see Bermudez 2010), I will focus in this chapter on the political linkages maintained with the home country.

Participation in Formal Politics: Elections and Political Parties

Dividing the group of 30 Colombian migrants interviewed in London among those with little or no involvement in transnational politics, those with some involvement, and those who are the most heavily involved, only seven interviewees, all women, belonged to the first group. Women also predominated among those with some involvement, while men were a majority of the most heavily involved (five men and three women). At the formal political level, there were at least 13 men and women who said they participated in the Colombian elections (voting) or in other forms of electoral activity and party politics. This is no surprise, since Colombians abroad have a wide array of political rights, including the right to vote in presidential elections (since 1961), and following the 1991 constitution, the right to hold dual citizenship, vote in elections for the Senate, and choose their representative in the lower chamber of Congress.[3] The studies available have highlighted how voting rates from Colombians abroad tend to be reduced, with voter turnout being particularly low among the community in the UK (see table 12.1). However, these election results have to be contextualized.

Table 12.1 Rates of participation in the May 2006 presidential election in Colombia and abroad

	Spain	UK	France	Italy	US	Canada	Venezuela	Ecuador	Total abroad	National total
Potential votes	39193	5632	3935	2563	126959	7268	81298	13575	319045	26731700
Total votes (%)	28.74	29.94	43.96	32.81	48.05	47.44	23.29	37.27	37.82	45.11

Source: Registraduría Nacional del Estado Civil, República de Colombia (2006)

Generally, for those countries that allow their nationals abroad to vote in elections, external participation rates tend to be lower than internal. In addition, electoral participation in Colombia has been historically low compared to other countries in the region. This is partly a reflection of certain aspects of the Colombian political culture, such as distrust of the state, low appreciation of political parties, and a generally negative perception of the political process (Guarnizo 2008; Guarnizo, Portes, and Haller 2003), as expressed by some interviewees in the research. But there were other reasons why Colombians in London did not vote in the elections. Some interviewees complained about lack of information, poor facilities for voting, and the bureaucratic problems they had encountered, while others said they had been travelling or sick at the time of the elections. Community leaders Ruth and Juan explained that having to go all the way to the consulate to vote on a Sunday, which for many migrants was their only day of rest during the week, was a disincentive.

Nevertheless, this did not reflect a general lack of interest in home-country politics. A majority of respondents regularly followed the Colombian news and talked about the situation in the country, whether they were more actively involved in transnational politics or not. Other studies have argued that participation in conventional or formal politics can also involve activities such as expressing political opinions or generally talking about politics (Desposato and Norrander 2005; García Bedoya 2005). This was best expressed by Mariano, a young refugee man, who said he had not been able to vote for bureaucratic reasons, but was politically active in other ways:

> I do not have my *cédula* [national identity card] yet . . . But I make noise in other ways . . . Speaking, arguing, standing outside the Colombian embassy playing drums, which is a form of discussion.

Referring now to those Colombian migrants in the sample group who said they voted in the elections, although they included both men and women, there were some differences in the ways they explained their reasons for doing it. Men, for instance, seemed to be more informed and were more likely to defend the need to uphold democracy or to participate in order to have a voice, as two Colombian journalists noted: "I always vote. I always exercise my democratic rights" (Pedro) and "You have to participate if you want to complain" (Omar). Women, on the other hand, in some cases said they had voted influenced by others or seemed less informed about the political situation, as was the case of Vanesa, a lower-middle-class woman from Cali, who said she had never voted before but had recently started participating following the recommendations of her brother in Colombia. In general, those migrants with refugee status were the less inclined to vote, given their reluctance to approach the Colombian authorities.

Gender differences were even more noticeable when looking at levels and types of participation in more collective forms of formal political action, such as through political parties or contributions to election campaigns. The extent of such activities within the London-based Colombian community was very limited, especially when compared to Colombians in the United States, which can be partly explained by the greater geographical distance, the reduced numbers, and more recent establishment of the community in the UK. Nevertheless, as the Colombian political parties have gradually woken up to the potential of the diaspora, their presence is also growing within the European context. The current research found evidence of some instances of electoral campaigning around the 2006 polls in London, especially led by two, newer, political parties: Polo Democrático Alternativo (Alternative Democratic Pole, PDA), a coalition of leftist groups, and MIRA (Movimiento Independiente de Renovación Absoluta— Independent Movement for Absolute Renovation), a political movement associated with a Christian church.

Migrant participation in the political parties and their campaigns, as expected, was very reduced, with men predominating within the sample group, especially as organizers or representatives, while women acted in more support positions. The representative of MIRA in London was a man who had migrated to London to work and had been a member of the church associated with this political movement in Colombia. He explained how despite having started to organize formally as a party only recently, the group was already very active, participating in public events and offering the Colombian migrant community services, such as English classes. The person who was trying to organize support for the PDA in London was also a man, a former human rights lawyer who had left Colombia because of threats to his life and had become exiled in London for the second time. The only two women interviewed in London who actively participated in Colombian party politics, but in more secondary positions, were Ruth, who in the past had helped organize support for one of the candidates to represent the Colombian diaspora in Congress, and Pilar, who had participated in the Liberal Party election campaign from London. These women, and especially Ruth, who had also helped found a political movement for Latin Americans in London, the Latin Front, and was also active in British politics, were exceptions to a general pattern that reflects wider gender inequalities in political participation and representation in Colombia (and throughout the world).

Community Organizations and Their Transnational Links

Apart from the individual and collective forms of involvement in formal politics described above, other studies have already analyzed the formation and activities of Colombian transnational migrant organizations abroad (Mejía 2006). Most of these are in the United States, but there is a growing presence in Europe as well. Many of these groups are organized around general collective interests, such as maintaining national or regional cultural identities, and offer a wide array of activities and services for migrants. However, others have a more specific focus, whether they are business, professional, artistic, or sport groups, or have a political or religious orientation (Mejía 2006).

The research in London also found evidence of migrant participation in this type of collective informal politics. Despite the relative marginality of the Latin American population in the UK, in London, its presence is becoming increasingly visible, through several annual festivals and other cultural activities, business enterprises, sport leagues, media outlets, and other community services.[4] Since Colombians account for a significant part of the Latin American community, they have played a key role in these initiatives, a reflection also of the activism of many refugees, especially in the organizations created to help migrants at the local level or to denounce human rights and the situation of conflict in the home country. According to Paula, another Colombian journalist, this was logical, since many of the refugees who had settled in London were more open to identifying the needs of the community and trying to help because of their prior political and social experiences. Thus, many of these organizations had their origins in the solidarity and support groups set up by refugees arriving in the 1970s and 1980s, mostly from Chile,

Argentina, and also from Colombia. However, as the Latin American migrant community grew larger and more diverse, these groups began to focus more on serving the local needs of migrants. These were the cases, for instance, of Coras (Colombian Refugee Association), Carila (Latin American Welfare Group) and IRMO (Indoamerican Refugee and Migrant Organisation), as summed up by a Colombian woman who worked for IRMO:

> IRMO used to be called *Chile Democrático* [Democratic Chile], but following the downfall of Pinochet, a lot of Chileans returned to their country and the Chilean community was reduced to a small minority . . . then, those who were in charge decided to restructure the group, created a new constitution and opened up the organization . . . which they renamed . . . Indoamerican Refugee Migrant Organisation.

Both Carila and IRMO, as well as Coras, served the Latin American community and the wider local migrant population, but were led and staffed by Colombians (among others); this pattern was replicated in other Latin American community associations. Their main focus was on providing advice on immigration, labor, health, housing, and education to migrants, offering translation and interpreting services, and organizing cultural or social events for the community. In some cases, services were targeted toward specific groups, the elderly, the disabled, youth, or women. In general, these organizations are seen mostly as service providers and oriented toward the settlement society. They have also been described as depoliticized, divided, in competition with each other, and incapable of innovating to address issues of "integration" that go beyond arrival (Peró 2007). However, as Goldring and Landolt (2009) argue in their study of Latin American community organizations in Toronto, such groups can also help create the necessary spaces for the political socialization and incorporation of migrants. In the case of Colombians in London, the woman leader of the Latin Front mentioned before had a long history of prior community involvement, both in the business and service provider sectors. At the time of the research she was also in charge of the London offices of Aculco (Asociación Sociocultural y de Cooperación al Desarrollo por Colombia e Iberoamérica—Sociocultural and Development Cooperation Association for Colombia and Latin America), a community organization based in Spain but with representations in several countries of origin and settlement.

As the two examples mentioned, that of IRMO and the Latin Front show, and contrary to what was observed at the formal political level, Colombian women in London play a key role in more informal community politics from below. The leader of Carila, for instance, was also a Colombian woman. These women came mostly from a middle- or working-class background, as opposed to those who were most involved in formal politics, who tended to come from a more upper-middle-class origin, and had been living in London for over ten years; some had arrived in the UK to claim asylum, while others had migrated to study or to travel and visit Europe. Gendered analysis of migrants' political activism has suggested that women become more active in improving their local conditions than in home-country politics. Although the organizations in which these Colombian women were involved practiced mostly what Østergaard-Nielsen (2003, 762–63) defines as "immigrant politics"—"the political activities that migrants or refugees undertake to better their situation in the receiving country"—these can also have a transnational scope. This was clearer in the case of Aculco, whose main aim was to work toward improving the situation of migrants at the local level, as well as the living conditions of the communities from which they came. Within such work, one of the objectives was to achieve full political rights for migrants in both the home and host settings. Also, the role played by Colombian refugees in some of these organizations meant that most still had some residual, or more significant in the case of Coras and IRMO,[5] involvement in home-country politics, especially around the issues of the armed conflict and search for peace.

Apart from these, there were other initiatives with a strong transnational dimension and in which Colombians in London played a key role. Examples of this were the development of a very dynamic Latin American media sector, as well as the Latin American evangelical churches and philanthropic groups. Peró (2007) classifies these as representing in many cases "conservative" forms of political engagement, as opposed to the more "progressive" nature of the other organizations outlined above.[6] Women played a predominant role in the charity initiatives, especially those from upper- and middle-class backgrounds (see below), while men, on the other hand, were a majority of those interviewed in connection with the ethnic media and the church.

Other Diasporic Initiatives from Below and Above

My study also found evidence of other transnational political activities at the collective informal level in which Colombian men and women in London were involved and that have received less attention in the literature. These include those actions more directly related with the situation of armed conflict and search for peace in Colombia, or what Østergaard-Nielsen (2003, 762–63) calls "diaspora politics"—"usually about political disputes over sensitive issues such as national sovereignty and security"—and participation in the initiatives launched by private and public interests in Colombian to strengthen ties with the diaspora (for exceptions, see Bouvier 2007).

As noted above, many Colombians had to migrate for reasons directly or indirectly related to the conflict, and the great majority still has family members in the home country who are affected by it. References to the current conflict and past instances of political violence in Colombia were common in the narratives of respondents in London, even among nonrefugee migrants. Some of these experiences had helped shape political allegiances and commitment, as in the case of Freddy, a refugee man interviewed, who had been a human rights lawyer in Colombia and in exile in London and was involved both in trade union activities in the host country and in left-wing party politics in the homeland. In addition, as was the case with involvement in formal politics, most respondents followed the news on the conflict and had something to say about it, although opinions differed greatly, a sign of the polarization present in Colombia as well.

Thus, it is no surprise that Colombians abroad have also become increasingly active in collective political actions related to this. The diaspora participated both in the 1990 plebiscite on constitutional reform and the 1997 *consulta por la paz* (peace referendum) (Serrano Carrasco 2003; see also Pérez-Brennan 2003). As part of the growing efforts of Colombian civil society campaigning for peace, migrants have also demonstrated outside consular offices to protest against human rights abuses, or marched around the world to demand the freedom of all people kidnapped by the guerrillas. In London, several organizations were active in raising awareness of the conflict and human rights situation in Colombia. The best example of this had been Coras, although at the time of the research they had lost their funding and were almost nonoperative.[7] IRMO and Nueva Generación (New Generation) had also participated in this type of work, and all three organizations had been a focal point of support for Colombian refugees. In addition, there were two organizations specifically focused on the human rights situation and search for peace in Colombia, one British-based but with some Colombian presence and links to the Colombian community, and another one with both British and Colombian members.[8] Their work involved mainly raising awareness internationally of the Colombian armed conflict and campaigning for a peaceful resolution, denouncing human rights abuses, and funding and supporting other similar organizations and projects in Colombia. Aside from these more formal organizations, my research also identified informal networks of Colombians, mostly refugees, working on these issues on a less institutionalized basis, for instance, through the convocation of meetings and talks organized on a word of mouth basis or through e-mail lists.

As is the case with the other community organizations researched, women had an active presence in these types of activities, especially if they had migrated because of the conflict. Men refugees were also particularly active in these types of political action, especially if they related to the more traditionally male-dominated spheres of leftist political parties and trade unions, as in the case of "Freddy" above. However, in general, as was the case with participation in party and electoral politics (beyond voting), these men and women represented a minority within the larger Colombian community. As other studies have suggested, this research also found evidence of mistrust of such political activities and a general sense of tiredness with the situation of conflict and hopelessness as to its resolution, a reflection of the deteriorating conditions in the home country. As Nelly, a community leader in London argued, "the impact [of our activities from here] is minimal . . . so it's better to spend our energy and time in our specific problems here." Nevertheless, the potential was there, and the contribution of Colombians abroad to civil society efforts at home to achieve a peaceful end to the conflict needs to be considered in detail, as studies in the context of other migrations to Europe have reflected (see Bermudez 2011; Zunzer 2004).

Finally, in the last few years, several initiatives have emerged from public and private interests in Colombia aimed at strengthening links with the diaspora (Colombia Nos Une—Colombia Unites Us; Conexión Colombia—Colombian Connection) or allocating it a special role (Colombia es Pasión—Colombia is Passion; Yo Creo en Colombia—I Believe in Colombia). Their activities include more social roles, such as informing and connecting people, and promoting diaspora philanthropy, but also more political actions such as promoting a specific image of Colombia abroad. The impact of these programs within the community in London was found to be minimal, partly because they were relatively recent and not many people knew about them yet. However, in the field work conducted within the Colombian community in Spain (Madrid and Barcelona), they seemed to be more active. Only two Colombian men who were in charge of promoting support for them were interviewed in London in connection with these initiatives. But upper- and middle-class women in London were also involved in these types of transnational initiatives, as Gabriel, the leader of I Believe in Colombia, explained:

> "[In the team] there are more women than men . . . although the idea motivates men and women equally, when it comes to commitment, women are more committed . . . I don't know, I think that may be women end up feeling closer to Colombia when they are abroad, and they are more motivated to do things for their country.

Other studies have analyzed the role of women in the formation of nations, and vis-à-vis nationalist and patriotic causes, and equally, women migrants have been found to be very active in transnational practices such as the sending of remittances to their families or in diaspora philanthropy, whether this is organized from below, as noted earlier, or from above as in the case of the Colombian initiatives explored here (see Glick-Schiller and Fouron 2001; Mama Cash 2006).

Conclusions

This chapter has focused on Colombian migration to London and the nature of their transnational political practices. In contrast with much of the existing work available, my study used a qualitative and conceptual approach that allowed for a broad definition of transnational political practices, both formal and informal, from above and below, and at the individual and collective levels, as well as a wide range of different types of migrants. This approach helped bring to the fore the different forms of transnational political participation among Colombian migrants, as opposed to the political apathy highlighted by other studies.

In addition, the research conducted contributes to the gender analysis of migrant transnational politics by highlighting how differences in levels and types of involvement by men and women are mediated not only by gender, but also by factors such as social class and type of migration. Among Colombian migrants in London, it seems that although men predominate in certain types of transnational political activities oriented toward the home country, especially the more formal ones, women also played an active part, especially in community and philanthropic initiatives (promoted from above and below). Thus, these results partly contradict the conclusions of other studies, and support the claims of alternative work (see Gammage 2004). As previous research on Colombian transnational practices had argued, this reflects in part the class composition of the Colombian community in London, with a significant proportion of middle- and upper-class migrants. These migrants were the most heavily involved in transnational political activities from above, which is no surprise, since these required collaboration with the authorities and access to Internet. On the other hand, men and women from working-class and lower-middle-class origins also played a key political role within the community, both in activities oriented toward the home country, and in host country politics. Here, the role of refugee men and women was very evident, and especially of women community leaders.

This chapter thus argues that the transnational political participation of migrants needs to be studied in further detail from a gendered perspective, seeking to understand not only how men and women might participate in different ways, but also looking at the influence of other individual factors, such as social class and type of migration, as well as the wider contexts in which these transnational practices are developed.

Acknowledgments

I would like to thank Cathy McIlwaine for her comments and revisions of the original paper. I would also like to thank the Economic and Social Research Council (PTA-030-2002-01565) who funded this research as part of my PhD at the School of Geography, Queen Mary, University of London.

Notes

1. Since the aim was not to find a representative sample, interviewees were recruited because of their involvement in different political activities, using previous contacts, identified groups, and snowball methods. The research focused on reasons for migrating, choice of destination, and life in the host society, and especially migrant political practices oriented toward the home country.
2. The information that follows is taken mainly from Guarnizo (2008) and Open Channels (2000).
3. This chamber allows for the election of five members as part of the *circunscripciones especiales* (special electoral districts): two for indigenous communities, two for Afro-Colombians, and one for Colombians abroad.
4. See the listings available in the *Directorio Iberoamericano* (Latin American Directory) [http://www.directoriol.com/indice.php?ciudad=LON&TPN=LAT] (accessed June 11, 2007).
5. Nueva Generación (New Generation) was a group linked to IRMO that worked with Latin American youth and arts. It started as a project

to help children that arrived with their migrant and refugee parents and the second generation being born in the country, but with time had acquired a more independent status and had established links with youth groups in Colombia, as well as in other Latin American countries and outside the region.

6. The Directorio Iberoamericano lists 13 written media outlets and seven radio stations serving the Spanish-speaking community in London. One of the evangelical churches identified during the research was the Iglesia de Jesucristo Internacional (Church of Jesus Christ International), linked to the Colombian political party MIRA. Within the charity sector two groups were explored, Children of the Andes, which worked mainly in Colombia and, despite being a British organization, had Colombian members of staff and volunteers, as well as links with the Latin American migrant community in London, and Friends of Colombia for Social Aid, a mixed organization mainly linked to the better off classes.

7. This organization has now ceased to exist.

8. These were Justice for Colombia and the Colombian Solidarity Campaign.

References

Bermudez, Anastasia. 2010. "Transnational Political Practices of Colombians in Spain and the United Kingdom: Politics 'here' and 'there.'" *Ethnic and Racial Studies* 33(1): 75–91.

———. 2011. "The 'Diaspora Politics' of Colombian Migrants in the UK and Spain." *International Migration* (forthcoming).

Bouvier, Virginia. 2007. "A Reluctant Diaspora? The Case of Colombia. In *Diasporas in Conflict: Peace-Makers or Peacewreckers?*, ed. Hazel Smith and Paul Stares, 129–52. Tokyo and New York: United Nations University Press.

Conpes (Consejo Nacional de Política Económica y Social, República de Colombia, Departamento Nacional de Planeación). 2009. Política integral migratoria. Documento Conpes 3603, August 24, Bogotá, Colombia.

Desposato, Scott, and Barbara Norrander. 2005. "The Participation Gap: Systemic and Individual Influences on Gender Differences in Political Participation." http://www.latinobarometro.org/fileadmin/documentos /articulos_y_documentos/The_Participation_Gap.pdf (accessed November 17, 2007).

Gammage, Sarah. 2004. "Exercising Exit, Voice and Loyalty: A Gender Perspective on Transnationalism in Haiti." *Development and Change* 35 (4): 743–71.

García Bedoya, Lisa. 2005. *Fluid Borders. Latino Power, Identity, and Politics in Los Angeles.* Berkeley, Los Angeles, and London: University of California Press.

Glick-Schiller, Nina, and Georges E. Fouron. 2001. *Georges Woke Up Laughing: Long-Distance Nationalism and the Search for Home.* Durham, NJ: Duke University Press.

Goldring, Luin. 2001. "The Gender and Geography of Citizenship in Mexico-U.S. Transnational Spaces." *Identities* 7 (4): 501–37.

Goldring, Luin, and Patricia Landolt. 2009. "Las organizaciones de migrantes latinoamericanos en Toronto: entre las políticas de base, y el imperativo de la etnización del estado multicultural." In *Migración y participación política. Estados, organizaciones y migrantes latinoamericanos en perspectiva local-transnacional,* ed. Angeles Escrivá, Anastasia Bermudez and Natalia Moraes, 203–34. Madrid: CSIC.

Guarnizo, Luis E. 2008. *Londres Latina: La Presencia Colombiana en la Capital Britanica.* México DF: Universidad de Zacatecas and Miguel Angel Porrúa.

Guarnizo, Luis E., and Luz Marina Díaz. 1999. "Transnational Migration: A View from Colombia." *Ethnic and Racial Studies* 22 (2): 397–421.

Guarnizo, Luis E., Alejandro Portes, and William Haller. 2003. "Assimilation and Transnationalism: Determinants of Transnational Political Action among Contemporary Migrants." *American Journal of Sociology* 108 (6): 1211–48.

Guarnizo, Luis E., Arturo I. Sánchez, and Elisabeth M. Roach. 1999. "Mistrust, Fragmented Solidarity, and Transnational Migration: Colombians in New York City and Los Angeles." *Ethnic and Racial Studies* 22 (2): 367–96.

Itzigsohn, Jose, Carlos Dore Cabral, Esther Hernández Medina, and Obed Vázquez. 1999. "Mapping Dominican Transnationalism: Narrow and Broad Transnational Practices." *Ethnic and Racial Studies* 22 (2): 316–39.

Itzigsohn, Jose, and Silvia Giourguli-Saucedo. 2005. "Incorporation, Transnationalism, and Gender: Immigrant Incorporation and Transanational Participation as Gendered Processes." *International Migration Review* 39 (4): 895–920.

Jones-Correa, Michael. 1998. *Between Two Nations. The Political Predicament of Latinos in New York City.* Ithaca, NY, and London: Cornell University Press.

Levitt, Peggy, Josh DeWind, and Steven Vertovec. 2003. "International Perspectives on Transnational Migration: An Introduction." *International Migration Review* 37 (3): 565–75.

Mahler, Sarah J. 1998. "Theoretical and Empirical Contributions toward a Research Agenda for Transnationalism." In *Transnationalism from Below,* ed. Michael P. Smith and Luis E. Guarnizo, 64–102. New Brunswick, NJ, and London: Transaction Publishers.

Mahler, Sarah J., and Patricia Pessar. 2006. "Gender Matters: Ethnographers Bring Gender from the Periphery toward the Core of Migration Studies." *International Migration Review* 40 (1): 27–63.

Mama Cash. 2006. "(she gives back) Migrant Women's Philanthropic Practices from the Diaspora. Research Report (she changes the world)." [Available from: http://www.mamacash.nl/site/docs)shegivesback _researchreport.def.pdf] (accessed June 18, 2007).

McIlwaine, Cathy. 2005. "Coping Practices among Colombian Migrants in London." London: Queen Mary, University of London (Available from: http://www.geog.qmul.ac.uk/docs/staff/4402.pdf) (accessed May 2, 2011).

———. 2008. "Challenging Displacement: Livelihood Practices among Colombian Migrants in London." London: Queen Mary, University of London.

McIlwaine, Cathy, and Anastasia Bermudez. 2011. "The Gendering of Civic and Political Engagement among Colombian Migrants in London." *Environment and Planning A* 43: 1499–1513.

Mejía, William. 2006. "Colombianos Organizados en el Exterior y Transnacionalismo. Paper presented at the 52th International Congress of Americanists, July 17–21, in Seville, Spain.

Open Channels. 2000. "The Colombian Community in London." Peterborough, UK: Open Channels.

Østergaard-Nielsen, Eva. 2003. "The Politics of Migrants' Transnational Political Practices." *International Migration Review* 37 (3): 760–86.

Pérez-Brennan, Tanya. 2003. "Colombian Immigration. Fighting Back: Activism in New York." *ReVista. Harvard Review of Latin America* 2 (3): 86–87.

Peró, Davide. 2007. "Anthropological Perspectives on Migrants' Political Engagements." Working Paper no. 50, COMPAS, Oxford: University of Oxford.

Piper, Nicola. 2006. "Gendering the Politics of Migration." *International Migration Research* 40 (1): 133–64.

Reed-Danahay, Deborah, and Caroline B. Brettell. 2008. *Citizenship, Political Engagement, and Belonging. Immigrants in Europe and the United States.* New Brunswick, NJ, and London: Rutgers University Press.

Serrano Carrasco, Angela L. 2003. "Colombia, la posibilidad de una ciuda- danía sin fronteras." In *Votar en la Distancia: la Extensión de los Derechos Políticos a Migrantes, Experiencias Comparadas,* ed. Leticia Calderón Chelius, 115–44. Mexico: Instituto Mora.

Smith, Michael P., and Luis E. Guarnizo, eds. 1998. *Transnationalism from Below.* New Brunswick, NJ, and London: Transaction Publishers.

Zunzer, Wolfram. 2004. "Diaspora Communities and Civil Conflict Transformation." Berghof Occasional Paper no. 26, Berlin: Berghof Research Center for Constructive Conflict Management.

Chapter 13

Everyday Transnationalism: Religion in the Lives of Brazilian Migrants in London and Brazil

Olivia Sheringham

While migration from Brazil to London is by no means insignificant, London's Brazilian community remains largely invisible within existing migration research and within the public consciousness. Such invisibility has been put down to various factors including the recentness of the flow, the tendency for migration research in the UK to focus on communities with direct colonial or historical links to Britain , the fact that many Brazilian migrants are undocumented and so choose to keep a low profile (Evans et al. 2007), and finally, the fact that, compared with many other migrant groups, there exist few examples of institutional or informal support networks to mobilize or unite the community . Yet there is little doubt that London's Brazilian community has grown rapidly in recent years, evident through the emergence of a growing number of Brazilian shops, restaurants, and, perhaps most significantly, a diverse range of religious institutions. This chapter explores the role of religion in the lives and imaginations of Brazilian migrants in London, their families "back home" in Brazil, and, furthermore, how it enables them to create and maintain links between the two. Conceptually, the relationship between religion and migrant transnationalism is one that has, until recently, been largely overlooked within academic research. Yet it has become increasingly clear that as cities such as London have become ever more "super diverse" (Vertovec 2007), multiple new religious spaces, beliefs, and practices have emerged, demanding greater understanding and engagement among both academics and policy makers (Smith 2000; Wills et al. 2009; Garbin, 2010). This chapter thus contributes to an emerging body of work that explores the relationship between migrant transnationalism and religion. It begins with a discussion of some of the theoretical debates on the relationship between religion, globalization and transnationalism, and more recent research that considers "everyday" religion. The subsequent sections discuss the key contextual factors surrounding the research, and its methodology. These broader arguments are then discussed in relation to the narratives of Brazilian migrants and their families in sending and receiving contexts, with reference to data collected through ongoing ethnographic research in both London and three towns in Brazil. While highlighting the important role of religious institutions in providing social and spiritual support for migrants and their families in new contexts, I argue that more attention needs to be paid to manifestations of religion beyond the institutional realm. For many Brazilian migrants, their individual faith in God is an integral part of the migration experience.

Religion across Borders: From the Transnational to the Everyday

While the historical links between religion and global transformations have been widely documented, recent research on processes of globalization has neglected the theme of religion. Indeed, emphasizing its economic, political, and, later, cultural dimensions, globalization tended to be theorized within a broadly secular framework, linked to modernity and a move away from tradition and hence religious adherence (Vazquez and Marquardt 2003; see also Beyer 2006). However, the irrefutable evidence of a religious resurgence in recent decades—most notably in the Global South and with increasing prevalence in major cities of the Global North (Freston 2001)—has challenged such secularizing or privatizing predictions and revealed a more multifaceted religious arena (Beyer 1990; Casanova 1994).

The religious field in Brazil is a key example of such religious complexity. An enduring remnant of the country's colonial past, Catholicism—brought by the Portuguese and established as the national religion—remains the predominant religion (Lehmann 2000; see also Deccol 2001). Yet Brazil is now also the second largest Protestant country in the world (Freston 2008), the world capital of Spiritism, and home to a myriad other religious movements, including Afro-Brazilian religions and Buddhism (ibid.; see also Pierrucci and Prandi 2000). While the presence of Afro-Brazilian religion has its roots in the slave trade, the significant spread of Protestantism—

and in particular Pentecostalism—across the country, dates back to the arrival of European migrants, and missionaries, in the nineteenth and, most notably, twentieth, century (Deccol 2001).

Thus the diverse and constantly changing religious field in Brazil, while undoubtedly influenced by, and adapted to, very specific local contexts, is inextricably linked with changes at the global scale. For Levitt (2007, 12), it is imperative that analyses of religion in the contemporary world take a global perspective as, she argues, "we must see the local Mosque or Pentecostal church as part of multilayered webs of connection where religious 'goods' are produced and exchanged around the globe."

So, despite the fact that "[r]eligious communities are among the oldest transnationals" (Rudolph 1997, 1), the prevailing literature across the social sciences relating to globalization, and more recently to transnationalism, has tended to ignore religion's crucial role (Ebaugh and Chafetz 2002, 190).[1] Some recent studies of migrants have responded to the need to "bring religion back in" to migration research, yet such research remains largely limited to the US context, and how migrants have contributed to fundamental changes in the US religious landscape (Diaz-Stevens and Stevens Arroyo 1997; Warner and Wittner 1998; Menjivar 2006; Vasquez and Marquardt 2003; Leonard et al. 2005; Levitt 2007). In Europe, the few studies that have considered the role of religion among migrants have focused mainly on Islam (Foner and Alba 2008), on transformations within contemporary religious institutions (Smith 2000), or on the extent to which religion encourages or inhibits migrant incorporation (Tubergen 2007).

Among scholars working on Brazilian emigration, religion has emerged as a pertinent theme (Martes 1999, 2000), yet the focus is, again, on Brazilian migrants in the United States—and in particular those emigrating from the town of Governador Valadares, in the state of Minas Gerais, the origin of Brazil's first significant emigration flow (Siqueira 2003). Interestingly, however, some recent studies of this particular migratory movement consider the impact of migration on the religious practices of family members left behind (Amorim, Dias, and Siqueira 2008), or people planning to emigrate (Duarte et al. 2008).

These studies are insightful as they reveal how the interrelation between religion and migration is manifested not just in the receiving context, but also the sending one (see also Hagan and Ebaugh 2003). However, as with Levitt's (2007) multisited research into migrant religion, the focus is predominantly on religious institutions, as opposed to the experiences of migrants themselves and how their religious practices and beliefs, beyond the church, influence, enable, and adapt to the experience of living across borders.

Elsewhere, however, some scholars have pointed to the need for more grounded work that considers how religion is actually lived (Orsi 2003; McGuire 2008) or practiced in the everyday lives of individuals and communities (see also Ammerman 2006). Thus, even if the declining "orthodoxy of belief and regularity of attendance" suggest that religion's significance is diminishing, the study of everyday religion reveals how "religious ideas and practices may be present even when they are neither theologically pure nor socially insulated" (Ammerman 2006, 4, 6). This broader meaning of religion reflects what Appadurai (1996, 7) terms "new religiosities," or what McGuire (2006, 187) describes as the ways by which "people make sense of their world—the 'stories' out of which they live." Indeed. the study of religion, as some have recently argued, requires less the "seizing" of religion as a point of investigation, than a two-way dialogue, in which religion "speaks back" through its own specificities (Yorgsan and della Dora 2009, 631).

As well as religious institutions, this chapter also considers how migrants (and their families) use religion in their everyday lives, in order to live transnationally, and to cope with the psychological or practical challenges of life in a new country. Yet, while not discussed here in detail, attention to the agency of migrants must not overlook other fundamental factors and actors that impact upon their everyday transnational lives, in particular the social and political strategies "for identifying who has access to certain places and under what conditions" (Silvey and Lawson 1999, 128). Indeed, large numbers of Brazilian migrants in London are undocumented and often forced to work in insecure, low-paid, and often exploitative conditions. The following sections will provide some background to the research, before going on to consider some of its empirical findings.

Contextualizing Brazilians in London

The exodus of vast numbers of Brazilians since the late 1980s represents a reversal of historical trends in a country that, up until the 1960s, had been a recipient of diverse flows of immigrants (Sales 2000; Beserra 2003). There is a general consensus in the literature that the first massive wave of emigration from Brazil occurred toward the end of the 1980s, known as the "lost decade" throughout Latin America.[2] The economic crises gave rise to what Sales (2000, 152) refers to as the "triennium of disillusionment": a time of hope and expectation at the return of democracy that was soon thwarted by inflation, unemployment, and recession. Since these initial outward waves, predominantly to the United States, Brazilian emigration has become a widespread phenomenon and in recent years, significant numbers have begun migrating to Europe, adding to rather than substituting the US-bound trend (Padilla 2006). Moreover, sending regions have diversified to the extent that, as Margolis (2008, 342) writes, "emigration has become a national phenomenon in Brazil."

While there is still a relative absence of research into the lives of London's Brazilians compared to other migrant groups, it is increasingly clear that they represent a significant "new migrant group" in the UK (Evans et al. 2007, 2011). Unofficial estimates, including an extensive study conducted by the Evelyn Oldfield unit, put the number in London alone at somewhere between 150,000 and 200,000 (see also Evans et al., 2007, 2011), while the Brazilian government estimates 180,000 Brazilians in the UK (MRE 2009).[3]

One thing that is very clear from existing research is that Brazilian migrants represent a highly diverse group in relation to factors such as generation, gender, occupation, migration experience, social class, region of origin, and religious affiliation (Patarra 2005). Despite such differences, the majority of Brazilians in London are economic migrants, coming predominantly to work and make money to invest back home (Evans et al. 2011). Moreover, the great majority are employed in low-skilled, low-paid service-sector jobs, often due to lack of language skills or appropriate documents as opposed to educational level, which is, in many cases quite high (McIlwaine, Cock, and Linneker 2011). Broadly reflecting the employment profile of Brazilian migrants in other countries, women are primarily employed as cleaners, while men tend to work in restaurants, as construction workers, or, notably, as couriers (ibid.).

London's sizeable Brazilian presence is reflected in the growing numbers of shops, restaurants, beauty salons, and community newspapers that exist, established predominantly by Brazilians to serve Brazilians. However, despite the presence of these commercial spaces, there exist only two community organizations that support Brazilian migrants. By contrast, churches of varying denominations represent crucial spaces in which Brazilian migrants come together and are able to be more visible in expressing both their religious faith and their cultural identity. According to recent estimates, there are approximately 70 Brazilian Protestant Evangelical churches, and Catholic Mass held in eight different churches across London (Evangelical Alliance).

The proliferation of Brazilian churches in London is in many ways unsurprising given the prevalence of different religious institutions in Brazil itself within a "religious field" that has undergone important changes in recent years (see above). After a brief discussion of my methodology, the following sections will consider religion in the lives of Brazilians in London, through recourse to empirical material.

Methodological Considerations

Since this study is concerned with the relationship between religion and the migration process, a methodological approach that could encompass both sides of the migration flow was considered crucial. This chapter thus draws on data collected through ongoing empirical research among Brazilian migrants in London between September 2009 and March 2010, and during two periods of research in the states of Minas Gerais and Goias in Brazil in June 2009 and between April and July 2010. The London-based research consisted of ethnographic research in two churches: one Catholic, which I refer to as St. Mary's (a pseudonym) and one evangelical that was founded in 1990 by a Brazilian Pastor who has now established another branch of the church back in Brazil. I refer to this one as the CE (Comunidade Evangélica), also a pseudonym.

These churches were chosen because they are two of the longest-standing Brazilian churches in London and have a large number of congregants. At the time of writing, a total of 40 in-depth interviews were conducted, with 15 members of each church, as well as religious leaders and other members of the Brazilian community. In Brazil I stayed with four different families—relatives of migrants interviewed in London, and who lived in towns where there were large numbers of people living in London. Living with families enabled me to be an active observer of and participant in informal conversations and everyday activities. Thus, I could observe first-hand the ways in which religion was (or not) incorporated into peoples' everyday lives through, for example, the presence religious objects in the home, religious music, television programs, or home-prayer groups. Furthermore, as well as five in-depth interviews with family members of migrants in London, I also interviewed 20 return migrants, and three religious leaders. Participants in both London and Brazil were accessed through existing contacts in the Brazilian community, through attending religious services and events at both churches in London, and, predominantly, through the use of the snowballing technique as participants would often introduce me to other potential respondents (Margolis 1998, xi).

All interviews were carried out in Portuguese and appear in the text, in italics, as my translation.

Thanks to London and to God: Religion across Borders

Churches Adapting to New Circumstances

The notion of adaptation in terms of how the church must adapt in order to respond to the diverse needs of migrants was one of the key issues that emerged in my conversations with church leaders (three Catholic Priests and two evangelical Pastors) in London. Thus, far from merely replicating churches in Brazil, these churches in the receiving society needed to be flexible and take on different roles in response to the new context. In the case of St. Mary's, Padre José described this as a kind of "broadening," or greater open-mindedness. He said that while the doctrines of the Catholic Church could never be changed, "the discipline" had to be loosened so as to address some of the challenges facing migrants. These included (in his words) the fact that many members were undocumented, and that there were couples living together outside marriage, as they were unable to marry legally in the UK. Furthermore, he said that he was fully aware that in the new context, many people attended church to address their practical as opposed to spiritual needs. He explained: "People come to church more here than in Brazil—out of need . . . The majority come to church because they feel a lack, be it of a sense of 'Brazilian-ness', of their language, of somewhere to live." Padre Omario mentioned the very different role for church leaders in the receiving context given the fact that many migrants were short-term residents, making it difficult to carry out any long-term "religious orientation." Thus, he suggested that the role of the priest in the receiving context often becomes that of providing more immediate "psychological support and advice": a shoulder to cry on, or a listening ear for people to recount the problems they face in London.

Pastor Nielton, from the CE, said that the "community" (meaning the religious institution) was theologically very open, a necessity, he believed, for a church in diaspora. Thus, while they didn't define themselves as Pentecostal, the service style included elements of a Pentecostal service, such as talking in tongues, as many of the members had been Pentecostal in Brazil. He said that members brought what he called "theological baggage" and that the church needed to respond to diverse expectations. The CE in London maintained ties with the branch of the church in Brazil, yet, he said, these were fraternal as opposed to institutional, as the London-based church needed to remain theologically independent so as to accommodate a certain doctrinal and practical flexibility in response to migrants' needs.

On the other hand, in contrast to St. Mary's, the CE seemed somewhat less open when it came to acceptance of members' behavior in a different context. While the Catholic leaders seemed to be openly supportive of undocumented migrants, the agreed line among the evangelical leaders was openly against migrants being undocumented, and people were encouraged to "regularize" their situation. The founding pastor, Pastor Marco, explained how such a stance had its roots in the teachings of the Bible and the teachings of the Apostle Paul under Caesar during the Roman Empire. He explained:

> Apostle Paul shows clearly that we must obey the authorities because there are no authorities that have not been established by God. So, based on these biblical teachings, we instruct people that they change their situations, that they regularize themselves.

Furthermore, among interviewees who frequented the church, some mentioned how they had not wanted the pastor to know that they were undocumented, as they knew that it was disapproved of. Juliana, who frequented the Brazilian branch of the CE, was in fact deported, having lived for three years as an irregular migrant in London. She talked about the guilt that she felt as she had known that the church had disapproved of her actions, but how now she was on a true, honest path back in Brazil, and was strongly supported by the church. Wagner, another return migrant, explained that he had returned home as his visa had expired and he felt too much guilt while living illegally in London and knew that this was condemned by the church. Yet, despite the CE's openly hard line, undocumented migrants were by no means turned away. As Pastor Neilton said, "we wouldn't let anyone go hungry or homeless." Rather, they were given support and guidance, both spiritual, through specific prayers, and practical, in their quest for regularization.

Such attitudes echo the findings of Duarte et al. (2008) in their discussion of evangelical churches in the Brazilian town of Governador Valadares. They describe how, while the churches' doctrines were openly against the emigration of Brazilians from the town, which they knew was illegal in most cases, they continued to provide support to both these migrants and their families who stayed behind. Thus the churches, by necessity, ended up adapting to the demands of their members. Even if, they remark, "they position themselves effectively against illegal emigration, the churches do not stop supporting those who partake in this process" (Duarte et al. 2008, 10, my translation). The CE seemed to hold a similar attitude, explicitly condemning illegal migration, yet still offering support to those such as Juliana and Wagner whose actions went counter to the official line. Thus, in both sending and receiving contexts, the realities of migration compel many churches to adapt both their practices and doctrines to address the new needs of their members.

Religious Practices in a New Context

Just as the churches themselves have to adapt their doctrines and practices so as to respond to the diverse needs of migrants in new circumstances, so the religious practices of migrants—the ways they "use" the churches—undergo changes in the new context. Among the majority of respondents in London, the church seemed to take on a different, and in some cases more important, role than in their home context. Indeed, within the descriptions of their experiences of living in London, there was a recurring notion of lack, or emptiness, a lacuna that the church played an important role in filling. This was often expressed with reference to the social dimension of religion—how the church represents a space in which to meet people, and to feel more at home in an otherwise unfamiliar environment. Dulce, from St. Mary's, remarked:

> It's just that here [in London] I feel an even greater need to go to church—because that's when you feel a lack—and you go through lots of problems here . . . I couldn't imagine myself here without having a community—in the church—in which to participate.

Indeed, for many interviewees, the church in London became their new family in a context where their real family was far away. This narrative was particularly pertinent among evangelical respondents from the CE, which could reflect the fact that the majority were young and single and thus not in London with any family members, compared with most of my Catholic respondents who were with at least one family member. Tania, for example, described the role of the church in her life here in London as

> very important . . . because I found a family here and I think this provides you with a base, it's like, you have to have some kind of structure behind you . . . I came here without my dad, without my mum, without anyone, and I've been here until now without anyone in my family . . . So here [at the church] I have a family structure, you see.

Similarly, Florencia, at the CE in Brazil, recalling her experience living in London for six years where she had frequented the CE there, remarked:

> Goodness! There we were like . . . a family . . . You would go to the church and say "I don't have any money for food", and the money would appear. You don't have anywhere to live and someone would say "come, you can stay at my house . . . " . . . It was like a real family—we'd get together on Sundays and all be together . . . Here it's not like that—here you have your family and you go to their house.

Yet, perhaps more importantly, the discourse of the CE itself evokes the community as a family—in communion with God. Thus members address each other as *irmão/irmã* (brother or sister), and, within the family structure, everyone has a role in what are called *ministérios* (ministries). There was, for example, a ministry of music (the largest and very important), a ministry of multimedia (in charge of broadcasting the *cultos* [services] and maintaining the church's Web site), and a ministry of teaching (in charge of organizing English and Portuguese classes). As Pastor Marco explained, the church encourages people to discover their "spiritual ability," or particular talent, which they can then contribute to the family structure.

Within the Brazilian branch of the church these ministries also existed, yet they seemed to play a less prominent role than in London. Beatrice, a return migrant at the CE remarked: You have other things to do here—clean the house, visit your family. Here I have less time to spend at the church." Another returnee, Wagner, explained that in London the transport was much cheaper and more reliable, which made it easier for him to go to church every day after work to participate in his ministry. Back in Brazil he went just once or twice a week for the culto, and to teach English on Saturdays.

Another recurring theme among the London migrants was that coworshippers met at the church were more likely to be "good" and trustworthy as compared to other people (usually other Brazilians) in London.[4] Paulo, who had not been a church-goer in Brazil, began frequenting St. Mary's in London because, he said,

> People who go to the church—of course we know that they're not perfect—but . . . without doubt you'll find good qualities in them, true words—you know? . . . It's the opposite of when you meet people in a bar, or in the street, in different places in London because . . . the people who are there—they're only there for pleasure . . . to drink, for women etc. When you are there [in the church], you are there to find God, to find peace.

Indeed, as this citation suggests, there is a sense that the church provides a moral framework to follow in an otherwise "immoral" city of pleasures. This moral discourse also points to a kind of insider/outsider dichotomy whereby those who are members of the church (in this case, Catholic), or who are believers, have the strength to remain within this moral framework, whereas many other Brazilians "lose themselves" (Ana) and have no clear path to follow. Religion, in this sense, provides a means by which to control any "immoral" urges. Ana's words illustrate such a view:

> I would say that without it [the church], without this communion with God, it is very difficult to live here without doing immoral things. Because the majority of Brazilians come here and they lose themselves . . . They become involved with drugs, with prostitution, sometimes even robbery . . . I think that the church becomes a way of not getting involved, of attempting to get out, or of attempting to avoid [such things].

The role of the church in the creation and maintenance of social networks also emerged as an important theme across the interviews, once again reflecting different "uses" of the church within the migration context. Thus, for many respondents, both Catholic and Evangelical, the church represented the first point of call for finding jobs, a place to live, or someone to look after your children, among other things. Lucas, a return migrant in Brazil, said that his life would have been "very difficult" without the church (St. Mary's), since

> the people at the church help a lot with overcoming problems—you can make new friends, meet other Brazilians. Before we went to church we didn't have much contact with people in London.

Sidney, another returnee, who had been brought up a Catholic, recounted how he began to attend the CE in London because his first, Brazilian, landlady in London attended the cultos (services), and invited him to go with her. When he was there he got talking to someone during the social gathering after the culto who offered him his first job. After this, he went every so often to a culto, but mainly to meet up with his friends, with people he knew he could trust. He described it as the "base" of everything for him in London: "friends, work . . . everything, the base for good friendships. When I went there I felt a sense of peace."

Unlike the majority of the evangelical respondents, however, he hadn't been "born again," and back in Brazil he did not frequent the church as he did not feel the same necessity as in London.

Thus, for many Brazilian migrants in London, the church seemed to take on a new role as a consequence of migrating. Whether it is merely to find a job or to socialize with other Brazilians, or whether it is to "nurture one's faith in the divine force of God" (Ana), for migrants whose lives are challenging, and often filled with fear, the church can represent a space in which they can gather together and create a familiar, safe, Brazilian space. However, while the above sections seem to concur with the findings of existing studies of migrant churches in terms of their role in creating a space of sociability and spirituality (for example, Vasquez and Marquardt 2003), it seems that, for many Brazilian migrants and their families, the church itself was by no means more pertinent than their individual faith that was manifested in diverse ways in their everyday lives.

Everyday Faith across Borders

Individual contact with God seemed to represent, for many, the ultimate solace in the face of the loneliness and hardship encountered in London. Nestor, who taught English at St. Mary's every weekday, explained how his faith inspired him,

> The most important thing for me isn't the Catholic Church, but my faith, what I believe in. Independent of me being in the church, I know that God is with me all the time . . . I always try to do the best that I can . . . these classes that I give, are for free. I know that it is good to help people . . . it's my religion.

Among respondents from the CE, the presence of religion in their everyday lives seemed to be reflected in the all-encompassing nature of their faith. Their narratives suggested that God was in charge of every aspect of their everyday life, and there was no separation between the sacred and the everyday—God is their everyday. As Lucia, replied when asked what she meant when she said that Christ was her priority: "It means wanting to follow God's will, do what he wants me to do with my life and not what I want. I can't do what I want anymore."

While the notion of God's presence in their everyday lives was also apparent in the narratives of many Catholic participants, the discourse seemed to be less about God working on them—transforming them, but rather, comforting and protecting them. As Maria, explained:

> I feel the presence [of God] all the time. When you're walking in the street you feel God's presence because he is protecting you from

someone, from a thief . . . from some kind of danger, a car, something that's out of control, a hole in the road, or something bad that might happen.

The relationship between faith and the migration experience—before, during, and after—was also an explicit theme throughout the narratives of both migrants and their families. Thus, many respondents explained how grateful they were to God for things having worked out in London. Ana remarked, "I also think that God opened these doors to us. Because when I came, I didn't speak any English at all. So . . . it was God who prepared everything." In other cases, respondents recounted how when things went wrong and they were on the verge of going back to Brazil, their faith gave them the strength to stay.

The notion of God bringing migrants closer to their families was also a very important theme. Dulce, from St. Mary's, commented,

> You're far away from your family, but I know that God is looking after me here, and God is looking after my sons over there [in Brazil] . . . So God connects us. Do you see? Because God is in our prayers . . . he's here in our prayers for them.

Similarly, Sofia in Brazil, a Catholic and mother of a woman who lived in London, explained how her faith had helped her enormously to deal with family separation:

> If I didn't have faith, I wouldn't be able to overcome my difficulties. My daughter is in London, my husband has always worked far away— God gives me strength to overcome this. I always turn to my faith and I know that, thank God, my daughter does too.

As discussed above, there seemed to be an opposing discourse among Catholic and evangelical leaders with regard to immigration status. Thus, while the CE was openly against undocumented migration, St. Mary's took a more tolerant stance and was in fact involved in various campaigns to defend the rights of undocumented migrants in London, such as the Strangers into Citizens Campaign (Peró this volume). The relationship between faith and immigration status was also an important element in the narratives of some interviewees themselves. For some, God protects the undocumented. Thus, as Paulo remarked,

> I think that I'm here because of God's plan, because the world is God's creation. It's not Tony Blair's, not Gordon Brown's . . . I believe that's it's due to a divine power that I have the right to be here as long as [I]

want to, but the rules of man say that I don't. I follow the rules of God so, as long as he allows me to be here, I will stay . . . If I have to leave tomorrow, it will be because of God's will.

For some, even the church was a space of fear, and so they chose not to attend. Anete, a return migrant who had lived in London for four years said that, although she was a devout Catholic and regularly attended Mass in Brazil, she had not frequented a church in London as she was terrified she could be deported. However, she described her migration experience as being successful primarily because of her faith in God. Without God's protection she would have been deported when five of her colleagues were, and she would certainly not have been able to earn the money to renovate her house back in Brazil, and pay for her daughter to go back to London. As she showed me around her newly refurbished house in a small town in Minas Gerais, she said it was possible "thanks to London, and to God." Thus, religious belief and practice in the lives of London's Brazilians were not just manifested within the space of the church. Rather, for many, God's presence was integral to their everyday struggles and feats.

Concluding Remarks

Charles Hirschmann (2007) summarizes the role of religion in meeting the needs of migrants in three words, "refuge, responsibility, and resources." Be it through attending religious services, going to church in order to find a job, or drawing on religious narratives in order to gain strength in the face of the challenges of migration, religion is a key factor in the everyday lives of many migrants. Indeed, as some scholars have observed, this amplified role is often in the absence of state or civil society organizations working to meet the diverse needs of migrants, who, in many cases, continue to live invisibly, marginalized, and outside the official reach of the state.

Thus, religion plays multiple roles in the lives of many Brazilian migrants in London, enabling them to inhabit spaces and develop practices that can facilitate a sense of belonging in London, while at the same time reinforce a sense of closeness to home in Brazil. This chapter has also pointed to the ways in which religious institutions, and migrants' "use" of such institutions, adapt to the new contexts. Churches—and by extension religious leaders—often take on important, supportive roles for migrants faced with the struggle of life, in an unfamiliar, potentially hostile, city, and for their families back home in Brazil who are left to cope with the absence of their loved ones. Yet, beyond the institutional realm, this chapter has also suggested how religious beliefs and practices manifested at the everyday level play a fundamental role in the migration experience. Indeed, for many, if it wasn't for the comfort and protection provided by God's presence every day, surviving in London would not have been possible.

Thus, while scholars of migration have begun to foreground religious themes, there remains a tendency to focus on the congregational realm (Warner and Wittner 1998), and to regard religion as somehow separate from other aspects of transnational migration processes. Yet, as this chapter argues, religious belief and practice are not tangible, measurable factors that are only relevant to the lives of migrants who frequent churches. Rather, the study of religion and transnationalism is about how religion is intertwined with the everyday lives and identities of a large proportion of the world's population, affecting not just those who migrate or belong to a religious community. Furthermore, it is about how religious faith is embodied, lived, and carried across borders where it may be renegotiated and transformed. Such transformations at multiple scales reveal how a consideration of the role of religion in the everyday lives of migrants may have implications that stretch far beyond what is perceived as merely a "religious field."

Acknowledgments

This research was funded by the Economic and Social Research Council. I would also like to thank Geraldo, Michel, Jesus, Neide, Ana Paula, Junia, and Darley for their support and hospitality during my visit to Brazil; Cathy McIlwaine for her extremely useful comments on drafts of the chapter and in particular; the Brazilian families and individuals who gave up their time to participate in this study.

Notes

1. MRE. Ministério das Relações Exteriores 2009. http://www .brasileirosnomundo.mre.gov.br/pt-br/mensagem_do_ministro.xml (accessed 11/01/10). "Transnationalism" and "globalization" are highly contested terms, whose meanings are far from clear, and are often overlapping. Yet scholars have pointed to important distinctions between the two. My use of the terms follows (broadly) Kearney's (1995, 548) distinction, in which "[w]hereas global processes are largely de-centered from specific national territories and take place in global space, transnational processes are anchored in and transcend one or more nation states."

2. The financial crises in the region were spurred by spiraling international debt, leading to rigid structural adjustment programs imposed by the international lending institutions, the IMF and World Bank (Bulmer-Thomas 2003).
3. See McIlwaine, Cock, and Linneker (2011) for a discussion of data sources for estimating the size of London's Latin American population, the problems with them, and how they relate to other, unofficial, estimation methods for measuring numbers of Latin Americans in London.
4. See Margolis (1998, 104–5) for a discussion of the "Brazilian paradox," whereby on the one hand Brazilians forge a collective identity to separate themselves from other ethnic groups, while on the other they seek to maintain their distance from other Brazilians whom they mistrust.

References

Ammerman, Nancy, ed. 2006. *Everyday Religion: Observing Modern Religious Lives.* Oxford: Oxford University Press.

Amorim, Aparecida, Carlos A. Dias, and Sueli Siqueira. 2008. "Igrejas Protestantes Como Espaço de Sociabilidade e Fé para os Familiares dos Wmigrantes em Governador Valadares." *Fronteiras* (Campo Grande) 10: 251–76.

Appadurai, Arjun. 1996. *Modernity at Large: The Cultural Dimensions of Globalization.* Minneapolis: University of Minnesota Press.

Baker, Chris. 2009. "Faith in the City? Negotiating the Postcolonial and the Postsecular. Paper presented at Centre for Research in Ethnic Relations, March 2009, University of Warwick, Warwick, UK.

Beckford, James. 2000. "Religious Movements and Globalisation." In *Global Social Movements,* ed. Robin Cohen and Shirin Rai, 178–84. London: Athlone.

Berger, Peter. 2002. "Secularization and Desecularization." In *Religions in the Modern World: Traditions and Transformations,* ed. Linda Woodhead, Paul Fletcher, Hiroko Kawanami, David Smith, 336–44. London: Routledge.

Beserra, Bernadette. 2003. *Brazilian Immigrants in the United States: Cultural Imperialism and Social Class.* New York: LFB Scholarly Publishing.

Beyer, Peter. 1990. "Privatization and the Public Influence of Religion in Global Society." In *Global Culture: Nationalism, Globalization and Modernity,* ed. Mike Featherstone, 373–97. London: Sage.

———. 2006. *Religion and Global Society.* London: Routledge.

Bulmer-Thomas. 2003. *The Economic History of Latin America since Independence.* New York and Cambridge: Cambridge University Press.

Cadge, Wendy, and Elaine H. Ecklund. 2007. "Immigration and Religion." *Annual Review of Sociology* 33:359–79.

Casanova, José 1994. *Public Religions in the Modern World.* Chicago: University of Chicago Press.

Cwerner, Saulo. 2001. "The Times of Migration." *Journal of Ethnic and Migration Studies* 27 (1): 7–36.

Deccol, René. 2001. "Imigração internacional e mudança religiosa no Brasil." Available at http://www.abep.nepo.unicamp.br/iussp2001/cd/ GT_Migr_Deccol_Text.pdf (accessed March 3, 2011).

Diaz-Stevens, Ana-Maria M. and Anthony M. Stevens-Arroyo. 1998. *Recognizing the Latino Resurgence in U.S. Religion: the Emmaus Paradigm.* Boulder, Colo.; Oxford: Westview Press.

Duarte Faria, Karla, Aparecida Amorim, Carlos A. Dias, and Sueli Siqueira. 2008. "Emigração e protestantismo: vivência religiosa de fiéis evangélicos em contexto emigratório." In Anais do XIII Seminário sobre a economia mineira. Belo Horizonte: UFMG/Cedeplar, 2008. v. 13.

Ebaugh, Helen R., and Janet S. Chafetz. 2002. *Religion across Borders: Transnational Immigrant Networks.* California: AltaMira Press.

Evans, Yara, Jane Wills, Kavita Datta, Joanna Herbert, Cathy McIlwaine, Jon May, Father José Osvaldo de Araújo, Ana Carla França, and Ana Paula França. 2007. *Brazilians in London: A Report for the Strangers into Citizens Campaign.* London: Department of Geography, Queen Mary, University of London.

Evans, Yara, Tânia Tonhati, Gustavo Tentoni Dias, Maria das Graças Brightwell, Olivia Sheringham, Ana Souza and Cleverson Souza. 2011. *Por Uma Vida Melhor: Brasileiras e Brasileiros em Londres, 2010.* London: Grupo de Estudos sobre Brasileiros em Londres.

Foner, Nancy, and Richard Alba. 2008. "Immigrant Religion in the US and Western Europe: Bridge or Barrier to Inclusion?" *International Migration Review* 42 (2): 360–92.

Freston, Paul. 2001. *Evangelicals and Politics in Asia, Africa and Latin America.* Cambridge: Cambridge University Press.

———. 2008. "The Religious Field among Brazilians in the United States." In *Becoming Brazuca, Brazilian Immigration to the United States,* ed. Clémence Jouët-Pastré and Leticia J. Braga, 255–70. Cambridge, MA: Harvard University Press.

Garbin, David. 2010. Embodied Spirit(s) and Charismatic Power among Congolese Migrants in London. In *Summoning the Spirits: Possession and Invocation in Contemporary Religion,* ed. Andrew Dawson, 40–57. New York: IB Tauris.

Hagan, Jaqueline, and Helen Ebaugh. 2003. Calling Upon the Sacred: Migrants' Use of Religion in the Migration Process. *International Migration Review* 37 (4): 1145–62.

Hirschman, Charles. 2007. "The Role of Religion in the Origins and Adaptation of Immigrant Groups in the United States." In *Rethinking Migration: New Theoretical and Empirical Perspectives,* ed. Alejandro Portes and Josh DeWind, 391–418, New York and Oxford: Berghann Books.

Jouët-Pastré, Clémence, and Leticia J. Braga, eds. 2008. *Becoming Brazuca, Brazilian Immigration to the United States.* Cambridge, MA: Harvard University Press.

Kearney, Michael. 1995. "The Local and the Global: The Anthropology of Globalization and Transnationalism". *Annual Review of Anthropology* 24: 547–565.

Lehmann, David. 2000. "Religion and Globalisation." In *Religions in the Modern World: Traditions and Transformations,* ed. Linda Woodhead, Paul Fletcher, Hiroko Kawanami, and David Smith, 345–64. London: Routledge.

Leonard, Karen, Jennifer Holdaway, Manuel Vasquez, and Alex Stepick, eds. 2005. *Immigrant Faiths: Transforming Religious Life in America.* New York: AltaMira Press.

Levitt, Peggy. 2007. *God Needs No Passport: Immigrants and the Changing American Religious Landscape.* New York: New York Press.

Margolis, Maxine.1998. *An Invisible Minority: Brazilians in New York City.* Boston: Allyn and Bacon.

———. 2008. "Brazilian Immigration to the United States: Research and Issues for the New Millennium". In *Becoming Brazuca,* eds. In *Becoming Brazuca, Brazilian immigration to the United States,* ed. Clémence Jouët-Pastré and Leticia J. Braga, 339–64. Cambridge, MA: Harvard University Press.

Martes, Ana Cristina Braga. 1999. "O trabalho das igrejas entre os imigrantes brasileiros em MA." In *Cenas do Brasil migrante,* ed. Teresa Sales and Rosana Reis. São Paulo: Boitempo.

———. 2000. *Brasileiros nos Estados Unidos: um estudo sobre imigrantes em Massachussets.* São Paulo: Editora Paz e Terra.

McGuire, Meredith. 2006. "Embodied Practices: Negotiation and Resistance. In *Everyday Religion Observing Modern Religious Lives,* ed. Nancy Ammerman, 187–201. Oxford: Oxford University Press.

———. 2008. *Lived Religion: Faith and Practice in Everyday Life.* Oxford: Oxford University Press.

McIwaine, Cathy, Juan Camilo Cock, and Brian Linneker. 2011. *No Longer Invisible: The Latin American Community in London.* London: Trust for London.

Menjivar, Cecilia. 1999. "Religious Institutions and Transnationalism: A Case Study of Catholic and Evangelical Salvadoran Immigrants." *International Journal of Politics, Culture and Society* 12 (4): 589–612.

———. 2006."Liminal Legality: Salvadoran and Guatemalan Immigrants' Lives in the United States. *American Journal of Sociology* 11 (4): 999–1037.

MRE. Ministério das Relações Exteriores. 2009. http://www.brasileirosno mundo.mre.gov.br/pt-br/mensagem_do_ministro.xml (accessed 11/01/10).

Orsi, Robert A. 2003. "Is the Study of Lived Religion Irrelevant to the World We Live In? Special Presidential plenary address, Society for the Scientific Study of Religion, Salt Lake City, November 2, 2002. *Journal for the Scientific Study of Religion* 42 (2): 119–74.

Padilla, Beatriz. 2006. "Brazilian Migration to Portugal: Social Networks and Ethnic Solidarity." CIES e-working paper No. 12. Available at https://repositorio.iscle.pt/handle/10071/175 (accessed February 2, 2011).

Patarra, Neide L. 2005. "Migrações Internacionais de e Para o Brasil Contemporâneo: Volumes, Fluxos, Significados e Políticas." *São Paulo em Perspectiva* 19: 23–33.

Pierrucci, António F. 2004. "'Bye Bye Brasil'—O declínio das religiões tradicionais no censo 2000." *Estudos Avançados* 18 (52): 17–28.

Pierrucci, António F., and Reginaldo Prandi. 2000. "Religious Diversity in Brazil: Numbers and Perspectives in a Sociological Evaluation. *International Sociology* 15 (4): 629–39.

Rudolph, Susanne H., 1997. "Preface: Religion, States, and Transnational Civil Society." In *Transnational Religion and Fading States*. eds. Susanne H. Rudolph and James Piscatori. . Oxford: Westview Press.

Sales, Teresa. 2000. "The "Triennium of Disillusionment" in International Migrations of Brazilians." *Brazilian Journal of Population Studies* 2: 145–163.

Silvey, Rachel, and Victoria Lawson. 1999. "Placing the Migrant." *Annals of the Association of American Geographers* 89 (1): 121–32.

Siqueira, Sueli. 2003. "O fenômeno da migração internacional em Governador Valadares." *Caderno do Neder, Governador Valadares* 1 (1): 1–35.

Smith, Greg. 2000. "Global Systems and Religious Diversity in the Inner City—Migrants in the East End of London. *International Journal on Multicultural Societies* 2 (1): 16–39.

Torresan, Angela. 1995. "Ser Brasileiro em Londres." *Travessia Revista do Migrante* 23 (Sept.).

Tubergen, Frank V. 2007. "Religious Affiliation and Participation among Immigrants in a Secular Society: A Study of Immigrants in the Netherlands." *Journal of Ethnic and Migration Studies* 33 (5): 747–65.

Ugba, Abel. 2008. "A Part of and Apart from Society? Pentecostal Africans in the 'New Ireland.'" *Translocations: Migration and Social Change* 4 (1): 86–101.

Vasquez Manuel, and Marie F. Marquardt. 2003. *Globalising the Sacred: Religion across the Americas*. New Brunswick: Rutgers University Press.

Vasquez, Manuel, and Lucia Ribeiro. 2007. "'A igreja é como a casa da minha mãe: religião e espaço vivido entre brasileiros no condado de Broward." *Ciencias Sociais e Religão* 9 (9): 13–29.

Vertovec, Steven. 2007. "Super-diversity and Its Implications." *Ethnic and Racial Studies* 30 (6): 1024–54.

Vertovec, Steven, and Robin Cohen, eds. 1999. *Migration, Diasporas and Transnationalism*. Cheltenham, UK: Edward Elgar.

Warner, Stephen, and Judith Wittner. eds. 1998. *Gatherings in Diaspora: Religious Communities, and the New Immigration*. Philadelphia: Temple University Press.

Wills, Jane, Kavita Datta, Yara Evans, Joanna Herbert, Jon May, and Cathy McIlwaine. 2009. "Religion at Work: The Role of Faith-Based Organisations in the London Living Wage Campaign." *Cambridge Journal of Regions, Economy and Society* 2:443–61.

Woodhead, Linda, Paul Fletcher, Hiroko Kawanami, and David Smith, eds. 2002. *Religions in the Modern World: Traditions and Transformations.* London: Routledge.

Yorgason, Ethan and Veronica della Dora. 2009. "Geography, Religion and Emerging Paradigms: Problematizing the Dialogue." *Social and Cultural Geography* 10 (6): 629–637.

Index